D1832923

STUDIES IN THE ANATOMY OF
A TRANSFORMATION :

AWADH

FROM MUGHAL TO COLONIAL RULE

STUDIES IN THE ANATOMY OF A TRANSFORMATION : AWADH FROM MUGHAL TO COLONIAL RULE

Saiyid Zaheer Husain Jafri

GYAN PUBLISHING HOUSE
NEW DELHI-110002

Studies in the Anatomy of a Transformation :
AWADH
From Mughal to Colonial Rule
(*History*)

ISBN : 9788121205979

All rights are reserved. No part of this book may
be reproduced in any manner without written permission.

© Saiyid Zaheer Husain Jafri

Reprinted in 2015 in India by
Gyan Publishing House,
5, Ansari Road, Darya Ganj
New Delhi-110002

Typesetting at : Elite-Art, New Delhi
Printed at Mehra Offset Press, Delhi

To My Mother
And
To The Memory Of My Father
Hazrat Saiyid Shah Muhammad Husain Jafri

رَبِّ ارْحَمْهُمَا كَمَا رَبَّيَانِى صَغِيراً ۝

"My Lord! Have mercy on them both as they did care when I was little!"

Al - Quran, xvii,24

Contents

CHANGES UNDER BRITISH RULE

RESISTANCE

List of Illustrations

Foreword

The name Awadh invokes several memories of the Kośala of Buddhist and Brahmanical traditions to the area of the efforescence of Urdu culture, annals of repression and constant breaches of commitment by the British regime, the revolt of 1857, the *ta'alluqadars'* increasing oppression and the anguished misery of its peasants, (Around 1900 over three - quarters of peasants in the Awadh districts were tenants-at-will). My own introduction to Awadh came from my father's lively recounting of anecdotes of its rural life; one of these stories may be read in his *Desecrated Bones and other Stories.* I was, therefore, very happy when Dr. Zaheer Husain Jafri decided to work for his Ph.D. degree on the agrarian history of Awadh from 1595 to 1856, with me as his Supervisor. He prepared a very informative thesis. I hope he would publish it soon.

During the course of his Ph.D. degree work, and later, during his successful career as a teacher, Dr. Jafri examined a large amount of documentary material, leading him into a number of by-lanes of Awadh's economic, cultural and social history. These he has explored in a number of published papers, and in a few others submitted at conferences and seminars. It is these papers that are now conveniently collected together in the present volume to give us welcome insight into the various facets of the changes in Awadh from the 16th century to the Revolt of 1857. Based extensively on Persian manuscript materials, Jafri's studies form an important addition to the contemporary historical literature on Awadh. And I hope that these would obtain the wide readership that they deserve.

PROF. IRFAN HABIB

Formerly Chairman, Indian Council of Historical Research and Professor (retd.), Centre of Advanced Study in History, Aligarh Muslim University, Aligarh.

1st May, 1998
Aligarh.

Preface

Awadh has a place in our historical memory owing to its contributions to our composite culture, and the British repeated acts of injustice against it, culminating in the Annexation in 1856. Its institution of the *ta'alluqadari* tenures came into limelight with the mutiny and Canning's proclamation. The heroic resistance offered by the people of Awadh forms a dramatic part of the Rebellion of 1857.

For a number of years I have been working on the several aspects of the history of Awadh from the period it was a *suba* of the Mughal Empire to the Revolt of 1857.

I became familiar with source material for Awadh when I worked on my doctoral thesis on the Agrarian Conditions of Awadh (1595-1856) at AMU, Aligarh, submitted in 1986, and which I hope to publish separately. My subsequent work on Awadh resulted in several studies on aspects other than (but including) agrarian history. These have been collected together in this volume since these now form fairly extensive explorations in the different aspects of the history of Awadh.

Some of these studies are based on archival and other material, often being used for the first time. Part of the documents and records pertain to *sufi* institutions. My access to Salon *Khanqah* papers has been of considerable help in elucidating aspects to social life of Awadh.

In preparing this volume I have immensely benefitted from the guidance and advice of my teacher and guide Professor Irfan Habib. He went through the typescript of this book and was gracious enough to write the foreword for this modest work.

I wish to express my gratitude to Professor Shireen Moosvi, who was my teacher in all the stages of my student career. Whenever in pursuit of these studies I went to Aligarh to check references, she as the Coordinator and Chairman of the Centre of Advanced Study in History, was kind enough to extend me the magnificent facilities available at the Centre under a short term visitorship.

I must thankfully acknowledge the help and encouragement I received from Professor M. Athar Ali, Professor D.N. Jha, and Professor K.M. Shrimali.

The maps included here have been drawn by Mr. Zahoor Ali Khan and Mr. Faiz Habib, Centre of Advanced Study in History, Aligarh Muslim University, I gratefully acknowledge their help.

I am grateful to many of my colleagues and friends for their keen interest during my researches and in the publication of this book. I must place on records the affection and kindness shown by my brother Saiyid Shah Ahmad Husain Jafri Islahi, the present *sajjadanasheen* of the *Khanqah-i Karimia* for allowing me access to the family documents and the manuscripts at Salon.

I am most grateful to my wife Tayyaba and to my son Tariq Miyan for their letting me be away from home in connection with this book. I hope this study will be deemed sufficient merit to deserve their indulgence.

Delhi University
21 Muharram 1419/18 May 1998

Saiyid Zaheer Husain Jafri

Previous Publication Details

1. Chapter I with three maps is from my unpublished Ph.D. thesis submitted at AMU, 1986, pp. 1-13.

2. Chapter II ('Administration of *Jagirs* in Awadh, 17th century', *U.P. Historical Review*, vol. 3, Allahabad, 1984, pp. 57-63).

3. Chapter III ('Two *Madad-i Maash farmans* of Aurangzeb from Awadh', *Proceedings Indian History Congress* (hereafter as *PIHC*) 1979, pp. 302-13).

4. Chapter IV ('Tension and Conflict in the Agrarian Society of Awadh during the 17th century — A Study of the Revenue Grantees', *PIHC*, 1990, pp. 354-61).

5. Chapter V ('Origin and Growth of *ta'alluqadari* Tenures in Awadh', *PIHC*, 1984, pp. 410-18).

6. Chapter VI ('Landed Properties of a *Sufi* Establishment — A Study of 17th-19th Century Documents from Salon in Awadh,' *PIHC*, I, 1986, pp. 417-31).

7. Chapter VII ('Armed *Zamindar* : The Power Play in Awadh, 1595-1858', *PIHC*, 1991-92, pp. 292-302).

8. Chapter VIII ('Inheritance, Succession and the Customary Law in a *Sufi* Establishment in Awadh', *PIHC*, 1992-93, pp. 321-27).

9. Chapter IX ('A *Sufi* Institution of Awadh', in *Ideology and Society*, ed. D.N. Jha, Delhi, 1996, pp. 269-89).

10. Chapter X ('British Intervention and Agrarian Instability in the Kingdom of Awadh', *PIHC*, 1993, pp. 545-52).

11. Chapter XI ('The Land-Controlling Classes in Awadh — A Study of Change in their Composition', *U.P. Historical Review*, vol. 5, Allahabad, 1989, pp. 22-39).

12. Chapter XII in the revised and enlarge version of my earlier paper presented in a *Symposium on 1857* at CAS, AMU, Aligarh, March 1988.

13. Plate Nos. I, II, III and V are included here for the first time, while plate no. IV has earlier appeared in Shah Hasan Ata's *Harir-i-Sang*, Karachi, 1964.

Introduction

There would be little support from any physical map for establishing Awadh as a region. The great alluvial plains of the Gangetic basin have no recognised barriers and rivers constitute links rather than obstacles. Yet historically what came to be the Mughal *suba* of Awadh, with its capital at Awadh (Ayodhya), stretching from the Ganga to the Gandak, had impeccable historical credentials.[1] By and large, it corresponded to the 15th century Sharqi kingdom with its capital at Jaunpur on the Gomti[2], and to the ancient Kośala, with its earlier capital at Sravasti and later at Ayodhya.

Within this region a dialect of Hindi, known as Awadhi, was in vogue in which Kabir, the great monotheist, who lies buried at Maghar, composed his verses and the famous Hindi poet Malik Muhammad of Jais, wrote his *Padmavat* during the 16th century. Tulsidas's celebrated *Ramcharitmānas* also is in the same dialect. It could, therefore, be asserted that the region had a distinct cultural personality as well.

As part of the Mughal Empire, Awadh had little reason to appear prominently in political or military history, after the suppression of the Uzbek rebellion in 1560s, since it did not lie directly on any axis of Mughal expansion and thus remained in political backwaters.[3] As a result, there were few nobles of high rank posted in Awadh during the 17th century; and this is reflected in the absence of any great Mughal monuments in its cities, after Mun'im Khan's Jaunpur bridge of the 1560s.

The 18th century saw a transformation in the position of Awadh, for two different reasons. As the Mughal emperors more or less confined their courts to Delhi from the time of Farrukh Siyar (acc. 1713) onwards, holding possession of adjacent provinces became very important for exerting influence at the Court. Thus the three successive governors of Awadh, Sa'adat Khan (1722-39), Safdarjung (1739-54), Shuja 'uddaula (1754-75), sought to use their control over Awadh and its resources as springboard for pursuing their ambitions at Delhi. Secondly, as the Mughal Empire began to contract, Awadh became subject to threats from the Afghans, Marathas and, finally, the English. For both these reasons Awadh re-entered and remained in the realm of political annals with a new prominence. Though Muzaffar 'Alam has not drawn attention to these extraneous circumstances for Awadh's rise to importance, his work, *The Crisis of Empire in Mughal North India*, the fact that he singles out Awadh and Punjab as the two key provinces for study underlines the alteration in its status that had now occurred.[4]

A basic shift in the position of Awadh took place with the battle of Buxar (1764), whereafter the centre of power under which Awadh worked was Calcutta, not Delhi. Under the new regime, Awadh became a veritable milch-cow for the English East India Company. One of the major contributions of Barnett's work on Awadh of this period is his study of the resources drained out of Awadh under various forms of tribute and impositions, until the size of the inflow being still judged insufficient, more than half of the area of Awadh was annexed by Wellesley in 1801.[5]

The subordinate principality (designated 'Kingdom' in 1814 with the Ruler of Awadh becoming entitled to the coveted address 'His Majesty' by an unintended stroke of Imperialist humour) was now again in political backwaters. The best Study of its position in the new phase (1801-56) is that by Michael H. Fisher.[6] This was the period when Lucknow became the centre of Urdu culture, a refuge of poets and courtiers from Delhi, as the Mughal court found itself bereft of all resources and the Emperor a mere pensioner of the British government after 1803. In the political and economic sphere, Awadh offered an example of abject tutelage, where the British had power but no responsibility. British ambitions, both political and financial grew apace, until Dalhousie enforced the Annexation in 1856, and eliminated a state that, since 1764, had never given any occasion for offence to the Paramount Power.

The annexation led to a short but heroic phase of resistance in the history of Awadh, when during 1857-59 it remained dogged in its support of the great uprising. On this the main work has been that of Rudrangshu Mukherji, unluckily it gives scant attention to Persian and indigenous sources, and this lacuna undoubtedly affects his interpretation.[7] The final essay in this volume seeks to put the record straight at least in respect of one important figure of the 1857 Rebellion.

The three centuries of transformation, from the Mughal occupation of Awadh under Akbar's commanders after his accession in 1556 to the Rebellion of 1857-59, form the period with which the studies collected in this volume are concerned. These essentially concern agrarian and institutional history, and touch on matters on which so far little has been written in the large literature that has been produced on Awadh. It will be seen that much greater use has been made of private documents, including those which have now found their way into official archives, than in most historical studies, which have relied on historical narratives or official correspondence and reports. It is, therefore, hoped that the importance of such material will be underlined by the information brought out by these studies; and it will receive attention from other hands as well.

Note on Sources

The earliest possible initial point for any agrarian history of Awadh is the statistical and topographical information contained in Abul Fazl's *Ain-i Akbari* (completed 1598). The Chapters entitled, *Ain-i Nuazdahsala,* we get the crop-wise revenue rates from 6th RY to 24th RY of Akbar for the province; and then in the *Ain-i Dahsala,* there are final rates for each locality (*dastur*-circle) within the *suba.* In yet another chapter, 'Account of the Twelve *suba*', there is not only a geographical description of the province, but in a separate statistical table information is provided for measured area (*arazi*), estimated revenue (*naqdi/jama'*), *suyurghal* (amount alienated in grants) caste of the *zamindars* and the number of their retainers (infantry and cavalry separately stated). The *Ain* stands unique for in the Mughal period at least it had no successor.

Subsequent to the *Ain,* we have a number of *Dastur-ul amals,* prepared during the 17th and early 18th centuries which provide summary statistics and sometimes give *pargana*-wise revenue and, in rare cases, area statistics.

The printed Persian chronicles of the Mughal period such as Abul Fazl's *Akbarnama* or Lahori's *Badhshahnama* or Kazim's *'Alamgirnama* provide only sporadic information about Awadh, referring to some appointments or to rebellions or expeditions. Similar facts can be abstracted from the *Akhbarat-i Darbari Mu'alla* of Aurangzeb's reign. These sources help in identification of a number of officials referred in various *Insha'* collections and other documents.

Another class of sources consists of collections of letters (*insha*) such as the *Insha-i Roshan Kalam, Munsur-ul Maktubat* and *Ausaf-i Asaf.* Their evidence relates to *zamindars'* rebellions, conditions of law and order, relations of the *zamindars* with the *jagirdars*, with some occasional references to the working of the *jagir* system and collection of land revenue.

The historical accounts of *Nawabi Awadh* are rather fewer in number and, with some exceptions, are loaded with political history, and little useful information could be exacted for other aspects of history. The typical representative of this class is Ghulam Ali Naqvi's *'Imadus-Sa'adat* (1808).

A valuable account of the administration of the Awadh kingdom exists in the *Mirat-ul Auza'*, penned by a court *waqainigar* Lalji during the decade before Annexation (1856). Since the author felt that the details of administration which led to the ruin of the kingdom might not be well received by the Lucknow Court he kept it secret. Valuable information pertaining to the revenue system, methods of realization and the armed power of the *ta'alluqadars* is provided here.

The most important sources of information lie in archival material consisting of *farmans, parwanas, sanads, mahzars* (statement of the facts) *chaknamas* (land demarcation papers), sale deeds, judicial decision, and private papers of various kinds. Most of them relate to the 17th and 18th centuries, and a few to the 16th. The principal repositories of these collections are the Research Library Centre of Advanced Study in History, AMU, Aligarh; the Central Record Office Allahabad; National Archives of India, New Delhi; and the Tagore Library, Lucknow University.

Some ecclesiastical institutions and families enjoying *madad-i-ma'ash* grants have preserved the documents relating to their claims as every subsequent confirmation depended on the evidence in support of their fiscal perquisites. *The Historical Documents Purchase Committee* and the *Indian Historical Records Commission* acquired these collections from various individual families. In spite of their success in this venture, a large number of documents still remain with the families connected with the mystic establishments or *qazis'* and other families. Some of them provide ready access to their prized collections, while others need to be pursuaded to show these records.

As some of these institutions were involved in long drawn litigation, we come across copies of some of these documents in the records of the judicial and the revenue files preserved in the record rooms of the District Courts and the Board of Revenue Library. These files tell much about the British policy towards the *ma' afidars* after

1857, and the multiplicity of land rights acquired by *ma' afi* holders. Between the Summary Settlement and the First Regular Settlement *(bandobast-i awwal)*, British officers compiled exhaustive reports examining the claims of the *ma' afidars* and the nature of their grants at the time of the annexation. The objects of such enquiries were limited to the terms at which new *sanads* were to be granted. The meticulously prepared *wajib-ul arz* of each village and *rawaj-e a'am* of each *pargana* recorded the customary laws of the then land-owning classes regarding a wide range of matters. Such documents are extremely valuable for giving us a peep into the society of Awadh during the earlier periods as well.

The *sufi* institutions have also 'created' some records having a bearing on a number of vital aspects to understand the inner dynamics of the 'world of spirituality'. The deeds of initiation into discipleship and nomination of successors like *shajra, khilafatnamah,* and *misal-i khilafat wa janashini* often used to spell out the *sufi* customs and traditions. Since the question of nomination was closely linked to the control of the landed property attached to the institutions by way of *madad-i-ma'ash,* such visualizations ultimately resulted in the change of the character of the grant. The institution of *waqf* was created in such establishments even when the grants were initially made for the personal expenses.

Records of this kind are to be found quite often scattered in the files of the Board of Revenue (records upto AD 1890 have now been transferred to UP State Archives, Lucknow) and in files of judicial proceedings. Many are, of course, still in private hands.

The printed works in English, are indispensable for any study of the agrarian life of Awadh during the first half of the 19th century. An outstanding source for us is the survey by Donald Butter of the southern parts of Awadh in 1830s. Though Butter does not explicitly refer to the official documents of the Awadh government, his detailed survey was hardly possible without some cooperation from local officials. His account appears a little biased against the Awadh government and he sometimes offers very severe comments, which are not always well grounded. We find him sharing the views of other British officials, that if Awadh was annexed to the British dominions, the people would be better - off.[8] Butter, however, offers valuable details of crops, agricultural production, implements, towns, markets and topographical information.

Charles Elliott's *Chronicles of Oonao*, deals exclusively with the history of the *zamindar* families of Unao, particularly the Bais clans down to AD 1861. The author consulted a large number of documents in the hands of leading *zamindar* families and also draw upon local traditions. It contains useful informations about the history of revenue-farms and the financial administration of the district. But surprisingly he shows little concern with purely economic matters such as the state of agriculture, crop pattern and trade.

Among the travellers' accounts, the most important are those of Heber and Sleeman. Bishop Reginald Heber visited Awadh in 1824, and had some pre-concived notions,[9] but he revised these after he made his personal observation[10] and also appears to have acquired some sympathy with the *Nawabi* regime. Indeed, he blames the non-cooperative attitude of the company's officials for the anarchy and misrule of the Kingdom.[11] His judgement about the people is the opposite to that of Butter, for he argued that "they prefer to be governed by their native *nawabs* rather than to be placed under the rule of the company."[12]

W.H. Sleeman's diary of his tour of Awadh which he made from December 1849 to February 1850 is now a celebrated historical text. He was then Resident at Lucknow, and the tour was made to supplement the report which he had presented earlier to Lord Dalhousie.[13] To him the basic fault in the political set-up of the Kingdom lay 'in the lack of effective central government' and the 'maladministration' which resulted from it.[14] Some of Sleeman's observations must be judged in the context of his explicit bias.

Whatever the reasons behind the compilation of Sleeman's diary, it still stands as a treasure house of facts relating to crops, agriculture, local administration etc. *Zamindars, 'ta'alluqadars* and *chakledars* find frequent mention in the diary, and this help us to form an idea of their power and role in local society and administration.

The people of Awadh and particularly the sepoys from the Bengal Army (many from Awadh), offered the stiffest resistance to the British during 1857-59. One of the central figures in organizing such an opposition was Maulavi Ahmadullah Shah, on whose activities and career as a leader of the resistance there is much interesting material calling to be explored and analysed. There is his versified biography, to be supplemented by the *Risala Fath-i Islam* (a representative piece on *Wahabi* ideology whose authorship is now attributed to the group led by Maulavi Ahmadullah Shah). These need to be used with much greater refinement and understanding than has been done, for example by Rudrangshu Mukherji and Gautam Bhadra. Fazl-e Haq Khairabadi's *Al-Sauratul Hindiya,* being the recollections of the chain of events by one of the chief ideologues of the period, has to be used to understand part of the ideological underpinning of 1857. His reading of the events is worth examining. An analysis of the proclaimations, letters, short notices, memoirs and the recollection of the contemporaries contain much useful information on the 'World of the Vanquished' than has been preserved in the 'Victors' narratives. The studies presented in this volume end with a study of Maulavi Ahmadullah Shah based on these 'indigenous' sources of enduring value.

References

1. For its exact boundaries in Akbar's time, see Irfan Habib, *An Atlas of the Mughal Empire,* New Delhi, 1982, Sheet, 8A.
2. Jaunpur itself was in the Mughal *suba* of Ilahabad, but became a part of the 18th century principality of Awadh.
3. Cf. M. Athar Ali, 'Provincial Governors under Shah Jahan: An Analysis' *Medieval India — A Miscellany,* III, pp. 80-112, and 'Provincial Governors under Aurangzeb-An Analysis', *Medieval India-A Miscellany,* I, pp. 96-133.
4. Muzaffar Alam, *The Crisis of Empire in Mughal North : Awadh and the Punjab, 1707-48,* Delhi, 1986, Cf. also Richard B. Barnett, *North India Between Empires : Awadh the Mughals and the British,* Berkeley, 1980, esp. Chapter I (pp. 1-41).
5. Barnett, *op. cit.,* Chapter V (pp. 127-63) and VIII (pp. 223-38).
6. Michael H. Fisher, *A Clash of Cultures : Awadh,* the *British and the Mughals,* New Delhi, 1987, pp. 90-246.
7. Rudrangshu Mukherjee, *Awadh in Revolt, 1857-1859, A Study of Popular Resistance,* Delhi, 1984.
8. Donald Butter, *Outlines of the Topography and Statistics of Southern Districts of Oudh and Contonment of Sultanpur,* Calcutta, 1839, Delhi Reprint, 1982, pp. 50-52.
9. "We have heard much of the mis-governed and desolate state of the Kingdom of Oude", cf Bishop Reginald Heber, *Narrative of a Journey Through the Upper Provinces, 1824-25,* London, 1828, Vol. I, p. 41.

10. "I have been pleased, however and surprised, after all which I have heard of Oude, to find the country so completely under plough, I cannot think that we should witness so considerable population." *Ibid,* p. 49.
11. *Ibid*, pp. 85-86,
12. *Ibid*, pp. 82-83,
13. RD Reeves (ed.), *Sleeman in Oudh*, Cambridge, 1971, see introduction, p. 13.
14. *Ibid.*

1
The Geographical Setting

The Natural Environment

The Mughal province of Awadh extended over the territory entirely consisting of alluvial plains, lying between 79.6° and 84° longitude E. and 26° and 28.4° latitude N. The limits of the *suba* are described by Abul Fazl in his 'Account of Twelve Provinces'. It was bounded on the east by the province of Bihar, and to the north lay the northern mountains; *sarkar* Manikpur of *suba* Allahabad was situated on the south of the province, while on the western side was *sarkar* of Kannuj of *suba* Agra. The distance from the limits of *sarkar* Gorakhpur to Kannauj was computed at 135 *kos*; while only 115 *kos* were said to separate the northern mountains and the southern boundary of the *suba*.[1]

To some extent, the boundaries of the *suba* took into account the physical features of the Upper Gangetic plains. Besides the Himalayan barrier to the north, the river Ganges separated it from the Mughal province of Agra and the river Sarju fixed the boundary line between *sarkar* Gorakhpur of Awadh and *sarkar* Jaunpur of *suba* Allahabad.

A number of rivers and their tributaries flowed through the province. Abul Fazl lists four principal rivers traversing the plains of the province. These were the Sarju, Ghaghra, Sai and Godi (Gomti).[2] But this list is a very short one. Butter lists the Ganges, Deoha (Ghaghra), Gomti, Sai, Tons and Lon rivers as the main water channels of the southern districts of Awadh alone. The distinguishing features of each of these rivers are well described by him.[3] The Ganges and Deoha had a low bed with an average width of four miles; and alterations occurred in the channels almost annually so much so that within a span of four or five years, the rivers considerably shifted their courses. Compared to these rivers, the smaller rivers had almost fixed narrow channels and little change occurred in their courses. Few of these rivers had depth enough to avoid overflow during the rainy season. The banks of these rivers were made up of high *kankar* ridges making them navigable; but it was noticed that as a result of the diminishing of these ridges during the summer, the depth of the rivers was adversely affected. Butter thought it a duty of the government of *Nawab-Wazirs* to clear out debris of such fallen ridges to keep the streams navigable.

In importance the river Gomti, though much smaller, was next only to Ganges and Deoha. Its right bank was made up of solid *kankar* giving the appearance of a mountainous range, while the left bank was low and sandy to the maximum extent of 3 miles being an arid waste. Beyond this zone the soil was quite fertile. The water was unfit for drinking because it was heavily loaded with yellowish clay. Fish abounded in all seasons. At some places, the Sai was as broad as the Gomti, but had only half of its depth. The Sai could accommodate boats of 300 maunds during rainy season, but because of its zig-zag course, it was avoided by navigators in favour of the Ganges and Gomti.

The Tons had its source in the Deoha, being essentially an arm of that river. It was shallow, and little navigation could be carried through it. The small river Lon flowed in the north-western portion of Awadh rising near Shahabad. It joined river Sai near Rae Bareli. During the summer it was of no consequence.

An important feature of the natural geography of Awadh in the 16th-18th centuries was the presence of large forest belts. It is possible to map the main forest tracts by drawing upon diverse sources.[4] We find that the Terai forest spread between the city of Gorakhpur and the Himalyan range, as shown in James Rennell's *Bengal Atlas* (1780). Ghulam Hazarat, in his memoir of the Gorakhpur district (1810), tells us that the city of Gorakhpur was surrounded by forests. He says that the *tappas* of *parganas* Anola, Bansi, Silhat, Basti, Maghar and Gorakhpur were desolate owing to the scarcity of peasants, the denseness of jungle and the inroads of the wild elephants. Owing to the depradations of these elephants, the peasants abstained from cultivation of the sugarcane.[5] Francis Buchanan who surveyed the district in 1807-11 estimated that out of the total area in the district of 7438 sq. miles, about 1450 sq. miles were covered with forest.[6]

Besides these forests, a number of patches studded with bush and long grass were to be found here and there.[7]

Another category of the forests consisted of jungle situated either on the low land (*kachar*) or on the higher grounds. These were carefully preserved from clearing by the *zamindars* of the area. These offered them a safe place of "asylum from the tyranny and the rapacity of the *chakledar*."[8] The face of the country was level plain, but river Gomti had cut the soil at some places creating ravines to the depth of 50 ft. These ravines were made use of by the *zamindars* who planted trees to create jungles and so made hide-outs for themselves. In the midst of these forests every landholder of consequence used to build mud forts (*garhis*) "surrounded by a ditch and dense fence of living bamboos, through which cannon shot cannot penetrate[9]." The *chakledars* were always helpless against such fortifications of the *zamindars*, as the *jungles* were too green to be set fire to and "being within the range of match-locks from the parapet, they cannot be cut down by the beseiging force."[10] Sleeman laments that such defences could easily be broken down but "Oude force had seldom either the means or the skill for such purpose."[11] Sleeman has listed twenty-four belts of forests in the kingdom of Oudh[12] (1850) which were being used by the *zamindars* to challenge the authority of the government officials. They were spread in all parts of the kingdom, and it was computed that about 882½ sq. miles of area were covered by such forests[12]. Sleeman offers us the figures for the estimated area under forest in the districts of the Awadh kingdom in square miles.[13]

Table 1

Forested Area in Awadh

Chakla (District)	*Forested area (in sq. miles)*
1. Sultanpur	279
2. Uldemau	102
3. Daruabad	76
4. Dewa-Jahangirabad	64
5. Bangar	72
6. Salon	72
7. Bainswara	30
8. Hydergarh	7½
9. Khyrabad Muhammadi	150
10. Baree and Muchreyta	30
Total	882½

The mud forts situated in these belts were said to number about 633.[14]

In order to increase revenue, and, perhaps, remove the *zamindars'* hideouts the clearing of the forests for the purpose of cultivation was generally encouraged by the government. A number of incentives were given to the peasants for carrying the work of reclamation. Forest-land was lightly assessed by the revenue officials of the *Nawab-Wazirs* "free for the first year of occupancy, charged at only two *anna* per *bigha*; the second year, four *anna*; the third year, six *anna*; the fourth year and fifth year, ten *anna*; beyond which, as an encouragement to the settlers, the rent is never raised."[15] In these lands the irrigation facilities were available abundantly as the water-table was found just at the depth of 10 feet, and wells and tanks could be dug quite easily. Butter describes the destruction of a *chiul jangal* which was twenty miles in length and eight miles broad, situated between Niwurdipur and Manikpur.[16]

However, due to the unremitting destruction of the forest, adverse affects were produced on the general climate. Butter thought that the annual average rainfall declined and the water-table went down, thus creating difficulties for irrigation. This situation could have certainly been controlled by a "systematic artificial planting to counteract the parching effects produced by the removal of these natural protectors of the soil."[17] But reclamation continued unabated. The agricultural statistics of 1885-86 show no forest area in those districts where, Sleeman estimates forest areas as 882½ sq. miles. It may be assumed, then, that by 1885-86 such extensive tracts of forest comprising about half a million acres had come under cultivation.[18]

Wild animals found their way into these deep and long stretches of green-belts. The *Tarai* forest of *sarkar* Gorakhpur was famous for containing numerous elephants, a menace to cultivation.[19] Tigers too were found in great number between the city of Gorakhpur and the mountains, and before the cession of this territory to the English their number was still larger. After 1801, due to forest clearing operations, a good many of them were hunted down by the English civilians as well as military officers. These animals lived so largely on cattle that in the year 1769, the year of the great famine, most of 'herbivorous' animals perished so that the tigers were famished.[20] The tigers in a large hoard fall upon the town of Bhewapor, and within no time killed about 400 of its inhabitants. The town remained deserted for a long period.

Wolves and jackals, too, were very common in these forests, posing a constant threat to the peasants as well as the domestic animals.[21] The wolf was quite a menace in the southern districts of Awadh when Butter compiled his survey. He says that they carried away a number of children from the small bazar attached to the Cantonment of Sultanpur. Superstition among the native population precluded their being killed; and their dens were observable along the sides of the 'ravines' throughout the country.[22]

Whether any change in climate occurred in the course of the two hundred and fifty years is a matter on which the information available is rather slight. In 1836 Butter was convinced of a "great change in the climate"[23] by which he perhaps meant a decline in rainfall. Butter has appended tables showing the diminishing pattern of the *rabi* as well as *kharif* crops. At the time of his writing the report (1836) even the 'produce in a good year' was much less than what it was 'before the great change in the climate.'[24]

Table 2[25]

***Kharif* Crops Sown in the Rainy Season**

Name of the crop	*Sers of seeds per bigha*	*Mans of produce in a good year*	*Mans of produce in a bad year*	*Former produce in mans*
1. Kodo	4	10 to 12	4 or 5	16 or 17
2. Makra	4	8 to 9	2 or 3	10 or 11
3. Sanwa	3	8	2 or 3	10 or 12
4. Asahan *kharif*	30	15	8 or 9	20

***Rabi* Crops Sown in the Winter Season**

Name of the crop	*Sers of seeds per bigha*	*Mans of produce in a good year*	*Mans of produce in a bad year*	*Former produce in mans*
1. Chana	30	14 or 15	5 to 8	18 to 20
2. Genhun	50	14 or 15	7 or 8	20 to 25
3. Jau	40	20 to 22	10 to 13	20 to 25

The average annual rainfall in Awadh according to him followed a very irregular pattern. At the same time it was, "steadily decreasing on an average of 5 or 6 inches year."[26] Butter attributed such a change to the destruction of the 'sylan vesture' by the peasants in order to bring more land under the cultivation. It was predicted that the country was under the slow but definite process of becoming 'barren ravines' as there were no forests left 'to ward off' the 'fierce rays of the sun' and 'dew deposition' thus creating 'springs of running water'. The green belts of the region had detained water in meshes, but such land was now 'ploughed into barren ravines'. As a result the province lost "its springs and parenial streamlets...the distance of water from the earth's increased — and its rainfalls, and the volume of its rivers diminished."[27]

The accompanying map drawn to show the isohyets clearly projects that the annual average rainfall of the province ranges from 54.7 inches to 25 inches.[28] It tend to be heavier as we move towards north-west, and lighter as we go west ward. Butter in 1836 estimated the average annual rainfall in southern Awadh at between "70 to 30 inches within a period of four months in duration; but is on an average of five or six years, steadily decreasing."[29]

The soil of the province was composed of different varieties. On occasions, it contained siliceous and calcoreous earth, the latter in the form of *kankar* which occurred in the limited horizontal layers at a depth of six to eight feet. The *kankar* ridges were generally found along the right banks of rivers[30]. At many places *kankar* constituted the surface of the soil as well. The sites of the 'primeval forests of Oudh' and the regions between Ganges and Deoha had the rich and dark soil. In the southern districts of Awadh, the soil of *pargana* Salon, Jais, Rampur and Manikpur was judged as the best and very productive in different varieties of the grain.[31]

Administrative Divisions

The Mughal province of Awadh came into being in the year 1580, when Akbar superseded the earlier divisions of the Lodi Sultans to make his own administrative arrangements.[32] This set-up entailed the formation of provinces (*suba*) with subdivisions, continuing under the older name of *sarkars*. Each *sarkar* contained a number of *parganas*. All the *sarkars* now included in *suba* Awadh are listed by Babur in his list of Lodi *sarkars*, but with Lucknow as Lakhnau-and-Balkar, and Gorakhpur as Saruar.[33]

The limits of the new territorial divisions were determined by a number of considerations, not all based on physical geography. C.A. Elliot, in his account of Onao district found that the *pargana* boundaries were traced in most irregular fashion, the proprietary rights of individual clans forming the basis for the limits of the *mahal*.[24]

The total number of the *parganas* included in the *suba*, as stated in *Ain-i-Akbari* 138, but those actually listed come to 133 *parganas* only.[35] Subsequent to the period when *Ain-i-Akbari* was written, many changes occurred in the internal administrative units of the *sarkar*, many new *parganas* were constituted so as to raise the number of the total *mahals* in each *sarkar*. Sometime during the 17th century, *pargana* Kant in *sarkar* Budaun of *suba* Delhi being transferred to *sarkar* Khairabad. But except for this minor adjustment between the limits of *suba* Delhi and Awadh, the territorial limits of the Mughal province of Awadh seem to have remained intact.[36]

Within the *suba* the *sarkars* were subject to change, though the changes were perhaps not many. One change was merely of nomenclature. *Sarkar* Gorakhpur was renamed Mu'azzamabad Gorakhpur after Prince Mu'azzam.[37] The *tappa* of *pargana* Pali was made a full-fledged *pargana* by the name of Shahabad[38].

A number of *parganas* in each of the five *sarkars* went on changing. A list showing such changes is worth giving:

Table 3
The Changing Number of *Mahal* in various *sarkars* of Awadh Province

	Sarkar Awadh	*Sarkar Gorakhpur*	*Sarkar Bahraich*	*Sarkar Khairabad*	*Sarkar Lucknow*	*Period*	*Source*
1.	21	24	11	22	55	1595	*Ain-i-Akbari* vol. II, p. 78
2.	21	31	11	24	55	c. 1656	Add. 6598, ff. 118b-19a
3.	21	35	12	25	56	c. 1720	Add. 6586 f. 96b.
4.	21	34	12	24	57	c. 1721	*Chahar Gulshan* (MS Abdus-Salam) ff. 80b-81a.

Awadh remained a relatively trouble-free province of the Empire throughout the 17th century. But things began to change during the second quarter of the 18th century, when Burhanul Mulk Sa'adat Khan was appointed the governor of the *suba* in 1722. With the general deterioration and slackening of central control, Burhanul Mulk (d. 1739) and later on his two immediate successors Abul Mansūr Safdar jang (1739-56) and Shuja'uddaulah (1756-75) were able to assert their independence from imperial control. However, this was a slow process.

In 1739, Sa'adat Khan joined the imperial forces to face Nadir Shah. Safdarjang and Shuja'uddaulah formally held the office of *wizarat*, and a number of other important posts under the Mughal emperors. The designation of *Nawab-wazir* was applied to them and their successors, at least till 1814, when Ghaziuddin Hyder designated himself King.

Attempts were made by the *Nawab-wazir* to get more and more area included under their jurisdiction. By 1728, their area of influence was pushed further east and south by the inclusion of fertile regions of Benaras, Ghazipur, Jaunpur and Chunargarh.[39] The western borders of Awadh kingdom were extended up to Kannauj by the use of armed power against the hereditary Rajput chiefs.[40] In 1735, Sa'adat Khan in addition to his duties, was invested with the *faujdari* jurisdiction of *sarkar* Kora Jahanabad to crush the activities of the rebel *zamindar* Bhagwant Singh, who was ultimately killed in a closely contested battle.[41]

Emperor Ahmad Shah conferred upon Safdarjang the office of the *wizarat* and assigned him the province of Ajmer in 1748, but the *wazir* exchanged his new assignment with *suba* Allahabad, which was contiguous to the province of Awadh; and he now established a hereditary claim over it.[42] The next important addition to the territorial limits of Awadh was made in 1774, when Shuja'uddaulah with the help of the East India Company annexed Rohilkhand, much of which formally belonged to *suba* Delhi. In addition Etawah was also controlled by him.

From the point of view of the extent, maximum limits were attained by the kingdom under Shuja'uddaulah. It comprised the Mughal province of Awadh, and much of the province of Allahabad (barring, of course, the Bundelkhand region), Rohilkhand and mid - Gangetic Doab including Etawah.[43] This compact region bordered the *Himalyan terai* in the north, the upper course of river Gandhak in the north-east, the river Son to the south, and the Yamuna in the south-west. In 1764-65, Shuja'uddaulah joined the armies of Shah Alam II and Mir Qasim in an unsuccessful attempt to invade Bihar and Bengal. After the defeat at Buxar and then at Jajmau, Shuja'uddaulah was compelled to seek terms. Although he was permitted to continue as a ruler of the Mughal *subas* of Awadh and Allahabad, certain areas (notably Allahabad itself) were transferred to Shah Alam II. The appointment of the English Resident in 1773 and the deployment of various contingents of British forces in the Ruhela war, whereby Shuja'uddaulah was able to annex Rohilkhand, made the kingdom of Oudh one of the first subsidiary-alliance states in India well before Lord Wellesley.

After the death of Shuja'uddaulah, the situation underwent important changes. A new treaty was concluded with his successor Asafuddaulah in 1775. Now the amount of subsidy imposed on Awadh was increased, the *zamindar* of Ghazipur was asked to pay the tribute to the Company in stead of *nawab*, and the entire region of Benaras was ceded to the Company. Later, in default of payment of the subsidies, the fort of Allahabad (which had been earlier retransferred from Shah Alam to Shuja'uddaulah) was annexed by the English.

Asafuddaulah died in 1797, and this provided an opportunity to the Company to conclude a new treaty with his successors, first with Wazir 'Ali and then with Sa'adat Ali Khan (1798-1814). The treaty concluded in 1801, marks the watershed in the history of relations of the Company with Awadh. Under this treaty the broken crescent formed by Rohilkhand, Farrukhabad, Kara, Kora, Etawah, Fatehgarh, Kalpi, Gorakhpur and Azamgarh, yielding an annual revenue of Rs. 1,35,00,000 was ceded by Awadh to the Company.

The limits of Awadh from 1801 onwards down to its annexation (1856) remained more or less fixed. The principality was bounded on the north and north-east by Nepal; on the east by the British district of Gorakhpur; on the south-east by district Allahabad; on the south-west by the Doab including the British districts of Fatehpur, Kanpur, and Farukhabad; and on the north-west by Shahjahanpur. These new limits extended from latitude 29°6 to 25°34, and from longitude 79°45 to 83°. The total area was computed at 23,923 square miles[44].

With the treaty of 1801, Nawab Sa'adat Ali Khan once more felt that he was the ruler of what territories were left under his control. He started with vigour and enthusiasm to streamline the administration and to introduce the new revenue system. The arrangements entailed a reorganisation of the older administrative divisions by dividing Awadh into *nizamats* and *chaklas.*[45] Of the five Mughal *sarkars,* Gorakhpur had been ceded to the Company. *Sarkar* Bahraich was now too small a unit to continue as a separate division, hence Gonda was added to create the Gonda-Bahraich *nizamat*. The limits of the old *sarkar* Awadh, broadly corresponded to the boundaries of the newly created Sultanpur-Fyzabad *nizamat* and *sarkar*, Khairabad was divided into Khairabad *nizamat* and *chakla* Shah Rah comprising of *parganas* Sandeela, Sandee, Palee, Shahabad and Bangarmau. Later on the *chakla* of Shah Rah was placed under the jurisdiction of two *chakledars*, having their headquarters at Sandee and Sandeela. *Sarkar* Lucknow was completely broken up; the Bainswara division was made a separate *nizamat* consisting of a number of *chaklas*, namely, Hydergurh, Rae Bareli, Purwa, Meangunj and Rasoolabad.[46]

The *chaklas* were put under the over all charge of the *chakledar* or *nazim*, while the smaller units were looked after by the *faujdar* and the *diwan*, receiving Rs. 25 and Rs. 15 each respectively as their salaries.[47] While the *chakledars* had no fixed salary, "the difference between the sum, which he has for the year engaged to pay into the public treasury, and the amount, which, with the military power of the state at his command, he can levy from the *zamindars* constituted his official income.[48]

Butter, gives the following list of *chaklas* in Awadh[49].

1. Sultanpur was made up of 6 *parganas*
2. Aldemau had 5 *parganas*
3. Partapgarh had 3 *parganas*
4. Pachhimreth also had 3 *parganas*
5. Bainswars contained the largest number, 13 *parganas*
6. Salon had 4 *parganas*
7. Ahladgunj too had 4 *parganas*
8. Goanda-Bahraich was divided into 5 *parganas*
9. Khairabad again contained the largest number, i.e., 13 *parganas*
10. Sandee also had 4 *parganas*
11. Rasulabad was divided into 5 *parganas*.
12. Lucknow was made up of 5 *parganas*.

However, sometimes during the last days of Awadh regime, the above arrangements, too were changed, and while retaining few previous divisions, new units were created for the purpose of revenue administration. The names of the new administrative divisions have not been provided by our authorities.[50]

References

1. Abul Fazl, *Ain-i Akbari*, ed. Blochmann, Bibliotheca Indica, Calcutta, 1867-77, vol. II, p. 78.
2. *Ibid.*
3. Donald Butter, *Outlines of the Topography and Statistics of the Southern Districts of Oudh, and the Contonment of Sultanpur*, Calcutta, 1839, pp. 10-14.
4. Among the Indian works, only the *Haft Iqlim* seems to refer to forests in Awadh. Cf. Irfan Habib, *An Atlas of the Mughal Empire*, OUP, Delhi, 1982, Sheet No. 8A (notes).
5. Mufti Ghulam Hazrat, *Kwaif-i Zila-i Gorakhpur*, (1810 A.D.), MS, Aligarh SubhanUllah Collection - 954/12, ff. 12a-b.
6. Francis Buchanan, District Reports, (1807-11) edited and abridged by Mantgomery Martin, *The History, Antiquities, Topography, and Statistics of Eastern Indias*, 3 volumes, London, 1838, Indian reprint, 1976, The Survey of Gorakhpur is in Martin's abridgement, vol. II, p. 512.
7. *Ibid.*, 513.
8. Butter, *op. cit.*, p. 5.
9. W.H. Sleeman, *A Journey Through the Kingdom of Oudh during 1849-50*, 2 volumes, London, 1858, volume II, pp. 279-87.
10. *Ibid.*
11. *Ibid.*
12. *Ibid.*
13. *Ibid.*
14. Foreign Secret Consultation Number 136/52 dated 31 August 1856, *National Archives of India*, New Delhi. Cf. A.A. Azmi, "Ta'alluqadars in the kingdom of Awadh, 1814-56". Paper presented at the session of *Indian History Congress*, (Allahabad Session, 1965), but only its summary was published in the proceedings (p. 323). For details, see the cyclostyled paper, Department of History, A.M.U., p.16.
15. Butter, *op. cit.*, pp. 7-8.
16. *Ibid.*, p. 7.
17. *Ibid.*, p. 48.
18. *Agricultural Statistics of British India*, 1885-86, Calcutta.
19. Ghulam Hazrat, *Kwaif-i-Zila-i Gorakhpur*, f. 9a.
20. Martin, *op. cit.*, vol. II, p. 500.
21. *Ibid.*
22. Butter, *op. cit.*, p. 56.

23. Butter, *op. cit.*, p.18.
24. *Ibid.*
25. *Ibid.*, pp. 57-58. The tables contain information about a number of other crops, but entries are provided against the last column only for the crops listed in our table.
26. *Ibid.*, p. 16.
27. Butter, *op. cit.*, p. 9.
28. Albert T.Walker, *Memoirs of the Indian Meteorological Department* (from Records up to 1920), vol. XXIII, pt. VII Calcutta, 1924.
29. Butter, *op. cit.*, p. 16.
30. *Ibid.*, pp. 25-26.
31. *Ibid.*, p. 27.
32. Abul Fazl, *Akbarnamah*, Bibliotheca Indica, Calcutta, 1873-78, vol. III, p. 412.
33. Babur, *Baburnamah*, English translation by A.S. Beveridge, London, 1921, vol. II, p. 521.
34. Charles Alfered Elliott, *Chronicles of Oonao*, Allahabad, 1862, p. 149 and notes.
35. Abul Fazl, *Ain-i Akbari*, vol. II, pp. 78-80.
36. See Add. 6586, f. 95a.
37. *Tappa* Shahabad included in *pargana* Pali was assigned to Diler Khan Afghan in his *al-tamgha jagir* by Emperor Aurangzeb in 1662 (the text of the *farman* has been reproduced by Muzaffar Husain Khan, *Nama-i Muzaffari*, 2 vols, Mujtabai Press, Kanpur, 1917 (vol. I, pp. 174-79), but in 1686, as we find in a *sanad*, Shahabad has been styled a separate *pargana*. *Ibid.* I, p. 266. See also Add. 6586, f. 95a.
38. Add. 6586, f. 94a.
39. Essentially these areas lay in the *jagir* of one Murtaza Khan, who had leased them out to the *nawab* for a payment of Rs. 7 lakhs per annum. A.L. Srivastava, *The First Two Nawabs of Oudh*, Lucknow, 1933, pp. 44-45
40. *Ibid.*, p. 46.
41. *Ibid.*, pp. 49-51.
42. *Ibid.*, pp. 128, 260.
43. A.L. Srivastava, *Shuja'uddaulah*, vol. II, Lahore, 1945, pp. 312-3.
44. Butter, *op. cit.*, p.1; Masihuddin Ahmad, *Oude: Its Princes and its Government Vindicated*, London 1857; reprinted as *British Aggression in Awadh* by Safi Ahmad, Meerut, 1969, p. 22; Walter Hamilton, *East India Gazetteer of Hindoostan and Adjacent Countries*, London, 1828, vol. I, pp. 348-49.

45. Butter, *op. cit.*, pp. 97-99: C.A. Elliott says that in Oude four large districts, Bahraich, Khairabad, Sultanpur and Bainswara, were called *nizamat*, while the smaller ones like Dareeabad, Sandi, Sandila, Meanganj and Rosulabad were called *chaklas*. *op. cit.*, p. 131(n).

46. C.A. Elliott, *op. cit.*, pp. 131-32.

47. Butter, *op. cit.*, p. 99.

48. *Ibid.*

49. *Ibid.*, pp. 97-98.

50. "The fiscal divisions (in Awadh) are arbitrary. Mr. Mad Lock in 1831 shewad 24, Dr. Butter in 1837 twelve; we have before us a list of 25 large and small districts, obtaining during the present year". 'The Kingdom of Oudh' *Calcutta Review*, 1845 (part III), (pp. 386-87).

A Sketch map showing the major administrative divisions of Awadh circa 1850

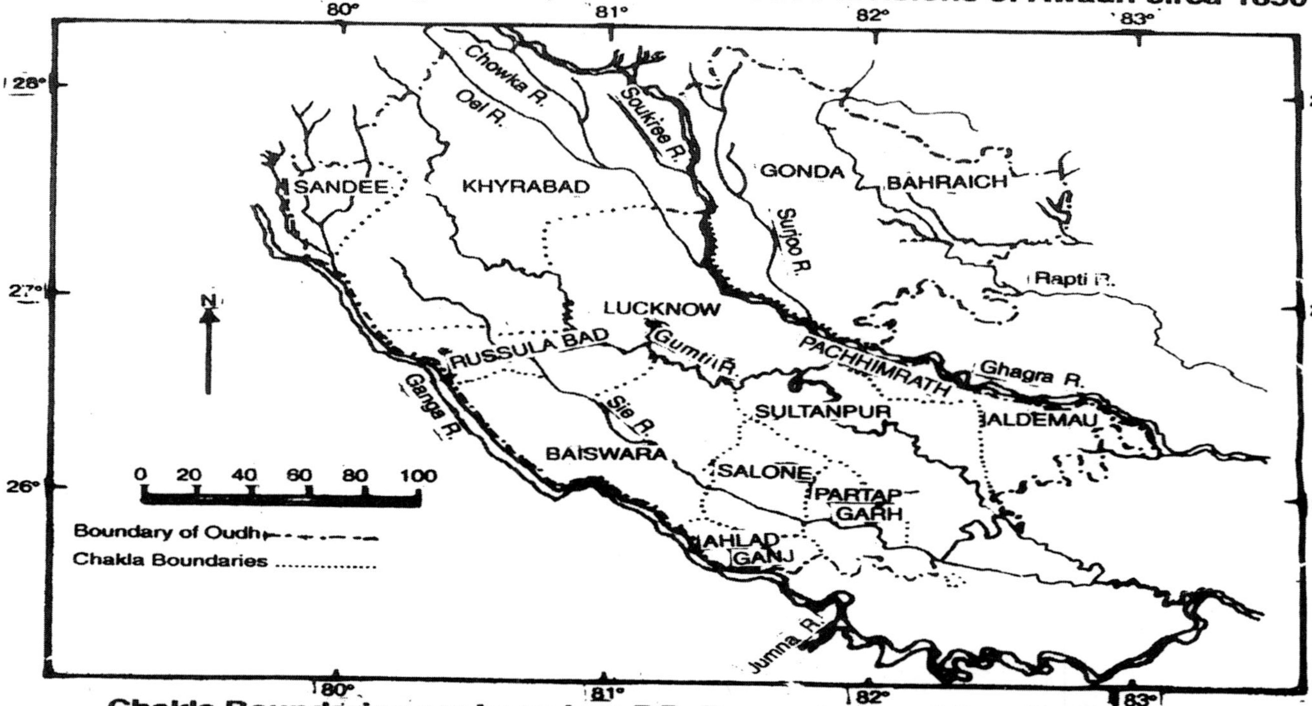

Chakla Boundaries are based on P.D. Reeves' map of Awadh, ibid. P. 303

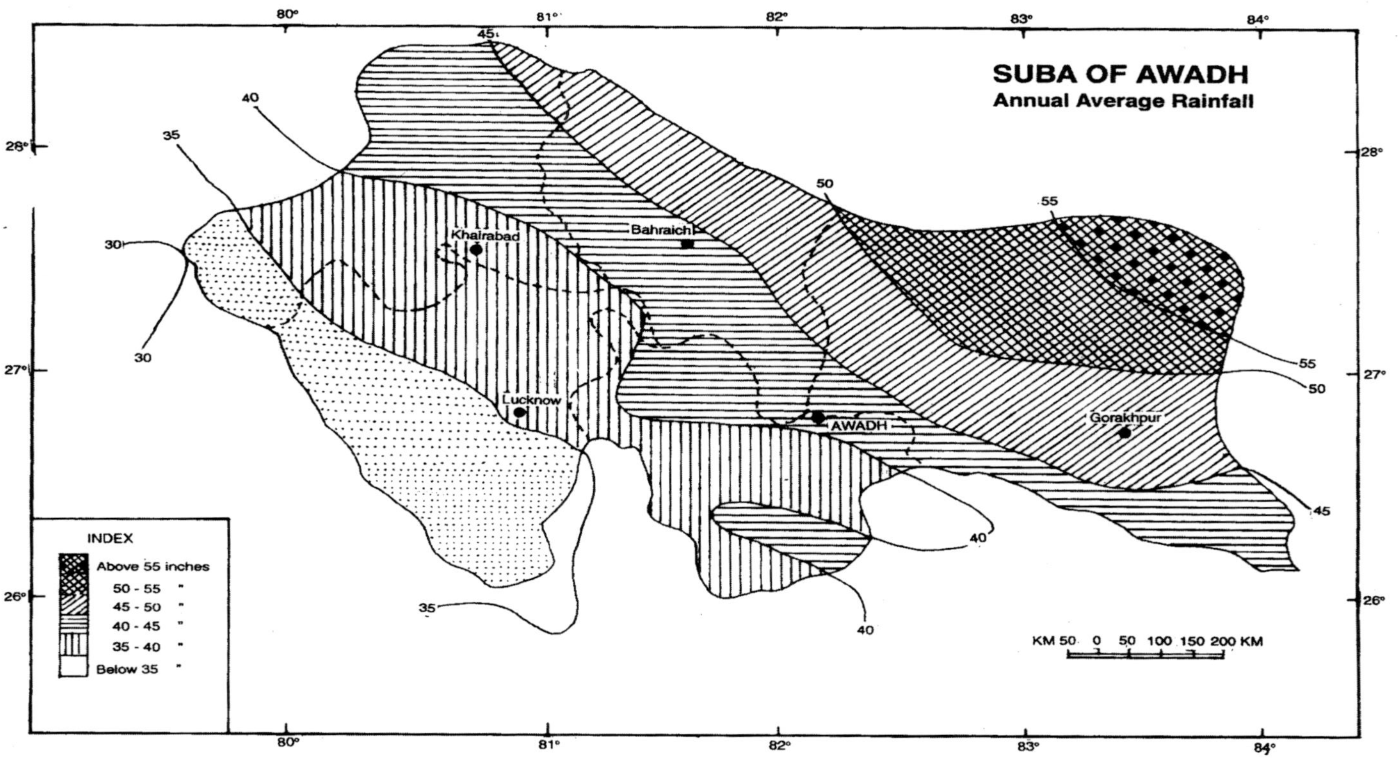
SUBA OF AWADH
Annual Average Rainfall
Khairabad
Bahraich
Lucknow
AWADH
Gorakhpur
INDEX
Above 55 inches
50 - 55 "
45 - 50 "
40 - 45 "
35 - 40 "
Below 35 "
KM 50 0 50 100 150 200 KM

MUGHAL AWADH

2

Administration of the *Jagirs* in Awadh during the 17th Century

If we examine the surviving documents from Awadh during the 17th century we would find that those relating to the *jagir* administration are very rare, while papers relating to the *madad-i-ma'āsh* grants and even the *zamindari* rights are quite numerous. This is obviously because the families that have preserved documents have been more concerned for maintaining their claims of the *ma'afi* and *zamindari* titles, while the *jagir* papers were of no interest from such motives, unless, of course, they are related to *inam* or *altamgha jagir.*[1] Nevertheless explorations at the Regional Records Office (Allahabad), Research Library of the Department of History (AMU) and National Archives of India (New Delhi), resulted in the discovery of a certain number of papers, which, studied together, help to give some picture of the *jagir* administrations as it functioned in Awadh during the 17th century.

A *jagirdar* receiving his assignment in an area would invariably be an outsider. The documents show that a *jagirdar* would either appoint his own agents to collect the taxes on his behalf or farm out the taxes of his *jagir* with a view to assuring stable revenue receipts. When the *jagirdar* made their own arrangements by appointing some agents, they used to take the latter's a *qubuliyat* (agreement) to collect certain amounts. Such deeds were executed keeping in view the *hasil* (previous revenue collection) figures of the *jagir.* The cost of the collection and other obligations of the *jagirdar* were always deducted from the amounts agreed to be paid by these agents. We possess an actual specimen in the form of *qubuliyat* deed executed in 1116F/1708 by one Dilawar for a *jagir* in *pargana* Sandila, having a *jama* of 41 lakh *dam*. In all, excluding the cost of maintaining the *sehbandi* troops and *peshkash* to *faujdar*, Rs. 22001 were to be paid to the *jagirdar* in two instalments.[2]

The *amils* generally belonged to the *jagirdar's* own staff, and were like their masters usually outsiders. One recalls that Charles Elliott on the basis of his own reading of documents relating to the Unnao district, gained the impression that the *amils* "were hardly ever natives of the *pargana*, and did not necessarily hold the office for more than a year."[3] The *amil* had to maintain an armed contingent for quelling any minor resistance to his authority, and in case he met stiffer opposition, he could call the *faujdar* for his help.[4] Very often the big *jagirdars* were also entrusted with the *faujdari* jurisdictions in their respective *jagirs*. The payments to the *amil* was done their by allowing him a certain percentage of the revenue-collection, or he received a fixed salary.[5]

The assistance of hereditary local officials such as the *qanungo* and the *chaudhari* was indispensable for the *amil* of the *jagirdars*. They used to present the previous year's assessments, which were accepted in toto, but in case the *amil* asked for a higher assessment, the revision of the previous figures was also done by these officials. Similarly, they helped the *amil* in collecting the outstanding balances from the peasants as per their records, against which there were no appeals.[6]

From early documents (c.1619 A.D.) from *sarkar* Bahraich, it appears that some *jagirdars* used to assign village of their *tankhwah jagir* to their troopers directly. If in such a village some areas had been already granted to the *madad-i-ma'āsh* holders, the troopers were directed not to interfere with such possessions.[7]

The small *jagirdars,* or those having their postings in a far-off area, always tried to farm out their *jagir*. Certain conditions were imposed upon these revenue contractors or *ijaradar*. There are actual instances where they were asked to treat the *ri'aya* (peasants) gently so that they might remain settled and carry on cultivation. It was thought to be the duty of the *ijaradar* to see that even "one *biswa* of cultivable land should not be left uncultivated".[8] It appears from the claim by a *patwari* (village accountant) that hereditary officials serving in the *ijara* villages were paid their salaries by the revenue farmers.[9] The system of *ijara* had become so popular during this period that even the *a'immadar* or the holders of the *madad-i-ma'āsh* grants started this system of the revenue realisation in their villages.[10] The *ijaradar* had no salary or land grant in view of the services performed by him; but, as Butter puts it, "the difference between the sum, which he has for the year engaged to pay into the public treasury" constituted his official income.[11] In case of natural calamities, the *ijaradar* could be provided some relief by being allowed a deduction, and by the *jagirdar* not insisting upon the full amount for which the contract was held.[12]

The terms on which *ijara* of a *jagir* was given are set out in a document of 1081 F. (1673 AD):[13]

"Agreement (*Qaul-o-qarar*): I, Mir Abu Turab, *mansabdar*, affirm that (tract carrying a *jama-i-dami* of) 2,100,000 *dam* from *pargana* Hisampur, *sarkar* Bahraich had been assigned in our *jagir* with effect from the beginning of the *kharif*, Udi il, 1081 '*amali*. Therefore, at my own will, I have given the said (territorial) assignment of *dams* in *ijara* (farm) to Mir Saiyid Muhammad 'Arif in fixed payment of Rs. 2,850 to continue so long as the *jagir* is retained by me, so that he may pay the said amount to me annually according to the following particulars. Should, God forbid, a natural calamity happen, then according to the (official) rate (of remission) for the said *pargana*, I will allow a deduction in the said amount. But, if, by God's grace, more is realized in excess of the said amount, that is left to the said Saiyid." The following figures follow :

(*Jama*)	
Comprising original	2,10,000 *dam*
enhancement	2,00,000 *dam*
Equivalent, for the year	10,000 *dam*
at 7 months, 7 days	Rs. 3,162
Deduct on account of *nankar* (salary of officials), *muqaddam's* pay, (illegible)	Rs. 312
(Balance)	Rs. 2,850

From this document, it is clear that the *ijaradar* pledged himself to pay a certain amount annually to the *jagirdar* — in this case, a fixed proportion of the *jamadami* (7 months, 7 days in the month-scalè). From this he was allowed a fixed deduction for payment to local officials, etc. This explains the claim of the *patwari* on the *jagirdar*.

The *jagirdar* allowed him the profits of the enterprise, as Butter defines them; but the *ijaradar* could claim a reduction of account of officially sanctioned tax-remissions for the locality.

While the *jagirdar* had to make arrangements locally to collect the revenue either directly or through contractors, he had to meet certain obligations to the government. For this purpose the more substantial *jagirdar*, at any rate, used to keep a *wakil* permanently at the imperial court to safeguard his interests and to receive the orders on his behalf. Two very interesting papers concerning a dispute between a *jagirdar* and his *wakil* have survived which shed light on this part of the functioning of the *jagirdar's* establishment. The two documents are translated in Appendix to this study.

One major obligation on the part of the *jagirdar* was the maintenance of a number of animals of standard breed for the imperial stables, providing the cost of feeding them as per schedules and furnishing a number of other supplies under the general name of *khwurak-i dawabb.*[11] It appears that the amount required for the purpose was sent by the *jagirdar* to his *wakil*. The *wakil*, in return paid the required money to the *ijaradars* (farmers) of the *Khwuark-Dawabb*, met the expenses for maintaining the animals (horses as well as elephants) and when the time for maintaining the animals was over, handed them over to the officials of the Imperial stables.

In addition to these duties, the *wakil* was called upon to look after the interests of his master at the court such as getting him a better *jagir*. In the present case the *wakil* was allowed the sum of Rs.300 by the *jagirdar* to be spent on the business (*muhimsazi*) of getting a new *jagir* assigned in *pargana* Amethi.

The accounts submitted by the *wakil* in connection with these expenses were subjected to rigorous scrutiny. He had to present all the original receipts under the seals of the *ijaradars* of *khwurak-i-dawabb* and the *mutasaddis* of *dawabb*, at the time of the audit by the *jagirdar's* officials.

In case of any dispute between the *wakil* and the *jagirdar* regarding the settlement of these accounts, the matter was apparently placed before some Imperial officials. Unfortunately, the exact designation of this officials is not given in our documents; he might well have been *diwan* or *faujdar*.

The present study does not pretend to give a comprehensive account of *jagir* administration in Awadh. Such an account, given the [illegible] of our documentary evidence, is perhaps not possible at the present moment. But the above information culled from various documents suggests that enough exists for us to start building a picture of how the *jagir* system as it operated in real life.

APPENDIX

(i) Allahabad-896

I, Buland Khan, *mansabdar* in the *biradari* (clan) of His Highness Diwan Khudadad Khan Jiv affirm as follows: Saiyid Muhammad 'Arif held the office of *wakil* at the Imperial Court on behalf of the said Khan. After the termination of his appointment as *wakil* the said Saiyid handed over the *tahihanama* (certificates of contingents) and other documents and papers of *jama-kharch* (income-expenditure) of the *khwurak-i dawabb* to Miyan Muhammad Yusuf, son of the said Khan. As a dispute ensued, the matter was taken up before Faulad Khan. On this account Saiyid 'Arif presented the receipt *(qabz)* of the farmer *ijaradar* of *khwurak-i-dawabb* and *dastaks* (certificates) under the seals of the officials *(mutasaddi)* of the imperial horse stables and elephant stables and other papers, to the agent of Faulad Khan and Ghasi Ram, the (new) *wakil* of Khudadad Khan. However, the case before Faulad Khan not having yet been settled, Diwan Khudadad Khan Jiv and Miyan Muhammad Yusuf maintained their dispute with the said Sayyid. Now that Miyan Muhammad Yusuf came to the town of Biswa, I took Saiyid 'Arif along to the town of Biswa. Muhammad Yusuf told Saiyid Muhammad 'Arif; "Previous to this you had given in writing a *tamassuk* (bond) for Rs. 3000/- for the expenses of *badarnavisi* (audit) from the beginning of your term as *wakil* to termination of appointment." Saiyid Muhammad 'Arif replied that *badarnavisi* has not been in accordance with proper norms *(be-hisab)*. Miyan Muhammad Yusuf told Saiyid Muhammad 'Arif : "The *jama-kharch* of *Khwurak-i-dawabb*, etc., of the period of your wakilship have been lost." Now he should submit copies afresh so that the account of his period as *wakil* might be settled. Saiyed Muhammad 'Arif produced copies of the *jama-kharch* of *Khwurak-i-dawabb* etc together with receipt *(qubuliyat)* of the farmer of *khwurak-i-dawabb* before Miyan Muhammad Yusuf, Ghasi Ram, Diwan of Khudadad Khan, Shaikh Habib-Ullah the *darogah* of the Court of Justice. Miyan Muhammad Yusuf allowed deductions *(mujra)* of Rs. 200 which the said Saiyid had paid to Miyan Muhammad Yusuf in *rew*[illegible] and also Rs. 565 that Shyam Das, *shiqqdar* of *pargana* [illegible] had forcibly realised from the village Bedaura of the property and *zamindar* possessions of the said Saiyid in excess of the *jama*, and had recorded under receipts *(wasul)*. Finally, after disallowing *bazyaft* the expenditure of Rs. 200 on account of Muhammad Khan, *mansabdar* and not writing off the expenditure of Rs. 300 on account of expenses for assignment of *pargana* Amethi, in all Rs. 1,480, annas 5, came out as the balance due to the said Khan, (itemised) as follows :

1. The sum the said Saiyid asked Udai Singh, banker (*sahu*) of Shahjahanabad, to pay to Muhammad Khan *mansabdar*, and entered as deduction in his accounts of *jama-kharch* not allowed by Muhammad Yusuf, and required to be refunded. — Rs. 200
2. The sum Diwan Khudad Khan Jiv had got paid to the said Saiyid for arranging the assignment of *pargana* Amethi, and the said Sayyid truthfully admitted that, without spending the sum, he had drawn the amount from the *jagir* and entered in the *jama* and *kharch* register; he sought condonation, but Miyan Muhammad Yusuf refused to condone it. — Rs. 300
3. The balance (*tattima*) in the accounts of the *jama* and *kharch* — Rs. 980 annas 5

(ii) Allahabad — 1232

Memorandum :

List of receipts of the *ijaradar* of *Khwurak-i-dawabb* and other papers which were given by Saiyid Muhammad 'Arif to the undersigned Ghasi Ram. 38 sheets received by the signatory, Ghasi Ram (seal).

Receipts (*qubuz-ul-wusul*) for Rs. 3128/- 11 annas under the seal and signature of Shaikh Firoz *ijaradar* of *Khwurak-i-dawabb* of the imperial establishment *khassa-i sharifa*, Rs. 3128/- 11 annas; 28 sheets. *Dastaks* under the seal of official of the *dawabb*, 6 sheets.

(i) For handing over 10 horses under the seal of Darab Khan, etc., one sheet.

(ii) For handing over one imperial elephant under the seal of Abdur Rahim Khan, one sheet.

(iii) For medicines for imperial elephants, one sheet.

(iv) For medicines for horses, one sheet.

(v) For the straw shed for the stable of horses, one sheet.

(vi) Repairs of the tiled roof for horses, one sheet.

The certificates for monthly payments to Shaikh Firoz, *ijaradar* one sheet. *Qabazul wusul* for Rs. 227/- received by the signatory, Ghasi Ram, according to accounts, one sheet.

Qabuzul wusul for 8 *asharfis* under the seal of officials of the office for fines on account of absence, one sheet.

Certificate (for receipt) of interest under the seal of the security *(malzamin)* of Miyan Khudadad Khan Jiv, Rs. 1900/-, one sheet.

References

1. A number of original documents relating to the *in'am-al-tamgha* grant of Diler Khan in *pargana* Shahabad have been reproduced extensively by Muzzaffar Hussain Khan in *Nama-i-Muzzaffari,* Lucknow, 1917.
2. Sec NAI-1487 (1116J/1708). This *qubuliyat* was executed in the presence of village official Jangash Das, *amin, shiqdar* and *mehta,* Kishan Das *waqai 'nigar,* Tilak Chandra, *karkun* and the *mutasaddi* of the Government. The instalments were not equal Rs. 13,200 were to be paid in *kharif* and Rs. 8,800 in *rabi* seasons.
3. C.A. Elliott, *The Chronicles of Oonao,* 1862, pp. 106-7.
4. *Ibid.*, p. 109.
5. *Ibid.*, pp. 106-7.
6. *Ibid.*, pp. 112-13.
7. *Allahabad-789.* The village Kapana was in *tankhwāh jagir* of Mirza 'Isa and he had assigned this village to four of his troopers. A *madad-i-ma'āsh* grant made over to a lady by imperial *farman* was to be exempted from their collections.
8. NAI-1574 (37th RY of Aurangzeb). This *qaul-o-qarar* relates to village Somb in *pargana* Sandila, *suba* Awadh in the *jagir* of prince. 'Azimuddin ('Azimushshan) at a total *jama'* of Rs. 445/- for the year 1101F/1693. The *qubuliyat* was given by Muhammad Qa'im, the *gumashta.* The total *arazi* (area) of the village was 445 *bighas.*

9. NAI-1287 (1254/1838). This *parwana* was issued to the *chakledār* of Sandila to enquire into the complaint of a village *patwari* regarding his pay claims against the *mustajir*.
10. *Firangi Mahal*-84 *(*4th RY of Farrukhsiyar*)*. The village in question belonged to Mulla Nizamuddin and was situated in *sarkar* Bahraich, while the grantee's residence happened to be at Lucknow. (This collection of *Firangi Mahal* documents is preserved in the Department of History, A.M.U., Aligarh.)
11. Donald Butter, *Topography and Statistics of the Southern District of Awadh and Sultanpur*, p. 99.
12. A *jagir* having a total *jama* 'of 4,40,000 *dams* belonged to Durvesh Beg *mansabdar* and others. It was situated in *pargana* Hisampur and Saiyid 'Arif held it on a *ijara* tenure. He had agreed to pay Rs. 7,332/- in two equal instalments. See Allahabad-885 (*1080 amali*). But the perusal of the receipt issued by the *jagirdars* to Saiyid 'Arif for the same year shows that he paid only Rs. 4000/- (1,60,000 dams). He was also exempted from any further obligation of any subsequent payment for the year, see Allahabad-889 (1080 'amali).
13. *Allahabad-884 (1081F/1675).*
14. For a discussion of these obligations, see; Irfan Habib, *The Agrarian System of Mughal India*, Bombay, 1963, p. 269 and M. Athar Ali, *The Mughal Nobility under Aurangzeb*, Bomabay, 1966, pp. 50-53.
15. The meaning of this terms could not be traced.

3

Madad-i-Ma'āsh : *Farmans* of Aurangzeb from Awadh

There exist two early copies of *farmans* issued under the seal of Emperor Aurangzeb conferring *madad-i ma'āsh* grants upon a religious divine of *pargana* Salon and his son. The earlier one was issued to Shaikh Pir Muhammad in the 19th R.Y./AH 1086 (A.D. 1676), while the other was issued to his son, Shaikh Muhammad Ashraf in the 22nd R.Y./A.H. 1090 (A.D 1679). I give annotated translations of these *farmans* in Appendices A and B.[1] The second of these *farmans* has certain uncommon features, which demand some attention. The documents also help us to understand the procedure followed in issuing such grants by the Mughal administration.

The first *farman* (translation in Appendix A) which was issued to Shaikh Pir Muhammad in A.H. 1086 (A.D. 1676) conforms to the routine text of such *farmans*. It has more or less followed the general form, which was set-out by the Mughal chancery for making such grants. However, there are two points which appear significant. First, this grant was not situated in an *a'imma* village (in the Mughal period grants were often concentrated in villages so styled),[2] but in *jagir* territory. The previous *hukkam* (officers, presumably *jagirdars*) of the village Mirza Bakhtiyarpur had already offered 200 *bigha* of land to the grantee and the imperial *farman* was issued really to confirm the grants, so that the grantee might not be harassed by any future *jagirdar* or any of his officials.[3] Secondly, the words, "an offering to the servants of one knowing divine truths" *(nazr-i-khadiman-haqaiqom 'ārif agah)* in the main the *farman* as well a *zimn*, show that the grantee was regarded as a mystic and hence considered deserving of the grant.[4]

The second *farman* issued to Shaikh Muhammad Ashraf in the 22nd R.Y. (A.D. 1679), is very important in many ways. First of all, unlike the usual *farman* conferring *madad-i-ma'ash* grants, it states the *jama* (estimated revenue) and not the area of the grant; it confers and entire village in grant.[5] The *zimn* furthermore gives the *hasil* (revenue realization) figure from the 4th to the 17th regnal year. This too is unusual.[6] The *zimn* to the *farman* also contains the statement that the grantee had previously settled in the village with the consent (*ba-razamandi*) of the *zamindars*.[7] This seems to imply that the *zamindars* had been unable to meet the revenue demand and so transferred their rights to Shaikh Muhammad Ashraf, who now sought tax-exemption from the authorities by way of *madad-i-ma'ash*. The village had been nearly abandoned, and its revenue-paying capacity greatly reduced, as figures which appear on the *zimn* on the *farman* show.

A—The total *jama* (estimated-revenue) of the village Singhwal in ientirety was 32100 *dams* (= Rs. 802.5)

B—Actual realisation *(hasil)*

Year	*Hasil in Rs.*
4th year	50.00
5th year	31.00
6th to 9th year.	91.00
10th year	21.00
11th year	26.00
12th year to 16th years	66.00
17th year	61.00

The fact that here the grantee was also now the *zamindar* of the area, might explain yet another feature of the grant, viz., its assignment to the grantee in absolute perpetuity, "generation after generation, and for all time to come".[9] This is interesting since it was only in 34th RY/A.D. 1690 that Emperor Aurangzeb made the *madad-i-ma'ash* hereditary by issuing a general *farman*,[10] whereas our *farman* was issued much before this measure, in A.D. 1679.

The beneficiaries of these grants were the founders of a family of mystics established at Salon (District Rae Bareli,Uttar Pradesh). The tomb of Shaikh Pir Muhammad still exists at Salon. The village Mirzapur Bakhtiyarpur in which he was given 200 *bighas* in 1676 cannot be traced, but Nasirabad, the headquarters of the *pargana* in which it lay, is about 14 miles from Salon. The tomb stone gives the date of his death as A.H. 1099/A.D. 1687[11] Shaikh Pir Muhammad must have thus been alive when his son Shaikh Muhammad Ashraf received the grant of village Singhwal renamed Ashrafabad. According to the chronogram on his tombstone he died in AH 1167/A.D. 1754[12] and a tradition recorded in H.R. Nevill's *Gazetteer* states that he was ninety years at the time of his death.[13] It follows that he was born in AH 1077/A.D. 1666-67. At the time of the grant Muhammad Ashraf then would been about 13 years of age. Probably he was named a beneficiary in the grant in lieu of his father, who already held a grant as a mystic. Shaikh Muhammad Ashraf's young age explains why no spiritual title is put before his name, contrasting with the respectful address used for his father.[14]

The village of Singhwal Ashrafabad (now called Ashrafganj Singhwal) is situated about 14 miles from Salon. Till the abolition of *zamindari* the family of Shaikh Muhammad Ashraf continued to enjoy *zamindari* as well as *ma'afi* rights over it, exercised through a scheme of administration drawn up by Mr. Fremantle, the Settlement Officer in 1896.[15]

The person who made copies of these *farman* seems to have been familiar with the styles in which official endorsements were put on the *farman*. Such endorsements are very difficult to decipher, and we are thus beholden to the copyist for presenting us with deciphered readings, which enable us to reconstruct the procedure followed in issuing the grants. Ibn Hasan has provided us with some details of the procedure to the point that the final draft of such *madad-i m'āsh farman* was made.[16] However the text of the *zimn* of our two *farmans* together with the endorsements shed much additional light on the procedure followed by the Mughal court and secretariat.

The *zimn* in the first *farman* shows that the procedure in preparing and issuing the *farman* was as follows: First of all an official (in this case, the governor of Allahabad, Himmat Khan)[17] made his recommendation for the grant. This recommendation was presented in written form *(risala)* by the *sadr*, Rizvi Khan[18] to the Emperor during the time of posting of the *waqia-nawis* Inayatullah,[19] on 5th Rajab 18th R.Y./25th Sept. A.D. 1675 when the Emperor signified his approval. In accordance with the *tasdiq* (or confirmed record of proceedings) the *yaddasht of waqi'a* (memorandum of proceedings) was prepared on 14th Rajab 18th R.Y/4th Oct. A.D. 1675. Thereupon the draft of the memorandum was sent to the *wazir (diwan-i-a'la)* Asad Khan[20] and then to the *sadr* Rizvi Khan and both of them verified it, ordering that it should be entered in the record of court proceedings *(waqi'a)*. The *waqia-nawis* then certified that the memorandum was same as the record of the proceedings *(waqi'a)*. The paper then again was sent to the *wazir*, who ordered that it be submitted a second time *(arz-i mukarrar)* for the Emperor's approval. This was done on 11th Ramazam, 19th R.Y./(29th Nov. A.D. 1675) as certified by the official in charge of *arz-i mukarrar*, Shaikh Abdul 'Aziz.[21] The memorandum now went to the *wazir* whose deputy Bahramand Khan[22] ordered that the *farman* be duly written. All this text along with some other details was first written out in *shikasta* hand on the back *(zimn)* of the paper that was to bear the *farman* on the front. The *farman* was then written out by the scribe in formal *nasta'liq* (with the stylised *tughra* written on top and Imperial seal affixed) on 5th *Shawwal* 19th R.Y./23rd Dec., A.D. 1675).

The *farman* was now sent to various offices again for verification and record before being handed over to the grantee. It was copied down at the *diwan-i sadarat* (the *sadr's* secretariat) on 12th Ziqad 19th R.Y./28th Jan., A.D. 1676, at the office of *a'imma* (land grants) on 9th Zilhij 18th R.Y./24th Feb., A.D. 1676, both offices entering their endorsements on the *zimn*. The *farman* was sent to the office of *taujih*[23] twice on 7th *Zilhij* and 9th *Zilhij* 19th R.Y. respectively. An interesting point is that the name of Khan Muhammad is mentioned in seven endorsements as the person presenting the *farman* at the endorsing offices. Was he the *wakil* (agent) of the grantee or an official ?[24]

From the second *farman* too it appears from the *zimn* that the same procedure for preparing and issuing the *farman* was followed. Here in this case first of all the *waqi'a-nigar* of *suba* of Allahabad, Mir Muhammad Raza Karvi conveyed to the Imperial court that the grantee has settled with the consent of the *zamindar* in the village Singhwal. The provincial *sadr (sadr-i juzv)* Saiyid 'Abdul' Rahim[25] also sent his recommendation and the reports were presented in written form by the *sadr* Rizvi Khan, to the Emperor during the time of attendance of *waqi'a-nawis* Daulatmand on 26th Ziqad 22nd R.Y./ 29th Dec. A.D. 1679, when the Emperor gave his approval. In accordance with the *tasdiq* (confirmed by the records of proceedings) the *yaddasht* of *waqia* was prepared on 21st Rabiul Awwal 22nd R.Y./ 21st April A.D. 1680. Thereupon the draft memorandum was sent to the *wazir* Asad Khan and then to the *sadr* Rizvi Khan for their verification and it was verified by them and ordered that it should be entered in the record of the court proceedings *(waqi'a)*. After being verified by the *waqi'a-nawis,* the *wazir* ordered that it should be submitted a second time *(ba arzi-mukarrar)* for the Emperor's approval. This was done on 12th Rabius Sani 22nd R.Y./12th May A.D. 1680 as certified by the official incharge of *arzi-mukarrar,* Lutfullah Khan,[26] whereafter it reached the *wazir* Asad Khan, who ordered that the *farman* be duly written. Here too in the *zimn* all this text along with other details was first written out in *shikasta* hand on the back of the paper, which was to bear the *farman* in *nasta'liq* hand on the front. The *farman* itself was written out by the copyist on 18th *Jamadul Awwal* 22nd R.Y./16th June A.D. 1680.

The *farman* thereafter was sent to various offices for verification. But unfortunately it is not possible to decipher these endorsements as they are much torn. However, the number of these endorsements is the same as in the earlier one. So it may be presumed that it went through the same channels before being handed over to the grantee.

The above-mentioned procedure goes to suggest that every possible precaution was taken before the passing of the order by the Emperor and later, for ensuring that the *farman* issued was in actual conformity with what was recorded so as to guard against fraud at any stage. It was undoubtedly a long procedure and in the case of these particular grants it took about 4 to 6 months' time before the *farman* could reach the grantee.

APPENDIX 'A'

In the name of the God, the beneficent, the merciful

(TUGHRA)

Copy of the square seal Abul Muzzaffar Muhi-uddin Muhammad 'Alamgir Padshah Ghazi, A.H. 1083. The names of his ancestors beginning with Timur *sahib-i qiran* in circle.

Whereas it had been submitted to the exalted court, that according to the deeds *(asnād)* issued by the officials *(hukkām)* 200 bighas of land from the village Mirza Bakhtiyarpur, *pargana* Nasirabad *sarkar* Manikpur, *suba* Allahabad had been made over by way of offering to the mystic Shaikh Pir Muhammad, resident of *pargana* Salon, and he is in occupation and control of the land above mentioned and entertains the hope that in this regard an Imperial *farman* may be issued; therefore the world-subduing order is issued that the aforesaid land at the old site, as per previous practice and upon conditions of (the grantee's) actual occupation and control, be given over to him in *madad-i ma'āsh* in accordance with the particulars on the back *(zimn)* so that he may, appropriating the revenues thereof for his own needs engage himself in praying for the long life of this ever more prosperous Empire—the present and future officials, revenue collectors, *jagirdars* and *karoris* should leave the land aforesaid in his hands and should never allow any transfer or aiterations herein and not harass (the grantee) on account of the land-revenue *(mal),* other taxes (*jihat*) and other ceses such as *qanungha, peshkash, jaribana, zabitana, muhsilana mahrana, daroghana, begar, shikar, muqqadami, qanungi* and *zabt-i harsala,*[27] or insistence upon cultivation, and all fiscal impositions and government dues whatsoever. They shall not demand a confirmatory order every year and if at some other place he (the grantee) has any thing (i.e. land grants), it should not be taken into account (to reduce the present grant). Written on the 5th Shawwal, 19th Regnal year.

Zimn

Copy of (court) proceedings, dated thursday 14th Rajab, 18th R.Y. Corresponding to A.H. 1086 (A.D. 1676-77) corresponding to Ilahi month, written upon the note *(risala)* of the honoured Saiyid (titles omitted), the highly elevated *sadr,* Rizvi Khan, during the posting as recorder *(waqi'a nawis),* Inayatullah, to wit; upon the recommendation of the governor (titles omitted), Himmat Khan, it has been conveyed to the exalted court that according to the deeds *(asnad)* issued by the *hukkam* (officials, or *jagirdars),* 200 bighas of land from the village Mirza Bakhtyarpur, *pargana* Nasirabad, *sarkar* Manikpur, *suba* Allahabad, has been made over as offering to the mystic Shaikh Pir Muhammad, resident of *pargana* of Salon, and he entertains the hope that in this regard an Imperial *farman* may be issued; therefore the world-subduing order was issued that we confer the aforesaid land at the old site as per previous practice and upon the condition of (the grantee's) occupation and control thereof for their *mada-i imad-'sh* and if at some other place he (the grantee) has anything (i.e. land-grants), it should not be taken into account. *Waqia* dated 5th Rajab 18th R.Y. Transcribed according to the verification of the memorandum.

Copy of the endorsement of the great minister (titles omitted) Asad Khan; "Enter in record of proceedings."

Copy of endorsement by the Saiyied (titles omitted), the elevated *sadr* Rizvi Khan : Enter in record of proceedings. Copy of endorsement by the Waqi'a Nawis : "True copy of proceedings".

Copy of endorsement of the great minister (titles omitted) (Asad Khan) : "Let it be submitted for the second presentation".

Copy of the note of the scholarly (titles omitted) Shaikh 'Abdul Aziz: "submitted for second presentation 11th Ramzan, 19th R.Y."

Copy of endorsement of (titles omitted) Bahramand Khan acting as deputy of the commander Jumdat-ul Mulk *(Mir Bakhshi,)*: "Let the Imperial *farman* be prepared."

"200 *bighas* of land old site be conferred as per previous practice."

Endorsements

1. The *farman* is written down according to the memorandum of the court proceedings.
2. Written down through the agency of Khan Muhammad.
3. Copied down in the office of *diwan-e-sadarat* through the agency of Khan Muhammad, dated 12th *Ziqa'da* 19th R.Y.
4. Verified the court proceedings on 14th *Ziqa'da* 19th R.Y. and compared with the entries of the diary dated 14th Rajab.
5. Entered in the *awarija* .
6. Copied down in the office of *a'imma* through the agency of Khan Muhammad dated 9th Zilhij 19th R.Y./A.H. 1086.
7. The copy of the Imperial order was sent to the office of *taujih* for details through the agency of Khan Muhammad on 9th *Zilhij* 19th R.Y.
8. Copy of the Imperial order was sent to the office of the *sahib taujih..........Ziqad* 19th R.Y./A.H. 1086/2nd of the Bahman Ilahi month.
9. Entered in the office of the........dated 27th *Zilhij* 19th R.Y./ A.H. 1086.

APPENDIX 'B'

In the name of the God, the beneficent, the merciful

(TUGHRA)

Copy of the square seal Abul Muzzaffar Muhiuddin Muhammad 'Alamgir Padshah Ghazi A.H. 1080. Also all the names of his ancestors beginning from Timur *sahib-i-qiran* in circle.

Copy of the exalted *farman* demanding obedience, bearing the seal of Abul Muzzaffar Muhiuddin Hazrat 'Alamgir Padshah Ghazi addressed to Shah Pir Muhammad Ashraf Saloni.

Wheras, at this time the exalted *farman* has been issued that the village of Singhwal in entirety, in the *pargana* of Salon within *sarkar* of Manikpur, of *suba* Allahabad, which has a *jama* of 32,100 *dams,* should be assigned to Shaikh Muhammad Ashraf, son of Shaikh Pir Muhammad, according to the *zimn,* from the half of Rabi harvest, Qui il, so that (the grantee) should spend all revenues for his own use and should busy himself in praying for the welfare of the everlasting Empire, therefore it is incumbent upon officers, administrators, revenue collectors present and future to leave the said village in his possession and recognize it as exempt from all taxes and demands. In this respect every year the renewal orders should not be demanded (from the grantee) and if at some other place he (the grantee) has anything (i.e. land-grant), it should not be paid attention to. Dated 18th *Jamadul Awwal,* 22nd R.Y.

Zimn

Copy of the (court) proceedings *(yaddashi-i-waqi'a)* dated Wednesday 21st Rabi-ul-Awwal, 22nd R.Y./AH 1090 Ilahi month........ by the honoured Saiyid (titles omitted), the highly elevated *sadr* Rizvi Khan, during the posting as recorder *(waqi'a-nawis) of* Daulatmand, to wit; and according to the letter of Mir Muhammad Raza Karvi, the *waqi'a-nigar* of the province of Awadh, it has been conveyed to the exalted court that Shaikh Muhammad Ashraf, son of the mystic Shaikh Pir Muhammad, resident of *pargana* Salon, *sarkar* Manikpur, *suba* Allahabad, who is adorned with perfection, has settled with the consent of the *zamindars,* in the village Singhwal under the aforesaid *pargana* and has renamed it Ashrafabad. Saiyid 'Abdur Rahim, the provincial *sadr (sadr-i-juzv)* of Allahabad, has also sent his recommendation. And Shaikh Muhammad Ashraf entertains the hope that world-subduing order be issued that the aforesaid village has been conferred in its entirety as his *madad-i-ma'āsh* for generations to come. And if at some other place he (the grantee) has anything (i.e. land-grants), it should not be taken into account *waqia*. Dated 26th *Ziqad*, 22nd R.Y. Transcribed according to the Register of proceedings (*fard-i-yaddasht*). Copy of endorsement of the great minister (titles omitted) Asad Khan, "Enter in the record of (court) proceedings (*yaddasht*)".

Copy of endorsement by the honoured Saiyid (titles omitted) highly elevated *sadr* Rizvi Khan, "Enter in the *waqi'a*." Copy of endorsement by the *waqi'a-nawis* "Is in accordance with the *waqi'a*" : Copy of the endorsement by (titles) Asad Khan : "Let this be put up for second presentation (*arz-i mukarrar*)". Copy of endorsement of (titles) Lutfullah Khan, "On the 12th *Rabi-ul-Awwal* 22 R.Y., submitted for the second time (*ba-arzi-mukarrar*) to the Emperor." Copy of endorsement of (titles) Asad Khan : "Let the Imperial *farman* be prepared".

(*Hasil* figures of the said village)

Year	*In Rs.*
4th year	50.00
5th year	31.00
6th to 9th year	91.00
10th year	21.00
11th year	26.00
12th to 16th year	66.00
17th year	61.00

References

1. I was introduced to these *farmans* by my late father Hazrat Saiyid Shah Muhammad Husain Jafri, the IXth *Sajjada Nashin* (1966-79) of the *Khanqah* of Salon. I had many useful discussions with him about the family history and other related matters. The documents are still preserved in my family collection. [see plate nos. 1 and 2]

2. Akbar in the year 1578, had issued an order by which he had concentrated all the existing grants in certain village, and ordered that all the new grants should also be made from the lands of these villages. It was a precautionary measure, to prevent the grantee from unlawfully acquiring grants in two places. Cf. Irfan Habib, *Agrarian System of Mughal India*, p. 301.

3. Since a *jagirdar* could assign a grant only for his term of assignment,

which was a few years duration, the new *jagirdar* might or might not respect the order of his predecessor. So this class of grantees lived in the greatest insecurity. They were, therefore, always anxious to obtain the confirmation of such assignment from the Court to escape eviction by future *jagirdas. Ibid.*, pp. 315-16.

4. See the text as well as the *zimn* in plate no. I.

5. All the *madad-i ma'āsh* grants were as a rule, made in terms of definite area stated in *bighas*. But there are some exceptions most of them from the earlier period. Two of Babur's *farmans* simply name the village and in one of them its *jama 'raqmi* is also stated. Akbar's *farman* of 1567 relating to Jalandhar, names the village and specifies its *jama'* but not the area. Aurangzeb's *farman* of 35th R.Y. relating to Pattan (Gujarat) omits area but gives both *jama'* and *hasil* of the village. (Irfan Habib, *op. cit.*, p. 301). A *farman* coming from a later period, of Shah 'Alam II issued in 21st RY/1779 A.D. relating to Pachcha, Tirhut omits the area and gives the total *jama*. K.K. Dutta, *Some farmans' Sanads and Parwanas*, Patna, 1962, p. 10.

6. Irfan Habib, *Agrarian System*. p. 301.

7. See the *zimn* of the second *farman* (Appendix B).

8. The grantees did not by virtue of their grant possess proprietary rights. They were obliged to pay the *huquq-i- milkiyat* to the *zamindars*. (Irfan Habib, *op. cit.*,) pp. 300-1.

9. See the *zimn* : Appendix B.

10. Irfan Habib, *op. cit.*, pp. 306-7.

11. The tomb is commonly known as the *Rauza-i-Ashrafi;* the chronograms on the tombstones are still to be seen. These have been published in Thomas Beale, *Miftah-ut-Tawarikh*, Nawal Kishore, Kanpur, 1867, pp. 286, 335.

12. See the preceding footnote.

13. H.R. Nevill, *District Gazetteers of United Provinces of Agra and Oudh* (Rae Bareli) Vol. XXXIX, Lucknow, 1923, pp. 100-3.

14. See the *zimn* and the main text in the two Appendices.

15. H.R. Nevill, *op. cit.*, Vol. XXXIX, pp. 102-3. After the abolition of the *zamindari* in 1952, an annuity was made of these *zamindari* and *ma'āfi* villages and now the expenditure is made by the present *Sajjada Nashin* Saiyid Shah Ahmad Husain Jafri Islahi in accordance with the scheme of administration drawn up by the Civil Judge, Rae Bareli (U.P.). (Regular Suit No. 1 of 1950 decided on 31-7-1953, Sunni Central Board of Waqfs, Lucknow vs. Shah Muhammad Naim Ata Sajjada Nashin).

16. Ibn Hasan, *Central Structure of the Mughal Empire*, Delhi, 1970, pp. 92-106.

17. The governor of *suba* Allahabad from 18th R.Y. to 24th R.Y (1675-81 A.D.)— Cf. M. Athar Ali, 'Provincial Governors under Aurangzeb,' *Medieval India—A Miscellany,* Vol. I, p. 108.

18. He was the *sadr-us sudur* of Aurangzeb during 10th R.Y. to 24th R.Y. and also held *mansab* of 3000 *zat* 500 *sawars. Ma'asir-ul Umara,* Vol. II, p. 558; see also in M. Athar Ali, *Mughal Nobility under Aurangzeb,* pp. 87, 237.

19. This officer might be the same as the famous Inayatullah Khan Kashmiri, who later rose to prominence and in 49th R.Y. got the *mansab* of 2500 *zat*/250 *sawar* Cf. Shah Nawaz Khan, *Ma'asir-ul Umara* tr. H. Beveridge Calcutta, 1941, Vol. I, pp. 680-82.

20. The well-known *wazir* of Aurangzeb held the *mansab* of 700 *zat*/7000 *sawars. Cf. Ibid.,* Vol. I, p. 271.

21. He held the *mansab* of 1500 *zat*/500 *sawars* during this period. Cf. *Ibid.* Vol. I, p. 34.

22. He held the rank of 7000 *zat*/7000 *sawars,* and was always assigned the financial and executive duties. Cf. Athar Ali, *op. cit.,* pp. 145, 217.

23. Where the office records of pay-assignments, etc., were kept, See Khwaja Yasin's Glossary, Patna, private collection (Rotograph in the Department of History, AMU, Aligarh No. 244).

24. See the *zimn* in the Appendix A.

25. No information on this official rocord has been found.

26. He held the rank of 1500 *zat*/500 *sawars.* In 2st RY he was made the officer-in-charge of *arz-i mukkarrar,* M.U., Vol. I, p. 838.

27. All these taxes and perquisites have been explained in B.N. Goswami and J S. Grewal, *The Mughals and the Jogis of Jakhbar,* Simla, 1967, and so do not require elucidation here.

بسم الله الرحمن الرحیم

ابو المظفر ... الدین محمد ... عالم بادشاه غازی

~~چون بعرض ... رسید~~ که بموجب اسناد حکام

سواری دو صد بیگه زمین از موضع مزبور بحساب

معموله پرگنه نصیرآباد تابع سرکار مانکپور مضاف صوبه اله آباد در وجه مدد معاش حقایق و معارف آگاه

شیخ پیر محمد ساکن قصبه سلون مقرر است و بر اراضی مزبوره قابض و متصرف اند امیدوارند که درین باب فرمان والاشان

مرحمت شود حکم جهان مطاع عالم مطیع صادر شد که زمین مسطور را بدستور سابق بشرط قبض و تصرف در وجه

مدد معاش آنها حسب الضمن معمور دانسته که حاصلات آنرا صرف مایحتاج خود نموده بدعای بقای دولت روز

افزون مواظبت نمایند باید که حکام و عمال و جاگیرداران و کروریان حال و استقبال اراضی مذکوره را در تصرف

انها بازگذارند و اصلا و مطلقا تغییر و تبدیل بدان راه ندهند و بعلت مال و جهات و اخراجات ... و قنلغه و شکار و

و جریبانه و ضابطانه و محصلانه و ... و ... و قانونگوئی و مقدمی و ...

و کل تکالیف دیوانی و مطالبات سلطانی مزاحم نشوند و درین باب هر سال سند مجدد طلب ندارند ...

شرح یادداشت واقعه بتاریخ روز چهار شنبه بست و کیم شهر ربیع الاول ۲۲ جلوس والا موافق ۱۰۹۰ ہجری مطابق ماه الهی برساله سیادت و نقابت پناه شرافت و نجابت دستگاه سزاوار عنایت بادشاهی قابل مرحمت شاهنشاهی صدر رفیع القدر رضویخان ونوبت واقعه نویسی کمترین بندگان درگاه خلایق پناه دولتمند قلمی میکردد که ازروی نوشته میر محمد رضا کروی واقعه نگار صوبه اوده بغرض والا رسید که شیخ محمد اشرف پسر حقایق آگاه شیخ پیر محمد ساکن پرگنه سلون سرکار مانکپور تابع صوبه اله آباد که بکمال آراستگی دارد برضامندی زمیداران در موضع سنکهول معموله پرگنه مذکور موطن گرفته انرا اشرف آباد نام نهاده وسید عبدالرحیم صدر جزو اله آباد نیز تجویز نامه داده امید وارست که سند درگاه مرحمت شود حکم جهانمطاع عالم مطیع صادر شد که موضع مذکور نسلاً بعد نسل ابداً موبداً دربست در وجه مدد معاش او مرحمت فرموديم واگر در محلی دیگر چیزی داشته باشد انرا اعتبار نکنند ...... واقعه ۲۶ ذی قعده ۲۲ مطابق تصدیق ...... یادداشت قلمی شد شرح بخط موتمن الدوله العلیه معتمد السلطنت ...... عمده وزراے رفیع الشان زبدهٔ خوانین بلند مکان شائسته انواع عنایت سزاوار اصناف مرحمت خان شجاعت نشان جمله الملک مدار المهام اسد خان آنکه داخل (واقعه نمایند) شرح بخط سیادت ونقابت پناه ...... دستگاه صدر رفیع القدر رضویخان آنکه داخل واقعه نمایند شرح بخط واقعه نویس مطابق واقعست شرح بخط شائسته انواع عنایت سزاوار صاحب مرحمت خان شجاعت نشان جمله الملک مدار المهام آنکه بعرض مکرر رسانند شرح بخط خانه زاد سزاوار عنایت والاحسان لایق الرحمته والامتنان لطف الله خاں آنکه دوازدهم ربیع الثانی ۲۲ جلوس میمنت مانوس مکرر بعرض مقدس رسید شرح بخط خان شجاعت نشان جملة الملک مدار المهام آنکه فرمان عالیشان قلمی نمایند بیض

شرح بخط جمله الملک مدار المهام آنکه ...... بنظر در آمد

شرح سیاهه یکموضع دربست مقرراً بیست ما دام

مقرراً تنخواه موضع سنکهول عمله و پرگنه سلون سرکار مانکپور صوبه اله آباد

موضع دربست

امال رقبه کل

مال [؟] وغیره

مقرراً ... م [؟] بقرار سراسری بیست ما دام دربست

ماے

بسم اللہ الرحمن الرحیم

طغرا (ابوالمظفر محی الدین محمد عالمگیر بادشاہ غازی)

مہر

یافتاح		یاواسع
	عالم گیر بادشاہ غازی محمد محی الدین ابوالمظفر ۱۰۸۳	
یارافع		یانافع

نقل فرمان واجب الاذعان بمہر ابوالمظفر محی الدین حضرت محمد عالمگیر بادشاہ غازی بنام شاہ پیر محمد اشرف سلونے آنکہ

درینوقت فرمان والاشان صادر شد کہ

موضع سنکھول دربست من اعمال پرکنہ

سلون تابع سرکار مانکپور مضاف بصوبہ الہ آباد کہ سی ودو ہزار یکصددام جمع آنست از نصف ربیع قوے ئیل دروجہ مدد معاش شیخ محمد اشرف ولد شیخ پیر محمد حسب الضمن مقرر باشد کہ حاصلات آنرا صرف معیشت خود نمودہ بدعاء بقاء دولت ابد طراز اشتغال نماید باید کہ حکام و متصدیان مہمات (عمال) حال و استقبال موضع مذکور را بتصرف او باز گزارند واز جمیع وجوہ و عوارض معاف و مرفوع القلم شناسند دریں باب ہر سال سند مجدد نطلبند اگر در محل دیگر چیزی داشتہ باشد آنرا اعتبار نکنند شانزدہم جمادی الاول سال بیست و دویم از جلوس والا نوشتہ شد۔

مواضع و چکوک و اراضی سکنی و زرعی که در پرگنات متعلقات سرکارات مانکپور و لکهنو مضا

اسناد حکامی و زمینداران بنام سالک مسالک طریقت واقف موقف حقیقت پیر محمد اشرف خلف الصدق

مسامحت احدی مقرر و معاف بوده آمده از ابتدای فصل خریف تنگوزئیل بدستور قدیم [illegible]

مواظبت و اتقا [illegible] باید که عمال و جاگیرداران و کروریان حال و استقبال در استمرار و استقلال این حکم معد

و بطنا بعد بطن خالدا مخلدا از مواد تغییر و تبدیل محروس و مصئون [illegible] بوجه المعاش مال و جهات و سایر اخراجات

صدد و بیتی قلبه کوئی و شکار بکار و غیره ابواب ممنوعه و درکاه و الاو کل تکالیف دیوانی و مطالبات سلطانی

یرلیغ کرامت تبلیغ [illegible] تخلف و انحراف نورزند و اگر در محصلید [illegible] داشته باشند [illegible] اعتبار نکنند بتاریخ [illegible]

فرمان

واجب الاذعان

اراضی سکنی و زرعی که در پرگنات متعلقات سرکارات مانکپور و لکھنؤ مضافات صوبه الٰه آباد و اوده بموجب فرمان اعلیحضرت فردوس

بداران نام سالک مسالک طریقت واقف مواقف حقیقت پیر محمد اشرف خلف الصدق و سجاده نشین قدوة العارفین شیخ پیر محمد سلونی قدس سره بالاستمرار کسب

معاف بوده آمده از ابتدای خریف ... قدیم ... الیه مرحمت فرمودیم که حاصلات از اصرف معیشت خود نموده بدعای بقای سلطنت

[illegible]

برسالۀ سیادت و نجابت پناه شجاعت و شهامت دستگاه [illegible]

تا بل حیات ظل الهی محمد [illegible] رفیع القدر بلند مکان [illegible] خان [illegible]

[illegible]

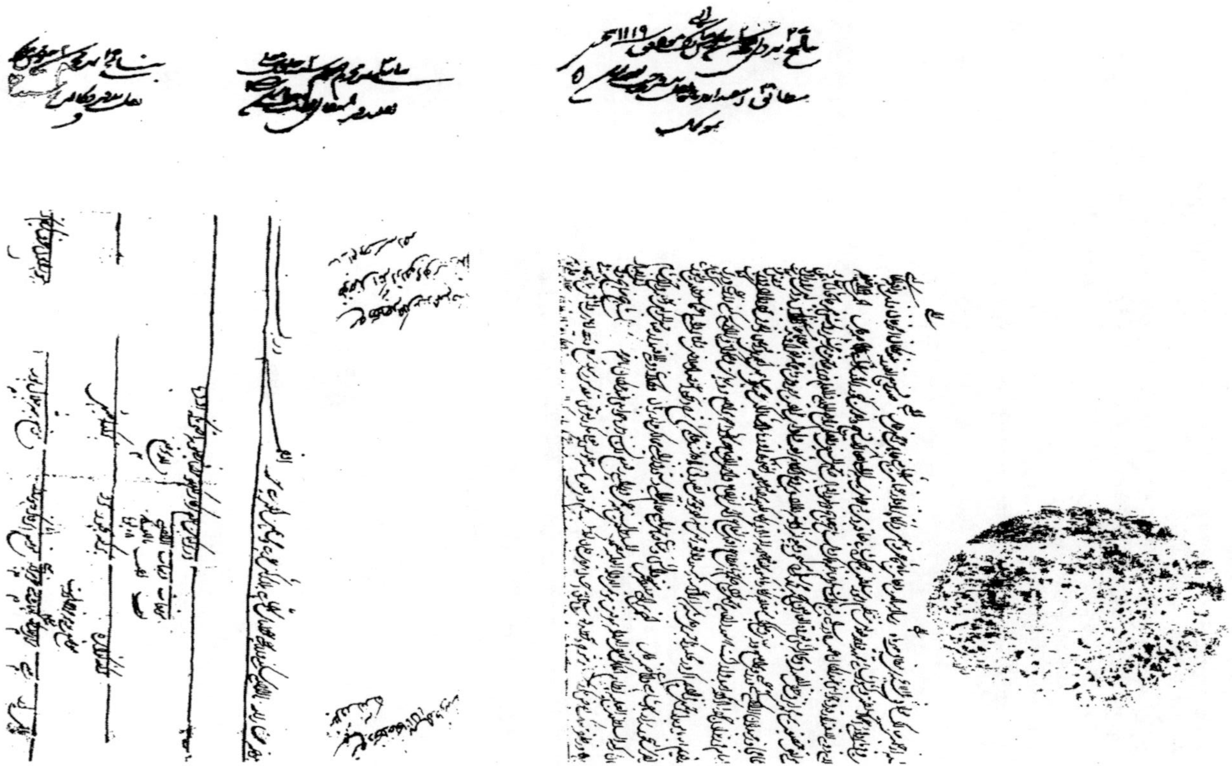

4

Tension and Conflict in the Agrarian Society of Awadh : A Study of the Revenue Grantees

The *madad-i ma'āsh* holders formed a minor segment of the agrarian society of Awadh during the Mughal period, but their conditions are illuminated by an extensive documentation. There appear to have been substantial conditions with these grants, in the beginning; later on these were dropped altogether and the grantees themselves were elevated to the status of the 'Army of the Prayer'. Still we find that the successive Mughal rulers insisted on confirmatory orders after the death of the original grantees. In matters of inheritance to grants the rules of *shari'at* were not applicable as *madad-i ma'ash* was supposedly an article of loan (*'ariyat)*.

At the same time we find that several of the state functionaries, particularly the ecclesiastical officers were holders of revenue-grants in lieu of their pay claims. Most of these grants were concentrated in particular villages. Often the induction of these outsiders as co-sharers of the social surplus in the agrarian society was resented by the *zamindar*. But their 'reservations' mostly related to trivial matters, which could be solved by the local officials.

An attempt is made here to examine some fresh evidence of the tension and conflict between the revenue-grantee and the *zamindar* as well as the elements of co-operation between the two classes.

The clashes mainly occurred between the grantees with positions in the official hierarchy and the rural elite. It is necessary to study the nature of the jurisdiction of these grantees as officials. We may take up as an illustration a single family. This family was established at *pargana* Sandila, *sarkar* Lucknow, since the heyday of the Delhi Sultanat. It enjoyed *madad-i ma'āsh* grants in lieu of its members rendering many ecclesiastical duties like *qaza, ihtisab* and *nirkh-nawis*, etc.

The association of the *zamindari* rights with domination of a particular caste in a *pargana* had been the most peculiar feature of the agrarian life in Awadh during the Mughal period. Any attempt to disturb this caste hegemony often resulted in an open clash between the local officials and the members of the affected castes. Since the genesis of these conflicts lay in the distribution of social surplus, the conflict often cut across religious lines.

A perusal of the *suyurghal* statistics in the *Ain-i Akbari's* account of the 'Twelve subas' shows that in absolute terms the number of persons holding *madad-i ma'āsh* rights in *parganas* with Rajput and other non-Muslim *zamindars* was larger than those holding these rights in the *pargana* having Muslim *zamindars*. An analysis of the data leads us to some interesting conclusions. In the five *parganas* of the various *sarkar* of *suba* Awadh where the *zamindars* happened to be Muslims, the percentage of total *naqdi* (cash) alienated by way of *suyurghal* ranged from 0.49% (*pargana* Utraula', *sarkar* Gorakhpur) to 12.6% (*pargana* Unam, *sarkar* Lucknow), while *pargana* Ibrahimabad, *sarkar* Lucknow by way of an exception records a high percentage i.e. 23.3% of the total *naqdi*.

In the other six *parganas* where Muslims are the co-sharers of *zamindari* rights with the Rajputs, the *jama'* alienated by way of *suyurghal* ranges from 1.78% (*pargana* Manwi, *sarkar* Lucknow) to 18.49% (*pargana* Sidhaur, *sarkar* Lucknow). While in another 72 *pargana* with no Muslim *zamindari* these grants constituted between 0.03% (*pargana*, Darijyapara, *sarkar* Gorakhpur) and 18.74% (*pargana* Sihali, *sarkar* Lucknow) of the total *naqdi*. The remaining 47 *parganas* recorded no *suyurghal* grants at all. This included *pargana* Anona, *sarkar* Awadh, where the *zamindars* were Chauhan Rajputs, newly converted to Islam. In Awadh, at least, the grantees appear to have been indifferent to the community of the *zamindars* while seeking grants.[1]

In any case, the total amount of the *jama'* alienated through such grants in 1598 was only 5.72% of the total *naqdi* in *suba* Awadh. But the fact that the *madad-i ma'āsh* grants as a rule were made out of the cultivable waste with the implicit purpose of making it cultivable; the standard formula used invariably in such orders was *zamin-i uftadal aiq-i ziraat kharij-az jama'*; at the most 1/3 of the total and at the later stages 1/2 of the total grant was put of the cultivated land (*mazru'*)[2]. It is to be remembered that the *suyurghal* figures of the *Ain-i Akbari* represent only the loss of revenue to the state through such alienations, and not the actual income from *madad-i ma'ash* lands. It might have included the amount distributed through cash allowances, but this is not clear. Holders of the *madad-i ma'āsh* rights *per se* posed no threat to the dominant elite of the area, neither could they ever claim any fiscal perquisites belonging to the *zamindar*[3]. The resistance to the induction of the grantees from outside by the local elements generally centered around questions like not relinquishing the cultivated land or, in *zortalab* areas, refusal by the peasants/*zamindars* to pay the land-revenue. A quick redressal of these matters even by the local officials could greatly relieve the grantees. Often a change in the area of grant was made in the same village or *pargana* under the usual administrative procedures. So the acquisition and possession of the prime land in the village and insistence on an uninterrupted flow of the revenues to the grantees was a major factor of tension, but it was kept in manageable limits. Such question could have seldom caused any major law-and-order problem.

But things assumed alarming dimensions when these revenue grantees happened to be the holders of ecclesiastical offices as well. Since such officers had a close proximity to the officials at the Centre and they had to perform many unpopular duties in the region, they could become easy targets of recalcitrant *zamindars.* These *zamindars* often thought of expelling such people from the area of their control.

A statement of the facts presented by the *qazi* family in the *faujdari* jurisdiction of Baiswara in the year AD 1662 sets the context of conflict quite unambiguously. It describes the situation obtaining there as follows:

> the region of Baiswara happens to be the abode of infidelity, and all the twenty-one *parganas* are the home of refuge of the Bais people. Out of these, six *parganas* have *qazis*, whereas fifteen *parganas* have netiher *qazis* nor mosques, nor do arrangements exist either for the *azan* or for the congregational prayers. The fact that the ancestors of this family of the *qazi* had supposedly exercised jurisdiction over all the twenty-one *parganas* earlier, and there had been on going

clashes between them and the Bais Rajputs, this way eighty years had passed and consequently the *qazis* lost their jurisdiction *('amal)* from 15 *parganas*. None has cared so far to eradicate the sources of infidelity; therefore the petitioner, Qazi Maudud, deemed it necessary to report the matter to the Emperor Aurangzeb."[4]

Not only the holders of the ecclesiastical offices were subjected to the *zamindars* wrath, but also the peasants residing in the villages of their *madad-i ma'āsh* were terrorised by the tumultous *zamindars* when they were out to settle scores with these officers. Cattle, prized possession of the peasantry, often attracted them, and villages were raided to lift livestock.

A petition from the family of the *qazi* from *pargana* Parsadepur in the year AH 1061 /AD 1652 complains of the raid in their *madad-i ma'ash* villages by the Kanhpuria Rajputs of *pargana* Salon:

> they raided the *madad-i ma'āsh* villages of the petitioners with a large number of their clansmen and carried away 940 oxen and buffaloes from the villages of Saleempur and Nizampur. This act was committed without there being any justification and with such impunity that, "they wounded even those two persons who had informed the Emperor of their misdeeds. The infidels are perpetuating such acts of oppression against the Muslims".[5]

The examples of such clashes could be multiplied, but it should not be assumed that the grantees holding ecclesiastical offices could be dislodged in this way from any region. They got protection from the Emperor in case of such clashes. There are instances, too numerous to be cited, when imperial *farmans* were issued to award exemplary punishments to the guilty in case of any loss sustained by the grantees.

One is naturally tempted to know about the actual working of the office of the *qazi* and other related offices in rural life, as to establish what duties they performed which brought them or had the potential of directly involving them in tussles with the *zamindar* of the area. The following relates to a case study of the establishment of a *qazi* family at Sandila, presently in Hardoi District of Uttar Pradesh.

A series of documents in the acquired collection of the National Archives of India enables us to study the ecclesiastical offices and the land grants held by the descendants of famous Chishti mystic Shaikh

Fariduddin Ganj Shakar. The founder of this branch settled at *pargana* Sandila *sarkar* Lucknow, was one Shaikh 'Ali Lahori, who was said to have been the grandson of the celebrated saint. He settled here, towards the close of the 13th century and was appointed the *qazi* of *shiqq* Sandila. The revenues of village Dhakua were assigned to him as *wazifa,* while other fiscal imposts, like *wujuhat* and *awarizat* of the village were assigned to him to meet the expenses for the occasion of the '*Urs* of the celebrated saint.[6] Thus we have here an example of a grant made for a specific purpose, rather than a personal grant.

The members of this family continued to hold the office of the *qazi* with many additional duties, and enjoyed fiscal perquisites attached thereto. The geneological chart showing the names and indicating their approximate tenure as the *qazi* of the *pargana* Sandila, has been worked out by Mr. Zakir Husain showing the continuance of the family down to the annexation of the kingdom of Awadh. The table spans over a period of about 600 years, but we stand on surer grounds with the accession of Akbar. As the family records are varied in nature, dealing with the working of the quasi-religious institution at the local level and the various problems encountered by them. Often their remunerations and perquisites were in jeopardy thus making them a vulnerable target of the *zamindars'* manipulations. This way they became more openly inclined towards the official side rather than identifying themselves with the local elements.

Documents from the reign of Akbar make one presume that qazi Nasrullah held the office of the *qazi* and *muhtasib* of *pargana* Sandila and its environs. These offices passed on to successive generations. In remuneration for their discharging the duties, a number of villages and other land grants by way of *madad-i ma'āsh* were made over to them. Still other grants were also given either on account of some public benefits which arose therefrom or as absolutely unconditional and unrelated to any obligation.[8]

The office of the *muhtasib* (censor of morals) and *nirkh nawis* (price-reporter) appear attached to the office of the *qazi,* also in the *farman* of Aurangzeb issued in favour of Shaikh 'Imaduddin on 11th *Rajab* 1091/A.D.1680. The duties connected with these offices too have been listed. These included:

> the delivering of judgments in matters of disputes and distribution of the (legal) shares among the heirs of the deceased, attestation of the *chaknama* (demarcation papers)

and other documents of legal nature, inducing the people to offer the (prescribed) prayers and to follow the religious injunctions, award of punishments, holding of the Friday and other congregational prayers, keeping an eye over the drunkards, miscreants and other bad characters; fixing the prices of essential commodities, standardization of the weights and measures, and dispatching the *roznamcha* (daily reports) containing a summary of the prices to the (imperial court?)[9]

Land-grants held by the members of the family reveal some interesting features. Qazi 'Imaduddin held an annual *wazifa* of Rs. 270/-, but sometimes afterwards the cash-grant was converted into a land-grant, and village Maner, *pargana* Sandila, with a total *jama'* of Rs. 203/- was assigned to him by way of *madad-i ma'ash* grant. This grant was confirmed on 13th *Safar* 14th R.Y./AD 1671[10] The previous officials (*mutassadi*) of the *jagirdar* and *khalisa-i sharifa* had in addition made over the revenues of the villages Siyamao and Maner, *pargana* Sandila, to Shaikh 'Imaduddin. This was confirmed by a *parwana* of 16th *Rabi I* 16th R.Y./1084/1673 A.D. Again, we find him receiving 200 *bighas* as *madad-i ma'ash* from village Mahsona. But in case of this grant a condition was imposed that the grantee was to continue in service (*khidmat*) and was not to realize taxes like *mehrana* and *nikahana*.[12] Another *sanad* of 15th *Shawwal* 22nd R.Y./ 1680 states that Qazi 'Imaduddin had been assigned the revenue of a village having the *jama' kamil* (maximum assessment) of Rs. 200/ - to Rs. 250/. This grant too was made in lieu of service.[13] In the 39th R.Y./1697, the revenues of village Khajari having total *jama'* of Rs. 440/- and the village Dhakua having a *jama'* of Rs. 5/-, were assigned to Qazi 'Imaduddin as *madad-i ma'āsh*. From yet in another *parwana* regarding village Mirzapur, *pargana* Sandila included in the *madad-i-ma'āsh* grant of *qazi* 'Imaduddin, the revenues of this village are said to have been misappropriated by others illegally, so that it had to be restored to him and an enquiry was ordered.[14] In 1095/1684, the revenues of village Maini *pargana* Sandila amounting to Rs. 270/ - annually were assigned to Qazi 'Imaduddin as *tankhwah* (salary).[15] This was possibly a temporary assignment.

These grants were made to the Qazi for fulfilling duties of his office. But he seems to have obtained further concessions by claiming to use his land for public benefit. In 1670 he was granted a plot of 8 *bighas* of uncultivated (*banjar*) land in the vicinity of *qasba* Sandila in order to raise a garden or orchard, "for the welfare of the general public.'[16] Again on 19th *Ramzan* 21st R.Y./1679, he was granted 10 *bighas* again in Sandila for the purpose of raising there an orchard, digging wells, and planting trees alongside the highway for the rest and relief of travellers and destitutes.[17] Interestingly enough such arrangements were resented by the owners (*malikan*) of the land (probably the *zamindar*) and hence the grantee had to request for the transfer of his grant elsewhere.[18] This was done with an increase of 7 *bigha* land, but with the additional obligation of establishing a mosque and *khanqah*. Fortunately, we possess the *chaknama* deed for the demarcation of these 17 *bighas*.[19]

A *parwana* issued in the 18th RY/1675 confirms a land grant of 294 *bigha* held by Qazi 'Imaduddin in *pargana* Nimkhar, *sarkar* Khairabad. This grant was designed to cover the expenses incurred by the grantee in feeding poor scholars and other destitutes at his *khanqah*.[20] The reference to *khanqah* confirms the mystic predilections of the *qazi*, who otherwise should have been an orthodox jurist. Similarly in 24th RY/1682 he obtained the revenue-free grant of village Mairat, *pargana* Nimkhar, *sarkar* Khairabad. This grant too was made by way of grant.[21] Apparently this family in the 17th century confined itself to income from grants and did not acquire *zamindari* rights of any sort.

The clashes between the revenue grantees and the superior fiscal right holders were mainly to control the flow of surplus and the prime land in the village. In no way could these clashes be termed as 'local battles between Hindus and Muslims' or 'the communal land wars'.[22] In fact we have seen that invariably the change in the area of grant was made within the same village and such arrangements were seldom opposed by the *zamindar*. One should also remember that such situations were confined to certain areas, the very regions which have acquired considerable notoriety for the recalcitrant attitude of their *zamindar*.[23]

APPENDIX A

Table 1

Sarkarwise Break up of the _Suyurgahal_ Statistics of _Parganas_ having Muslim _Zamindari_

I	II	III	
No. of the parganas	*Total jama' (dams)*	*Suyurghal (dams)*	*% III as to II*
4	(a) *Sarkar* Awadh 45,00,922	3,06,288	6.8%
1	(b) *Sarkar* Gorakhpur 13,97,367	6,935	0.49%
	(c) *Sarkar* Bahraich (No *pargana* with Muslim *zamindars*)		
	(d) *Sarkar* Khairabad (same as in C)		
7	(e) *Sarkar* Lucknow 1,75,84,829	17,40,280	9.89%
12	**2,34,83,118**	**20,53,503**	**8.74**

Table 2

Sarkarwise Break up of the _Suyurghal_ Statistics of _parganas_ without Muslim _Zamindari_

16	(a) *Sarkar* Awadh 3,63,37,212	13,77,877	3.79%
5	(b) *Sarkar* Gorakhpur 52,56,242	99,280	0.80%
5	(c) *Sarkar* Bahraich 2,02,42,182	1,06,482	5.24%
	(d) *Sarkar* Khairabad 39,41,541	16,56,100	4.15%
29	(e) *Sarkar* Lucknow 5,34,54,089	28,74,330	5%
71	**11,92,31,266**	**61,14,069**	**5.44%**

References

1. See Appendix 'A' for the tables. The figures of the tables are based on the two Mss. of *Ain-i Akbari*, Br. Museum Add, 5645 and Add 6552.
2. Irfan Habib, *Agrarian System of Mughal India*, p. 302 and notes.
3. It was only with the increasing monotization of the proprietary rights during the 17th century that the grantees could purchase such rights and could become *ijaradars*. In *pargana* Hisampur, *sarkar* Bahraich, see the example of Saiyid Muhammad Arif, who was originally a revenue-grantee, and made a considerable fortune. (Irfan Habib, *op. cit.*, pp. 150-52).
4. *NAI/2618/6*. This representation has as many as six seals of high officials, two of them of the *jagirdar*. It uses the word *ta'alluqa*, which appears to be the earliest reference to this institution in the proper context. Apart from this, topographical details have also been provided. The length of the *faujdari* of Baiswara *nizamat* in the east-west direction between *pargana* Dalmau and Harha was 25 *karoh*, the width in the south-north, lying between river Ganges and the bank of Sai river, was 15 *krohs*. Also the names of all six *parganas* under the jurisdiction of the *qazis* as well as of the 15 *pargana* from where they have been expelled are given.
5. Abdul Qadir Collection No. 4; U.P. State Archives, Lucknow. This petition has 7 seals three of them of the *jagirdar* of the area; and 14 signatures (5 of them in Devanagiri script). It is dated 3rd *Jamad* AH 1061/A.D.1652
6. Any textual references to this branch are not forthcoming from the sources. Similarly the documents relating to Shaikh Ali Lahori have not survived the ravages of time. However, Mr. Zakir Husain has been able to study the early fortunes of this family during the Turco-Afghan period. See 'Some Original Tughlaq Documents and their Significance. *PIHC* (1989) pp. 219-29. A cursory account of this family has been given by Raja Durga Prasad, *Tarikh-e-Sandila*, (Urdu) Lucknow, 1915, pp. 266-68.
7. Zakir Husain, *op. cit.*, p. 221.
8. *NAI-1386* (974 AH/1566 AD). This **hukm** (order) was issued to confirm the earlier imperial grant of 60 *bighas* of *madad-i ma'ash* land in village Khanjaura, *qasba* Sandila, in favour of Qazi Nasrullah and Qazi Mubarak. It was asserted that the grantees were to be treated as the *jagirdar* of the area.(?) (*NAI*-1585). A significant circular issued by Shaikh Abdul Nabi (though undated, but datable from the fact that it was issued after Shaikh had performed *haj*) records the facts of the division of the *madad- i ma'āsh* land in the family of the *qazi* which was again transferred to the main line after the death of other co-sharers without any heir. For other citations in favour of Qazi Nasrullah, *See NAI-1255*.

The *madad-i ma'āsh* grants attached with the office of the *qazi* continued to increase. A *parwana* (1081 AH/1670 A.D.) records 200 *bighas* in village Todakpur and 100 *bighas* in village Kasmandi, *pargana* Sandila in favour of *Qazi* 'Imaduddin, NAI-1382.

9. *NAI-1434* (1091/1681) After Qazi 'Imaduddin, one Ahmad Beg was appointed *Qazi*. His connection with 'Imaduddin's family is not established. He was for some reason removed, and a *farman* was issued on 6th Rajab 44th RY/1700 conferring the office of the *qazi* on Sharafuddin, son of 'Imaduddin with 100 *bighas* as *madad-i ma'āsh* on the condition of the service and non-realization of the dues as *mehrana* and *nikahana*. See NAI-1385 (1112/1700).

10. *NAI-1381.* The *jama'* was less than the cash grant, being is perhaps what is to be expected, since the grantee could in time raise the revenue through the extension of cultivation.

11. *NAI-1271*

12. *NAI-1273*

13. *NAI-1374*

14. *NAI-1274*

15. *NAI-1408*

16. *NAI-1341*

17. *NAI-1343*

18. *NAI-1651*

19. *NAI-1389*

20. *NAI-1272*

21. *NAI-1593*

22. C.A. Bayly, 'The pre-History of Communalism ? Religious Conflicts in India, 1700-1860', *Modern Asian Studies* 19(11), 1985 pp. 172-203. In fact in his zeal to absolve the colonial rulers from creating Hindu-Muslim divide in India, he reaches many hilarious conclusions, e.g. "the form of these land wars was often a savage attack by the totality of rural society against the small town headquarters of the Muslim gentry". This has hardly any basis. Moreover, his assumption that the grantees were generally town-based is again open to question. His other conclusions require some consideration. The destruction of the family graveyards was often referred to in most of these petitions. Should we consider such acts as "a straight forward piece of communal savagery" ? "But the complaints of this nature were preferred against the Muslim *zamindar* as well, even the destruction of the books of theology and religion is mentioned in these *mahzars*. Whether these occurrences were the order of the day cutting across religious lines or such things were mentioned only to attract the imperial attention or both is difficult to say.

23. For further details see Zahiruddin Malik, 'Problems of *faujdari* jurisdiction in Baiswara; *PIHC*, 1973, pp. 211-15.

UNDER NAWAB-WAZIRS

5

Origin and Growth of *Ta'alluqadāri* Tenures in Awadh

Considerable controversy exists about the rise of the *ta'alluqadāri* tenures in Awadh. It has been assumed that it was a part of the well-defined policy of the British after the tragedy of 1857 to "preserve this class (of *ta'alluqadārs)* for useful purpose, and to prevent its impoverishment by idleness".[1] Although Lord Canning did not have a favourable opinion about the growth of these tenures, he yet thought the continuance of such tenures necessary for "obtain(ing) a hold over the country which shall be beneficial to all the classes of its people".[2] But his view of their origin was that it lay in a delegation or usurpation of government claims to revenue and not in any previous existing allodial property. A relevant extract from Lord Canning's letter is worth reproduction:

> When we assumed the government of Oude in 1858, the greater part of the province was held by the ta'*alluqadārs* who resented it. They have been called 'Barons of Oude.' But this term applied to them as a class is misleading. Some had received titles from the kings of Oude, for service rendered or by court favours, some few are the representative of ancient families, but the majority are men distinguished neither by birth, good service or connection with the soil, who having held office under the native government as *nazims* or *chakledars,* or having farmed the revenues of extensive tracts, had taken advantage of the weakness of the native government and its indifference to all considerations of justice, so long as it received revenues, had abused the authority confided to them

> by that government, and by means of deeds of sale, sometimes extorted by violence sometimes obtained by fraud, had become the nominal proprietors and the actual possessors of the village, or the majority of the villages which formed what they called their *ta'alluqa* or estate.[3]

Indeed such an impression was popular enough to receive the attention of Marx as well. He discussed the issue of the ownership of land in Awadh at some length in his despatches to *New York Daily Tribune*. Although he made certain untenable assumptions in this regard, e.g., that "the property of the land was in the village corporation, in which resided the power of allotting it out to individuals for cultivation", he asserted explicitly: "the *zamindars* and *ta'alluqadārs* were noting in their origin but officers of the Government appointed to look after, to collect and to pay over to the prince the assessment due from the village.[4]" Marx was led to the inevitable conclusion that the proprietary rights claimed by the *ta'alluqadārs* and the *zamindars* originated, "in usurpation at once against the Government and the cultivators". The period (1856-57) between the annexation of Awadh and Mutiny was to prove a testing ground for the future survival of *ta'alluqadārs*. The government made every effort, "to get rid of them, as an incubus on the real cultivator of the soil and for the general improvement of the country". Still the fact remains that under the feeble reign of the *nawabs*, they were able to establish, somehow, their legal claims over the land, and it was but natural for the settlement officers to be engulfed in an "acrimonious controversy with them as to the extent of their rights". Ultimately this resulted in a state of discontent and "led them (the *ta'alluqadārs)* to make common cause with the revolted sepoys".[5]

This view of the position of the *ta'alluqadār* preceded the annexation. In 1849 it was contended that the *ta'alluqadārs* enjoyed their rights as a result of the delegation of the rights by government officials in respect of revenue-collection. The *ta'alluqadār* was a "person previously unconnected with the spot, and (were) permitted to realize on his own account the share of the produce otherwise due to the state".[6]

On the other hand, it was argued that the class of the *ta'alluqadār* did not solely consist of the people elevated to their position by the rulers, but a good number of them were the representative of the hereditary chiefs, in possession of large estates in their own rights. And recognition was accorded to their superior proprietary right by successive governments. This school took the view that the *ta'alluqadār* could not just have been favoured outsiders.[7] Charles Elliott, in *Chronicles of Oonao*, examined the issue at some length and concluded that a number of big *ta'alluqadāri* houses in the district of Oonao, Fyzabad and Sultanpur were the descendants of old hereditary chieftains. But at the same time, he too admitted that on occasions, it so happened that the revenue-officials seized the opportunity of acquiring superior proprietary rights by way of *ta'alluqa* arrangements.[8] It would be unhistorical, argued Elliott, to regard Rajā Daya Shankar Dikshit of Purenda, or Gulab Singh, the Purihar of Surosee, or Dost Ali, the Saiyid of Oonao, as persons having acquired their possessions without any previous background of their own.

On the Indian side Lalji, a well-informed critic of the Awadh regime prior to annexation, analysed the question in detail under a separate chapter in his *Mirat-ul-Auza* entitled, "Reasons for the ability of the *ta'alluqadār* to increase the *malguzari*".[9] Besides broadly confirming the impressions of the English officials he describes the actual mechanism through which a *ta'alluqadār* applied fraudulent or forcible means to enlarge his landed possessions at the cost of the government and weak neighbours. He says that most of the villages included in the estates of the *ta'alluqadār* actually belonged to those *zamindars* who had little means of defending their villages. They even did not bother to get any sort of deed executed in their favour. Similarly, some *zamindars*, in order to escape the high-handedness of the *amil*, sought the help of the *ta'alluqadār* by putting their possessions under 'farm'. But this often subverted the *zamindar's* own position. For, after a year or two, the *ta'alluqadār* used to take *tamassuk* from the *zamindar* under the pretext that so much amount had been paid to the *amil* on his account. Ultimately such fictitious amounts would grow too heavy for the *zamindar* to repay and then the *ta'alluqadār* would get them to transfer their lands to him by a fictitious sale. If the aggrieved *zamindar* ever thought of approaching the court, he would receive no remedy. It was through the use of such methods, comments Lalji, that Beni Mahdho Buksh *ta'alluqadār* of Shankarpur, Raghunath Singh of Khajuragaon (in Baiswara Distt.), Harpal Singh of Sapehi in Sultanpur, and Ram Dutt Pandey of Gonda had been able to seize innumerable villages yielding them lakhs of rupees.

The *nazim* and the *chakledar,* too did not lag behind in making their fortunes by such methods. Lalji, especially points out the case of Raja Darshan Singh and his family. They had seized the villages of the defaulting *zamindars.* In return for large sums of pretended balances of the revenues, the zamindars were forced to execute sale-deeds. Any scrutiny of the titles of the family would reveal, says Lalji, that only a negligible portion of the entire estate, was held by them as a hereditary. The rest was acquired in the above described manner. However, a few exceptions to the generally prevailing chaotic conditions have also been recorded. Lalji informs us that the *ta'alluqadār* of Tulsipur and Balrampur, Debi Buksh, the *ta'alluqadār* of Gonda, had already held hereditary *zamindari* worth lakhs of rupees.

Thus the two categories of *ta'alluqadārs,* one of hereditary *zamindars,* the other outsiders, came to be firmly established in the Kingdom of Awadh. It is necessary to enquire about their origin, and privileges during the 17th and 18th centuries, so as to understand the degree of power which they attained subsequently.

Etymologically the word, '*ta'alluqa*' means connection but technically it was, "used in the sense of land or area over which any kind of right was claimed"[10]. Nothing can be said with certainty as to when this term came into ordinary use. The *Ain-i Akbari* does not use the word at all. But from the 17th century, it begins to appear in documents. The testimony of Patrick Cornegy. "who have seen them (the terms) mentioned in a deed of the year 1642, under the seal of the Emperor Shahjahan"[11] is difficult to prove or disprove. In Awadh, the earliest reference where the assessee has been styled as *malik-wa-ta'alluqadār* of a certain village, comes from a *qaul-o-qarar* executed in *sarkar* Bahraich in 1685 A.D., from amongst the large number of documents that I have seen.[12] It seems that in case of the village in question the assessee possessed both the rights of *zamindari* and revenue payment. This contention is further supported by the explanation in Khwaja Yasin's *Glossary* which says that *ta'alluqadār* is a kind of "*zamindar* who contracted to pay revenue not only for his own *zamindari,* but also for the *zamindari* of other persons."[13] Generally such arrangements were made by the *'amil* and later on by the *nazim* or the *chakledar* owing to the convenience of revenue collection through big *ta'alluqadār,* in stead of making the same with a number of intermediaries, or small *zamindars*.

The *ta'alluqadār* might have the *zamindari* rights over a few villages of his *ta'alluqa* as well, but in case of the remaining villages, in which he was only an intermediary, *zamindari* rights would be vested with other persons. Thus to be a *zamindar* was something more substantial than to become simply a *ta'alluqadār* of the same area.[14]

Similarly Ghulam Hazrat in *Kwaif-i-Gorakhpur* describes three types of *zamindari* tenures, and says that the *ta'alluqadār*, or the owners of the *ta'alluqa* are like *rajas*. Theoretically, they were recognised as the owners of the villages included in their jurisdiction. In most of such villages the *birtiyas* also existed, and they always claimed *jalkar* and *bankar*, while they paid only the land revenue to the *ta'alluqadār* and at the time of assessment these. *Birtiyas* were entitled to *do-biswi* (rights), or 10% of the revenue.[15] It seems that *ta'alluqa* arrangements in *sarkar* Gorakhpur were made on an extensive scale during the 18th century. A letter in the *Mansur-ul-Maktubat* explicitly mentions that Nawab Badr-ud-din Khan, son of Nawab *Wazir-ul-Mumalik* (?), had become a wandering ascetic, and his exact whereabouts were unknown. He was heard of last, when he went to "*pargana* Hansi and Gorakhpur in the *ta'alluqa* of the *Banjaras*".[16] We known for certain that it was during the 18th century that the *Banjaras* emerged on the political horizon of the eastern part of the Awadh kingdom. The origin of their landed possessions lay exclusively in their numerical strength and the use of violence against the hereditary chiefs.[17]

One is struck by the fact that barring a few stray and often insignificant references, there is little information about the growth of the *ta'alluqadāri* tenures and the actual position of *ta'alluqadār* in the Awadh kingdom during the 18th century. Persian texts and documents have used the word *ta'alluqa* often in connotations different from those in which it was used during the first half of the 19th century.[18] Certainly, *ta'alluqadār*, begin to be heard of quite frequently by the close of the 18th century.[19]

As such the *ta'alluqadāri* tenures grew in Awadh at a massive scale as a result of the slackness which creeped into the administrative machinery of the kingdom after the death of Nawab Sa'adat A'li Khan in 1814. Elliot points out that as a result of the *ijaradari* system of the revenue collection, things had become quite favourable for the growth of *ta'alluqa* tenures. As long as the *amani* system was practised, "the collector of the revenue had no need to be over bearing if the harvest failed or sickness broke-out, he had but to state the impossibility of the collection and the amount was remitted". But under the contract system, the revenue contractor was bound to pay the entire stipulated amount irrespective of natural calamities or difficulties of collections. Often it happened that some new speculator without having an accurate knowledge of the revenue paying capacity of the area might enter an agreement with the government. On such occasions he was forced in self-preservation extort more than was due from the payers. The native government was not to be blamed for all the malice, as it placed, on the other hand, unlimited powers in their hands by, "shut(ting) its eyes to the way in which they reimbursed themselves". Under such circumstances it was thought to be more useful for the collectors of the revenue to avoid dealing with small *zamindars* and to convert big *zamindars* into *ta'alluqadārs* or intermediaries between the smaller *zamindars* and the government. As such the cost of collection too was minimized "beside making the receipt of the revenue much safer."[20]

As a necessary corollary to such arrangements, there was always a possibility that the power and the influence of the respective *ta'alluqadār* might grow to great proportions, and in case of their going to rebellion. "Large amount of the revenue would be imperilled". In case of any such eventuality, the *chakledar* and other government officers were often compelled to accommodate their ambitions. Even underhand methods were applied to keep 'peace' with the *ta'alluqadār* as to reduce the risk to the minimum, "by throwing him a sop of an extra village or two at judicious movements", while the *ta'alluqadār* "were nothing loth to accept these sops". As a result of such state of affairs, the "old *ta'alluqas* waxed fat, and new ones sprang up on all sides under this vivifying influence."[21] Such a policy in the long run had the result of continuously enlarging the *ta'alluqa*. In the pargana of Fyzabad in 1814, there was no *ta'alluqa* which could pay a revenue of Rs. 10,000, but by 1856, one estate was capable of paying an amount of Rs. 2 lacs to the treasury, and 2 estates paid Rs. 70,000 each, one had Rs. 50,000 as its rent roll and there were several estates yielding

Rs. 30,000 annually to the state treasury.[22]

It is necessary to point out that the British presence in Awadh and English Resident's interference in day-to-day affairs of the kingdom, indirectly helped the growth of the *ta'alluqadāri* tenures. To begin with, the treaty of Buxar had stipulated a drastic reduction of the native army and a strong exception was taken to every reported move of the *Nawab-Wazir* to reorganise his forces. Consequently, the *Nawab* had to look for the British authorities to carry on the work of revenue collection. As a result the forces maintained by the *Nawab* for the purpose known as *mutaayyana* and the *seh bandi* were always thought to be inadequate for quelling rebellion of the landholders, in case the latter refused to pay the land revenue. Although the revenue-officials, at least in theory, were fully entitled to ask the commandant of the English forces for "sending him the aid of two battalions and heavy artillery,"[23] yet the English officials were directed to exercise the utmost caution before they "comply with the requisition of the *aumil*".[24] In 1808, Lord Baillie, the Resident at Lucknow, informed the Governor-General that, "he sanctioned it (use of British troops) after a careful and minute investigation of each and every case."[25] It was thought by the English officials that the help extended by the English forces to the revenue-officials was so throughly misused that it had devastating effects on the countryside, and in 1833 Patan suggested that such assistance be discontinued.[26]

The genesis of the *ta'alluqa* tenures essentially lay in the growth of the power of elements from amongst the *zamindar* class during the weakening of Mughal power (as represented in Awadh by the *Nawab -Wazirs*) in the 18th century. Although some of the *ta'alluqadārs* had a hereditary basis for their allodial rights, they too also applied force, fraud and violence to enlarge their landed possessions in the form of *ta'alluqa* tenures. However, the British presence and interference in day to day affairs of the kingdom also aided the extension of *ta'alluqadāri* tenures. The Awadh government had to look for the English help even for the purpose of the revenue collection and the maintenance of law and order. Such conditions helped the local magnates and other speculators to usurp more at the cost of their weaker neighbours, the state exchequre and the very system which had sustained them so far.

References

1. *Report of the UP Zamindari Abolition Committee,* Vol. I, Allahabad, 1950, p. 111.
2. *Ibid.*
3. *Ibid.,* pp. 111-12.
4. Karl Marx, 'Lord Canning's Proclamation and Land Tenure in India', *New York Daily Tribune* No. 5344 of 7th June 1858; included in *The First Indian War of Independence,* Progressive Publishers, Moscow, 1952, pp. 140-42.
5. *Ibid.,* pp. 141-42.
6. C.A. Elliott, *Chronicles of Oonao,* pp. 155-56. The passage has been quoted by the author from an article published in *Calcutta Review* (Dec. 1849), p. 422.
7. Elliott, p. 156.
8. *Ibid.*
9. Lalji, *Mirat-ul-Auza* Ms. in Mulana Azad Library, AMU, Aligarh Collection (supplementary) *Farsi Tarikh-60,* ff. 74b-75b.
10. Irfan Habib, *Agrarian System of Mughal India,* p.171 and notes.
11. Patrick Carnegy, *Notes on the Land-revenue Assessment of Upper India,* London, 1874, pp. 69-70. However, a petition seeking redress against the high-handedness of the *chaudharis of pargana* Bilgram refers to the word, *ta'alluqa* as early as 1668, but in a different context. See *Bilgram Documents* in the Department of History, AMU, Aligarh No. 4.
12. *Allahabad Documents, 897.*
13. *Add. 6603,* ff. 54b-55a.
14. A reference in *Fathiya 'Ibriya* lends support to this assumption. The claimant to the throne of Arakan joined the Mughal banners during Shaista Khan's Chittagong campaign in the hope that at least, "if they could not become *rajas,* they might become *zamindars,* if not *zamindars,* then *ta'alluqadārs*" ff. 155b-156a, Cf. Irfan Habib, *op. cit.,* p.172.
15. Mufti Ghulam Hazrat, *Kwaif-i-zila-i-Gorakhpur,* 1810 A.D., Aligarh, Subhanullah 954/12, ff. 14a-b.
16. Awadhi Lal, *Insha-i-Mansur* or *Mansur-ul-Maktubat.* It consists of the letters drafted by Santokh Rai, *munshi* of Safdarjung. These letters were addressed to Emperor Muhammad Shah and Wazir Qamruddin Khan. The only known copy of this important manuscript is at Tagore Library, Lucknow University.
17. Banjara depredators had acquired considerable notoriety and in course of time they not only carved out a territory for themselves, but become

a scourge for almost the entire region. No individual chieftain was able to withstand their onslaught. To meet the threat posed by these *Banjaras*, the Bisin Raja of Majhauli had abandened a large portion of his estate to the newly established estates of Tamkhauli and Padrauna. Thus, he created a powerful buffer zone between his domain and that of the Banjaras. These conditions came to an end with the cession of this territory to the East India Company. (H.R. Nevill *District Gazetteers*, Vols. 44-45).

18. *'Imad-us-Sa'ādat* uses the word *raja* for Mohan Singh of Tiloin, who had his skirmishes with Sa'adat Khan Burhanul Mulk, while *Mirat-ul-Auza'* explicitly calls him the *ta'alluqadār* of Tiloin (f. 76a). It is quite possible that the local chieftains who enjoyed considerable power were by now reduced to the mere status of *ta'alluqadārs*.

19. See *Akhbarat* in Central Records Office Hyderabad-AR-*No. 5746* (dated 20th *Rajab* 1213 AH/28th December 1798). Some of these have been published along with English translations by Yusuf Husain Khan, *News Letters; 1767-1799*, Hyderabad, 1955, p. 66.

20. Elliott, pp. 133-34.

21. *Ibid.*, p. 134.

22. *Ibid.*, note.

23. *Foreign Secret Consultations (iii) 8th Jan. 1778*, NAI, Delhi.

24. *Ibid.*

25. Jagdish Raj, 'The Revenue System of the Nawabs of Oudh' *Journal of Economic and Social History of the Orient*, 1958, p.101.

26. *Ibid.*

6

Landed Properties of a *Sufi* Establishment—A Study of Documents from Salon in Awadh

The various original documents as well as the letters of Mughal and Nawabi periods preserved in the private collections of the family members of the mystic establishment at Salon (situated in Rae Bareli district, U.P.) relate to *madad-i-ma'āsh* grant held by Shaikh Pir Muhammad and his successors from the 17th century to recent times.[1] Since here we have an authentic account of the land-rights of a mystic family setting its roots in the soil from below, the documents and the history they expose, are of great interest. They also shed light on administrative policies from time to time. Here and there, however, our subject is also illuminated by the narrative sources and recorded traditions. A study of these documents provides us with a number of interesting details and leads us to new aspects of social life which are otherwise missing from the chronicles and other works. Important extracts of some of these documents are appended at the end of this chapter.

Procedure of Grant

The family of the mystics established at Salon claim to be Faruqi Shaikhs, and say that while their original home was Yemen, they had settled in Nagor, the celebrated Qazi Hamiduddin of Nagor belonging to this branch. The family is said to have migrated from Nagor to Jaunpur during the period of the Sharqi Sultans. Makhdum Shaikh Addhan became famous as a *sufi* saint, and from him the family members acquired the name of Addhani. One of his descendants,

Shaikh 'Abdul Nabi settled at Salon and here in AH 996 /1578 Shaikh Pir Muhammad was born. After early education, he went to Manikpur for higher studies in rational and religious sciences. He became a disciple of Shaikh Abdul Karim, the *sajjada-nashin* of the *Khanqah* of Shaikh Husam-ul-Haq Manikpuri. After remaining there for some time under his spiritual guidance, and according to his instructions, Shaikh Pir Muhammad returned to Salon and according to a later tradition took up his abode here along with a *sanyasi* hermit.[2]

It appears that Shaikh Pir Muhammad soon acquired prominence sufficient to merit the attention of local officials. They made over to him, 'by way of an offering for (God's) servant knowing mystic truths' a grant of 200 *bighas* land in village Mirzapur Bakhtiyar, *pargana* Nasirabad, *sarkar* Manikpur, *suba* Allahabad. Since presumably the grant was initially made by one of the *hukkam* or *jagirdars*, and so temporary in nature (co-terminal with the *jagir*-assignment), so an imperial *farman* was issued on 5th *Shawwal* 19th RY/1676 recognizing the *madad-i-ma'āsh* rights of the grantee on these 211 *bighas* and requiring that the grantee should not be harassed by future officials. (No. 1).

Shaikh Pir Muhammad's son, Muhammad Ashraf was assigned the revenues of a village Singhwal, *pargana* Nasirabad, by the *zamindars* of the village. A perusal of the *hasil* figures of the village from 4th RY to 17th RY suggest that the revenue paying capacity of the village was greatly reduced, hence the *zamindars* were unable to meet the revenue demand and so transferred their rights to Shaikh Muhammad Ashraf who now sought tax exemption from the authorities, soliciting a *madad-i-ma'āsh* grant. The assignment to grantee was ultimately made in absolute perpetuity on 18th *Jamad I* 22nd RY/1679.

Emperor Aurangzeb, before proceeding to the Deccan, is said to have invited Shaikh Pir Muhammad to pay a visit to Delhi, but the offer was politely refused.

Subsequent to the above grants Aurangzeb is said to have assigned the revenues of the village Palhipur to Shaikh Muhammad Ashraf in 1109/1697 as the *waqai'-nawis* of the area informed the court that the present income of the mystic was not sufficient to meet his expenses. Probably with similar considerations and procedure Emperor Bahadur Shah assigned the revenues of village Kishandaspur to Shaikh Muhammad Ashraf in 1119/1707.[3]

It appears that Shaikh Muhammad Ashraf came to possess a

number of residential plots and superior land rights in a number of *chaks* (land strips) and villages in *sarkar* Manikpur, *suba* Allahabad as well as in *sarkar* Lucknow, *suba* Awadh either through imperial favour or through local officials and even by the *zamindar*. All these acquisitions were now confirmed by Emperor Muhammad Shah on 19th *Rabi II* 10th RY/1729 through an imperial *farman*.

The next imperial *farman* was issued by Emperor Shah Alam II who is said to have held Shah Muhammad Panah in high esteem. The latter requested the emperor for a comprehensive *farman* in lieu of all other *farmans* and *parwanas* he had received from time to time. He sent all the copies of such orders along with a list of his possessions which included a large number of villages, *chaks*, gardens and residential quarters (*havelis*) situated in *subas* Allahabad and Awadh. It was also solicited that the new *farman* be issued in the name of his son Shah Karim Ata. Accordingly, when the emperor held his *darbar* at Allahabad, the desired *farman* was issued on 15th Safar 6th RY/ AH/1178/A.D.1764.

The exact details of the manner in which favours were bestowed upon these mystics by the local chiefs and *zamindars* are unfortunately missing. Still some idea can be formed by the perusal of some statements termed *wajib-ul 'arz* (spelt 'wajib-ool urz') compiled during the course of first regular settlement of the province of Oudh after the events of 1857. These papers recorded the history of the village from the earliest period to which it could be conveniently traced. On the basis of this villagewise information the history of the families and clans was arranged and finally incorporated in the settlement reports.

A few *wajib-ul 'arz* statements of the villages which were included in the revenue grants of these mystics are available. A perusal of these statements (dealing with the history of the village concerned) gives some idea of the procedure adopted in these grants. The following may serve as examples.

1. Village Dhankesra, *pargana* Parshadepur and village Barwaliya, *pargana* Salon belonged to Raja Balbhadra Singh, the Kanhpuria chieftain of Tilain. He donated the revenues of these two villages for feeding the poor, mendicants, and visitors to the *khanqah* of Shah Muhammad Panah in AH 1171/1763. These grants were confirmed by imperial *farmans*.

2. The Rajas of *ta'alluqa* Bhadri, *pargana* Behar, had allotted

two tracts of forest land to Shah Muhammad Panah. The grantee was to get the forest cleared and the area settled with peasant castes especially the Kurmis. One tract was named Panah Nagar, and another Hayat Nagar (after the name of his deceased brother Shah Muhammad Hayat).

3. A tract of forest land was also granted by Emperor Shah Alam II to Shah Karim Ata. The grantee got the land cleared from forest, settled the population (mostly Kurmis) and named it after his father as Panah Nagar.

The existence of a large number of the villages having nomenclatures similar to that of the family members of the mystic establishment leads us to conclude that large tracts of waste and might have been cleared by these grantees to settle the population and, in turn, raise their income.

Donald Butter gives a detailed account of this establishment in 1836. He says that the original proprietors of the town of Salon were Kanhpuria Rajputs who were deprived of their estate in Salon khas by Nawab Asafuddulah; it was then bestowed upon the mystic family for perpetual support of the religious ''eleemosynary'' establishment.

The establishment seems to have been the largest of its kind in the southern parts of Awadh. The annual income was estimated by Butter (1836) at Rs. 30,000, all of which was utilized in entertaining *bairagis* and *faqirs* without making any distinction of religion. The visitors used to flock to the *khanqah* in quite large numbers and at a time there were about 100 mendicants. They were attended to and looked after by the *sajjada-nashin* of the *khanqah*. The head of the institution (*sajjada-nashin*) was held in high esteem by the local officials. His reputation was such that whenever the *chakledar* came to Salon, he always paid a visit to the mystic and offered him a few hundred rupees.[4]

The keeper of the establishment did not have any sympathy for the religious zeal of the *wahabis* under Saiyid Ahmad of Rae Bareli. He was told by the *zamindar* of the area and the *sajjada-nashin* that they considered aiding the poor, maim, and blind as more pious than indulging in holy war. Similarly they refused to abandon the ceremonies associated with *muharram*.[5]

W.H. Sleeman, while undertaking his tour in the kingdom of Oudh

(1849-50) refers to this establishment as the prime mystic institution of the kingdom. Shah Panah' Ata, the then *Sajjada-nashin* of the *khanqah* was looked upon with great reverence by both Muslims and Hindus for the sanctity of his ancestors and the institution. He did not go out of the *khanqah* but remained there to receive the homage and distribute food to the needy travellers of all religions. Sleeman estimated the annual income from the grant held by him in A.D. 1850. at about Rs. 25,000.

In addition to the income from revenue-free grants assigned by the Awadh rulers, the local officials as well as princes in the distant places such as Bhopal and Sironj made substantial offerings. This way the actual income of the establishment was calculated to amount to about Rs. 50,000 a year. Complimentary letters were sent to 'Shah Puna Ata' by the Governor-General of India, and Lieutenant, Governors of the NW Provinces. When Sleeman was passing through the district of Salon 'Shah Puna Ata' sent him "letter of compliments and welcome with a present of a tame antelope, and some fruits and sugar". This goodwill gesture was reciprocated by Sleeman, who got the impression that his character was held in high esteem by all classes of the people, of whatever creed, caste or grade.[6]

After the annexation of Awadh an enquiry was instituted to examine the credentials of these grantees. Major Barrow was appointed to conduct it. The then grantee Shah Husain Ata deposited 30 *farmans, sanads,* and *parwanas* with the authorities on 15th June 1856 and obtained a receipt for them. But all these documents were destroyed during the Mutiny. The second enquiry could start only after the events of 1857. The details of the enquiry conducted by W.C. Wood, new forms a historical narrative giving the family history, details of the income and expenditure and the status of these grants. On the basis of this enquiry Lord Canning issued a *sanad* to Shah Husain Ata on 26-9-1862, recognising his allodial rights over the 22 villages of his grant. The *sanad* was issued subject to the condition that the grant was to continue so long as the income was devoted to the maintenance of the *khanqah* buildings, tombs, mosques, the running of a school of 'Muhammadan Education' and the continuation of the charities as detailed in the *sanad.*[7]

Law of Succession and Family Custom

Apart from a number of spiritual duties, the office of the *sajjada-nashin* was determined by a well-defined system of custom and conventions. Inheritance in matters of landed properties attached to the *khanqah* took a definite form after undergoing a number of experiments. There appears to have been no problem till Shah Karim 'Ata succeeded his father Shah Muhammad Panah, as before this time all the prospective claimants had predeceased their fathers. Since Shah Karim 'Ata had five sons (two of whom died in infancy), there arose the necessity to set out certain norms for future succession. At an earlier stage he himself had divided all his possessions including, buildings, villages, *chaks*, gardens, books and even relics, equally among his three sons, reserving one village for his daughter.[8] But, partly due to the fact that such an arrangement was not liked and approved by the Awadh Court, and also since his eldest son Shah Ashraf 'Ata expired after sometime, the earlier arrangement had to de annulled and a new *iqrarnamah* was executed by Shah Karim 'Ata in favour of his second son Shah Panah 'Ata on 6th *Jamad I* AH 1248/ AD 1832.

This document is of utmost importance for spelling out the *waqf* character of the properties attached with the institution and the position of the other members of the family in relation to the *sajjada-nashin*. In fact an institution was sought to be established as the new arrangement entailed that all the books, relics and the buildings of the *khanqah*, tombs, mosques and the *madarsa* were to be maintained and looked after by the incumbents to the office of *sajjada-nashin*.[9] The successor to this office could hitherto be theoretically chosen from amongst the sons, relatives, devotees and even strangers. The news of such nomination was to be always communicated to the Mughal emperor. This practice seems to have continued during the days of the *Nawab Wazirs* also. The approval was sought from the government for appointing a successor as *sajjada-nashin* and *mutawalli* (custodian). It seems that by the first half of the 19th century the office of the *mutawalli* came to be possessed by the spiritual head of the institution (*Sajjada-nashin*) himself. Our documents do not provide any clue as to when the existing difference between these two offices was done away with. Both offices were made hereditary and permanent. (Doc. No. 7 of the Salon papers).

The customs and the conventions peculiar to the family of the mystics were recognised by the British authorities during the first regular settlement of the province of Awadh after the annexation. These were made part of and incorporated in the *Rawaj-e-aam* document of the *pargana* where the *maafi* villages of the grantee were situated. In the preamble of the *Rawaj-aam pargana* Parshadepur *tehsil* Salon, it is explicitly admitted by the *ta'aluaqadārs, numbardars* and the *maafidars*, that the "legal settlement of the villages belonging to us had been made for a period of thirty years and hence all the privileges particulars to us had been described in detail, while the general rules applicable in the region had been omitted. We agree to abide by these." The superior land-right holders were asked to state their family custom with regard to six sections, subdivided into twentytwo questions. The main features of the family of *sajjada-nashin* were as under:

(a) The lawful heir and the legal representative of the *sajjada-nashin* could only be a *sajjada-nashin*. The latter was to be nominated by the previous incumbent in his life-time by observing certain customary ceremonies and rituals in a prescribed manner as detailed in the document itself.

(b) The other heirs of the *sajjada-nashin* including his widow, were not entitled to any share in the properties having *waqf* character left by the deceased. These heirs could claim only a subsistance allowance known as *guzara*. The widow and unmarried daughters of the deceased were to be looked after by the future incumbent of the office of the *sajjada-nashin*.

(c) The *sajjada-nashin* was only a custodian of the properties either held as *waqf* or *maafi* and thus he was not empowered to effect any change by way of sale or mortgage or by oral gift.

Nawab-Wazirs' Policy towards *a'imma* holders

Ghulam Ali Azad Bilgirami criticizes Burhanul Mulk Sa'adat Ali Khan and Safdarjung for resuming cash and land grants *(wazif-o-suyurghalat)* of the old and the new families. As a result of this he says, Muslim learning suffered very heavily in both Awadh and Allahabad provinces. He does not himself attribute this explicitly to any sectarian motive on the part of the two Awadh rulers; and it is possible to argue that the motives were purely financial. The members of scholarly families, says Azad Bilgirami, had to take to the military profession as a result of these measures, a curious statement which suggests that a connection was always maintained between the grant-holders and the army.[10]

Elsewhere it has been argued that as a result of the laxity in the administrative machinery during the first half of the 18th century quite a few grants were obtained by fraudulent means and perhaps the *nawab-wazirs* tried to weed out such grants and to confirm only the genuine ones.[11]

But a perusal of some 18th century documents of the family in the private collection of Shah Muhammed Hameed 'Ata (now residing at Karachi, Pakistan) suggest that an open policy of resumption of the *a'imma* grant was pursued by the first three *nawabs*, and it was a matter of rare favour if some of the *a'imma* grants escaped confiscation or the grantees were given back their grants after the resumption. A letter addressed by Shah Muhammad Panah to Burhanul Mulk Sa'ādat Khan clearly mentions that in compliance of his orders regarding the resumption of the a'imma (*bar-zabti-i-a'imma-i subajat*) grants the troops have been posted by the *amil* in every nook and cranny including the villages of Panah himself. Although he was in possession of a *parwana* for all the villages, still the *gumashtas* (agents) of Murshid Quli Khan were demanding a fresh *parwana* addressed to them (Doc. No. 8).

The fact that the policy of resumption was pursued by Safdarjung in full vigour is borne out by two of his *parwanas* issued to the local officials regarding the affairs of the villages included in the grant of these mystics. In a *parwana* addressed to Raja Ram Narain in the first RY it was conveyed that the revenues of village Barwaliya in entirety along with the *chaks* was granted to meet the expenses of the mendicants residing at the *khanqah* of Shaikh Muhammad Ashraf. It should be recognised by the *amil* of the area and no interference be allowed (Doc. No. 9). Another *parwana* waṣ issued in the 6th RY to Zainul 'Abidin Khan (?) stating that the village Barwaliya, which was earlier resumed and included in the *khalisa*, had been restored to the possession of Shaikh Muhammad Ashraf and Shah Pir' Ata. Now the descendants of the former *a'immadar* who held the land previously were interfering with the above mentioned village and *chak* attached thereto, which was illegal. They had to be asked to keep off the village and it was to be recognised as the *a'imma* (land) of the lawful grantees. Confirmatory orders did not have to be demanded from them every year (Doc. N. 10).

The resumption of revenue grants continued during Shujaud-Dulah's period also. In a letter addressed to Shah Muhammad Panah the nawab especially says that no orders have been issued to any amils for the resumption of the *a'imma* land of the grantee. If inadvertantly any interference had been committed, a *shuqqa* is being sent by hand which will further eliminate any such possibility (Doc. No. 11).

An acute financial crisis seems to have been responsible for the *nawab-wazirs'* resolve to bring all the land under *khalisa* and put it under their direct administration. We know for certain that almost all the Mughal *jagirdars* had leased out their *jagirs* to Burhanul Mulk on *ijara* tenures as they themselves found it quite difficult to collect the land revenue from their assignments.[12] Similarly, Safdarjung had reportedly instructed his *wakil* at the Mughal court to invite imperial attention towards the heavy expenditure incurred by the nawab in the administration of the two provinces, and hence no new *jagirs* were to be assigned in these provinces.[13]

CALENDAR OF DOCUMENTS

Doc. No. 7

***Farman* of Nasiruddin Haidar, 27th Rajab 1250 AH**

Addressed to Maulvi Shah Muhammad Panah 'Ata. Be it known to the present and future *mutassadi*, *pargana* Salon that Shah Karim 'Ata had three sons, of whom he nominated Shah Panah 'Ata as *Sajjada-nashin* and *mutawalli* of all the landed possessions. Approval of the sublime court was sought (for these acts) which was granted. The villages, *chaks*, gardens, and buildings situated at the *parganas* of Salon, Parshadpur, Jais, manikpur, and Bihar held by the grantees as *madad-i-ma'ash* from olden times, for meeting the expenses of *A'aras-i aimma-i athar*, *Khanqah* and mosques are now confirmed in the name of Shah Panah 'Ata and thereafter his son *Sajjada-nashin* Shah Husain 'Ata in perpetuity and for all times to come. It is incumbent upon the present and future *nazims*, *jagirdars*, *muiassadis* of the said *parganas* to abide by this order. The grantee should not be harassed on account of the taxes like *bhent*, *begar*, *jaribana* and *nazrana*. He should not be asked for the dues on account of *faujdari*, *tehsildari*, and *pattadari*. Confirmatory *Sanad* should not be demanded from him every year.

Doc. No. 8

Letter of Shaikh Muhammad Ashraf to Burhanul Mulk, undated

After due regards and salutations expresses his happiness and satisfaction over the extermination of Fateh Singh, the rebel of

(Tiloin ?). Congratulations to the *nawab* that by the grace of Almighty God he is able to establish the tenets of Islam in this region (?). Invites his attention to his orders for the resumption of *a'imma* (grants) of the *suba* (Awadh and Allahabad); consequently everywhere the *sawar* and *piyada* have been posted by the *amil* of the *nawab* including the villages of the grantee (the petitioners). Says that despite the fact that he has the *parwana* of *nawab* for all his villages, the *gumashtas* of Murshid Quli Khan are demanding a *parwana*, addressed specifically to them. Solicits the issue of a *parwana* (to the *gumashta*) of Murshid Quli Khan to the effect that no interference be committed in the villages of Muhammad Ashraf. If this is not done, the maintenance of the *khanqah* and the mendicants will become difficult.

The endorsement of the *nawab* at the right-hand margin on the top of the letter is as under:-

Whereas due to the grace of the innocent *Imams*, the Muslim saints and companions, the extermination of the rebel was possible, it will strengthen the cause of Islam. With regard to the villages you have submitted, a *parwana* (to the *gumashta*) by name is being sent.

Doc. No. 9.

***Parwana* of Safdarjung, 15th Ramzan 1st RY/AH 1167**

Addressed to Raja Ram Narain, the *wazir*, that village Barwaliya in entirety with the *chak*, *pargana* Salon was granted for the expenses of the mendicants of Shaikh Muhammad Ashraf. Zainul 'Abidin Khan solicited a *parwana* in his name and stood as surity (?). Therefore it is ordered that the *'amil* of that place should consider the said village in the grant of Shaikh Muhammad Ashraf and should not interfere with them so that they may engage themselves in praying for the welfare of the principality.

Doc. No. 11

Letter of Shuja'uddaulah to Shah Muhammad Panah, undated

Acknowledges the receipt of the gift sent by the mystic. Says that no orders have been issued to any of the 'amil for the resumption of the villages in his *a'imma* grants. If any interference has been done inadvertantly, a *shuqqa* is being sent by hand to eliminate the chances of further interference. The addressee should not worry on this count.

References

1. Apart from the family manuscripts, there are a few biographical notices of Shaikh Pir Muhammad in the 18th century chronicles and *tazkirahs*. This is obviously because of the fact that his grandson, Saiyid Sadullah of Salon obtained greater prominance subsequently as a theologian and a *sufi*. In all biographical notices, he is referred to as the grandson of Shaikh Pir Muhammad who in turn is called the great mystic and theologian of his times; See Khafi Khan, *Muntakhab-ul-Lubab,* Bib. Ind. 1860-74, Calcutta, Vol. II, pp. 559-60: Ghulam Ali Azad Bilgirami, *Ma'athir-ul-Kiram,* 1913, Hyderabad, Vol. I, p. 217. For independent references to him see Muhammad Bukhtawar Khan, *Mirat-ul-Alam* (edited by Dr. Sajida Alvi), 1979, Lahore, Vol. II, p. 417. Abdul Hai, *Nuzhat ul-Khawatir,* (Arabic) 1911, Hyderabad, Vol. V, pp. 97-98. The 19th Century British officials and travellers traversing Southern Awadh, have left notices of this establishment. See Donald Butter, *Topography and Statistics of Southern Districts of Awadh,* 1839, Calcutta, pp. 138-39 and 164-65 (Delhi, reprint 1982); W.H Sleeman, *A Journey through the Kingdom of Oudh in 1849-50,* 2 Vols, 1950, London, Vol. I, pp. 232-34; *A Gazetteer of the Province of Oudh,* 3 Vols., 1877, Vol. II, p. 290; H.R. Nevill, *District Gazetteer of United Provinces* (Rae Bareli) Allahabad, 1923, Vol. 39, pp. 100-103. Beside these printed works, there is a good deal of information in the files of Board of Revenue, Allahabad (now shifted to Lucknow) relating to the period of First Regular Settlement of Awadh in 1861.
2. *Nuzahat-ul Khawatir,* Vol. V, p. 97.
3. The texts of these *farmans* could not be traced, but they have been discussed by W.C. Wood in his despatch to the Commissioner of Baiswara Division in the course of his examining the credentials of the grantees and the validity of their claims to hold a number of villages in revenue free tenures. See letter no. 504, dated 13 July 1861, File Nos. 173 & 1870/1861-2 (Rae Bareli District) Board of Revenue, Lucknow (Hereafter as Wood's Despatch).
4. Butter, *op. cit.,* pp. 138-39.
5. *Ibid.,* p. 165.
6. Sleeman, *op. cit.*
7. The copy of the *sanad* is available with the present *sajjada-nashin* of the *Khanqah-i-Karimia,* Saiyid Shah Ahmad Husain Jafri Islahi.
8. *Iqrarnamah* of Shah Karim 'Ata in favour of Shah Ashraf 'Ata dated 11th *zilhij* 1238AH/1822, in the personal collection of the present *sajjada-nashin* of the *Khanqah.*
9. Copy of this *iqrarnamah* is also in the above personal collection.

10. Ghulam Ali Azad Bilgirami, *Ma'athir-ul Kiram*, 1913, Kanpur, Vol. 1, pp. 221-22.

11. See my unpublished thesis, *Agrarian Conditions of Awadh under the Mughals and Nawab-Wazirs: 1595-1856*, submitted at AMU, Aligarh, 1985.

12. Ghulam Husain Khan, *'Imad-us Saadat*, Nawalkishore, Lucknow, 1897 pp. 7-8.

13. Santokh Rai, *Insha'-i-Mansur* or *Mansur-ul Maktubat*, letters on behalf of Safdarjung and Burhanul Mulk addressed to Emperor Muhammad Shah and *wazir* Qamaruddin Khan. These were collected by one Awadhi Lal in AH 1212/AD 1803. Probably the only copy of this manuscript is preserved at Tagore Library, Lucknow University, Lucknow. See ff-46b-47a.

7

Armed Zamindar: The Power Play in Awadh (1595-1858)

Superior proprietary rights in land had an intimate connexion with the domination of particular clans over an area. Elsewhere it has been argued that the major *zamindari* clans were able to maintain their territorial hold broadly unchanged between 1595 to the annexation of Awadh. Although it has been pointed out that such stability was essentially due to the late date at which Awadh was annexed by the British,[1] one should not forget that such an uninterrupted possession of rights also depended upon the capacity of each particular clan to maintain its hold with the help of armed power. "Armed force appears as the first historical pre-requisite for the establishment, as well as the retention, of *zamindari* right."[2]

Use of armed power by various clans to keep their possessions intact and/or to acquire new possessions had been a continuous process in Awadh throughout the medieval period. The traditional account of the *chakla* Gorakhpur bears testimony to this fact:

> In ancient times the dominion and *raj* of the neighbourhood of this city belonged to the caste of *Doms*. Thus remains of their forts at Batyalgarh, Ramgarh, Bhindiagarh, Domangarh etc. in the area adjoining the city are found to this day. And in the villages the caste of *Tharus, i.e.* the hillmen of the race of those who are now settled at the foot of the hills, had their settlements. The markets of Batwal for the sale of goods from the hills was held in Gorakhpur. From the time of the establishment of the rule of the Muslims, the markets and settlements of the *Tharus* gradually disappeared and exist now only in the *Terai*. Some Srinet Rajput natives of Srinagar

having extirpated them, established their power and are uptill now known as Raja Gorakhpuri. Thus, their descendants hold the *zamindari* of some of the villages of Silhat and of the *pargana* of the environs of Gorakhpur in accordance with the deeds of the Gorakhpuri Raja. Afterwards in the time of Akbar, the ancestors of the *ta'alluqadari* of Kachhar, formerly residing in the *pargana* of Bhauwapora with their kinsmen seized the *zamindari* of the environs of Gorakhpur and Silhat which till now is in the hands of their descendants.[3]

Apart from such traditional accounts, Abul Fazl has given detailed statistical information in the 'Account of the Twelve *Subas*' about the military resources of the *bumiyas* or *zamindars*, viz., cavalry, infantry, number of elephants in each *pargana*. The *sarkar*-wise information is tabulated below."[4]

Table 1

Military Resources of the Zamindars

Sarkar	*Elephants*	*Cavalry*	*Infantry*
1. *Sarkar* Awadh	23	1,340	30,400
2. *Sarkar* Bahraich	-	1,170	14,300
3. *Sarkar* Gorakhpur	-	1,010	22,000
4. *Sarkar* Khairabad	-	1,160	27,800
5. *Sarkar* Lucknow	36	2,680	77,050
Total	59	7,360	1,71,550

Almost all the *parganas* of the *suba* possessed cavalry and infantry. This makes it almost certain that every landholder of consequence maintained armed retainers. By the 17th century, they invariably had built mud forts (*garhi* or *qilacha*) in the villages of their *zamindari* to station these retainers. An interesting petition from *pargana* Hisampur, *Sarkar* Bahraich, reports a night attack by certain malefactors on a village included in the *zamindari* possession of one Saiyid Muhammad 'Arif. He speaks of a *qil'acha* he had built to protect his possessions[5]. In another document a reference is made to the razing of a *qil'acha* by some usurpers and it was ordered that the same be rebuilt by these who had destroyed it[6]. In the *Insha-i Roshan Kalam* a number of expeditions against such forts of recalcitrant *zamindar* are mentioned. R'ad Andaz Khan and his deputy Sher Andaz Khan boasted of their services in destroying and capturing various *garhis* of the *zamindars* of Baiswara[7]. In one '*arzdasht* it is said that the Chauhan *zamindar* of *pargana* Kanjura had refused to pay the land-revenue and with the help of 8 or 9,000 men had attacked *pargana* Shahpur. In retaliation, a number of their forts (*garhis*) were captured and many of the rebels were put to the sword. Finally, they sued for peace and agreed to pay the land-revenue to the agents of the *jagirdar*.[8] In the similar manner rebellious *zamindars* of *pargana* Bijnore and Zaidpur were suppressed. A number of their forts were taken and handed over to the agents of the *jagirdar* in lieu of arrears of land-revenue.[9]

Any *zamindar* of consequence always tried to keep his hold over his fortresses and seize those of his weaker neighbours. The rebel *zamindar* of *pargana* Harsha had captured the fort of Murtazanagar from its Saiyid owners based in Unao. Later on its possession was restored to the owners with the help of imperial forces.[10] Similarly new forts were built by *zamindar* at places of strategic importance with the help of professional soldiers. Kharsen, the *zamindars* of *pargana* Jajmau, employed Salim Afghan and building a fort named it Salimgarh. But the Mughal forces stormed the fort, and a number of soldiers, including Salim Afghan, were killed[11]. Fortified houses situated alongside the highway were also used by the *zamindars* to block the passage of the imperial troops. The capture of such places and their control by the imperial officials was thought to be very necessary for establishing their control.[12]

A number of *mahzars* seeking redress against the wrongs suffered by the petitioners and imperial officials containing a recital to the same effect also provide important clues to the strength and the use of armed power by local *zamindars*. It seems that established hereditary *zamindars* usually resented the induction of any new element, such as land grantees, within their territory. During the reign of Shah Jahan and Aurangzeb, the holders of *madad-i ma'āsh* grants were therefore often faced with harassment from local *zamindars*, who enforced a non-payment of the land-revenue to the grantees or ensured a refusal of payment of the revenues to them by the peasants (*ri'aya*).

Two *farmans* of Aurangzeb from *pargana* Sadarpur *Sarkar* Khairabad direct the officials to investigate the allegation of the petitioners and report accordingly : it was contended that one Samar Singh *zamindar* of Mannauti, *pargana* Fakharpur had a number of mounted and foot soldiers, and had became a freebooter. He had raided and burnt the villages of the petitioners, mosques, and tombs being razed to the ground. A number of inhabitants were killed; money amounting to Rs. 8213 and 6376 heads of livestock had been taken away[14]. Similarly, the *madad-i ma'āsh* holders of a village in *pargana* Hisampur, *sarkar* Bahraich presented a *mahzar* in AH 1125/AD 1717 complaining that the residents (*zamindars?*) of the neighbouring villages had attacked their *a'imma* (grant) villages with the help of 500 persons. In the raid many inhabitants were killed, their property looted and destroyed, while the women had committed *jauhar*; even the corpses were not allowed to be buried. Moreover, the family grave-yard of the petitioners was brought under the cultivation by the malefactors.[15] Similarly the Muslim *zamindar* of *pargana* Fatehpur Devi and of *pargana* Sehali in *sarkar* Lucknow had attacked and killed the head of what later came to be known as the house of Firangi Mahal, Mulla Qutubuddin. The incident occurred in the 35th Ry/AD 1690 of Aurangzeb.[16]

Often the *zamindar* defied the administration by refusing to acknowledge the authority of the local *qazi*. It seems that the holders of the religious offices and *a'imma* holders were most vulnerable to the armed power of the *zamindars* since they had no force to back their claims; hence their existence in any area depended upon the help from the military officials of the area. A petition by the family of the *qazi* posted in Baiswara especially mentions the tussle between their ancestors and the Bais (*zamindars*) of the area which was going on for the last 80 years. The *qazi* had all the 21 *parganas* of Baiswara under their jurisdiction, but due to the hostility shown by the inhabitants, they had been driven away from 15 *parganas* and now only 6 *parganas* actually remained within his judicial jurisdiction.[17]

During the first quarter of the 18th century, the local chieftains and the *zamindar* had acquired much power and were in possession of considerable resources. When Sa'adat Khan Burhan-ul Mulk was appointed the *subedar* of the province, he had to fight a number of battles with these chiefs in various parts of the province. Prior to his appointment as the governor of the *suba*, these chiefs and the *zamindars* were strong enough to undermine the authority of the *nazim* and the agents of the Mughal *jagirdars* to make the work of revenue collection nearly impossible. But Sa'adat Khan dealt with these refractory elements with such firmness that in the very first year of his tenure, the total amount of collection increased from barely 70 lacs to 107 lacs of rupees. On realizing his ability and competence, the Mughal *jagirdars* too leased out their *jagirs* to him on *ijara* tenures. In the next two years the total collection reached two crores of rupees[18].

The traditional account of the capture of Lucknow from the hands of the Shaikhzada *zamindars* may well contain a considerable amount of exaggeration. However, from our point of view the importance of the episode lies in the fact that even the newly appointed governor had to resort to dubious methods to reach the provincial capital which happened to be in the hands of local *zamindar*;[19] or one may think of the power gained by the Kanhpuria chief of Tiloin, Raja Mohan Singh, by plundering the Saiyid owners of Mustafabad and the Bais chieftain of Khajurgaon. When Burhanul Mulk decided to end the growing pretensions of these chiefs, battle took place. Mohan Singh was killed and all his possessions which lay in the jurisdiction of *suba* Awadh were seized.[20]

Burhan-ul Mulk was able to keep the recalcitrant elements of the province in check, but with his death the local chieftains began to reassert their power. His successors, Safdarjung's letters to Muhammad Shah are full of references to the rebellions of the *zamindars*. It was alleged that with the help of their strong forts and numerous armed retainers, they refused to pay the land revenue and undertook depredations all round.[21] The *nawab-wazir* had to be constantly on the march; and the *nawab-wazir* offered this as an excuse for omitting to heed urgent summons from the imperial court.[22]

In Safdarjung's letters addressed to *wazir* Qamaruddin Khan, it is stated that due to the rebellious attitude of the chieftains, additional troops had to be maintained in order to carry on the work of revenue collection and keep the malefactors under effective control. This had enhanced expenses while the actual income (from the *jagirs*) had fallen, and the *nawab-wazir* had claims outstanding for which he had no *jagir*. An another place he says that he had instructed his *wakil* (at the imperial court) to be present at the time when new *jagir* assignment orders were issued for the province of Awadh, so that he may invite the attention of the *wazir* towards the acute problem faced by the *nawab-wazir* in administering the turbulent province of Awadh.[23]

The *zamindar* and local potentates were always prone to take to banditry. Roads and highways were considered to be quite unsafe, and it was always considered necessary for heavy armed escort to accompany the treasures passing through the territorial limits of Awadh.[24]

Among the major rebellions by the *zamindar* during Safdarjung's reign, was a fresh one by the Kanhpuria chieftain of Tiloin. He had collected together a numerous body of armed retainers and possessed a very strong fort. It was surrounded by a deep ditch and extensive belt of dense and thorny jungle. But the forces of *nawab-wazir* were strong enough to defeat the Rajput forces and to capture the fort in 1739.[25] Another important uprising was that of the Gaur *zamindars* of *sarkar* Khairabad. It appears that they had refused to pay the land-revenue and took to banditry. Safdarjung, through forced marches reached their strongholds, the forts of Nabigarh and Katesar. These forts fell after a siege of eleven days and with some difficulty the Rajputs were defeated and the area was brought under control.[26]

After the battle of Buxar Shuja-ud Daula was forced to reduce his regular army, and strong exception was taken by the Company officials at the reported attempts of the *nawab* to reorganize the army. As a result, the work of revenue collection could proceed only with the help of the British forces. Such help was always available to the local officials of the *nawab-wazir* as the Company was entitled to receive large sums of money out of these collections. Indeed, the English looked askance at the *zamindar's* refusal to pay revenue for the amounts so withheld were sure to be "expended on those numerous forces which the *zamindars* raised and (?) up only to support them in their resistance to Government."[27]

The revenue contractors had constantly to face armed resistance of the *zamindars* in their respective jurisdictions. Often they were ruthless in suppression of the uprisings. The atrocities committed by Almas Ali Khan against the *zamindars* of Doab were reported to Middleton in 1778. Whatever he did was with the help of the British forces.[28] But it was thought that the destruction of the forts of the *zamindars* in the Doab, "will have many ill consequences" and accordingly the *nawab-wazir* was advised to adopt, "more conciliatory mode of proceeding" when using British forces against such elements.[29]

In the early years of Asaf-ud Daulah's reign, the *zamindars* of Gorakhpur went into rebellion. The intensity of these disturbances was such that the *nawab-wazir* had to proceed in person to suppress the rebellion.[30] A group of bandits made a night attack on the royal treasury, when it was going to Lucknow from Baiswara. A good number of Company sepoys accompanying the treasury were killed.

Obviously such an attack could have been made only with the help of local *zamindars.*[31]

The death of Asaf-ud Daulah in 1797 marks a watershed in the history of Awadh. It offered an opportunity to the Company to conclude new treaties with his successors first with Wazir 'Ali and then with Sa'adat Ali Khan (1798-1814). Now, the subordination of the kingdom of Awadh to the Company was complete in every respect. The army had to be disbanded and even the work of revenue collection was to be done only with British help. The help had mixed results. It was alleged that the "country was pillaged under the sanction of the British name and under the terror of sepoy bayonets" and also, "the more parties (of the sepoys) were sent out in support of the *amin*, the more were called for."[32] To remedy such a situation, it was suggested by the Resident that the 'crown dues' be leased out to the *zamindars* for a number of years in stead of being collected by *amin*. Under this system 'proofs' were to be furnished by the king for the outstanding dues against the erring *zamindars* before military help was given by the British to coerce them into making payments[33]. Such a tedious process could only further encourage the *zamindars*. The king, accordingly remonstrated that, "all his difficulties have arisen from his entire confidence in the friendship of the Company. That this induced him and his ancestors to disband an excellent army and thus they have become unable without help to enforce payment of their ancient revenues[34]. Under these circumstances the *zamindar* had acquired such power as to make the king plead for his own survival, "from the only enemies he has or is likely to have his rebellious *zamindars*."[35] The 'judicious care' and 'scrutiny' of each and every case by the Resident, before the requisition of the king for sepoys was met, adversely affected the fortunes of the kingdom. The king was unable to face the rebellious *zamindars*, as they had driven away many of his officials from their areas and in this process, "the chief actual sufferers at the present movement are the king, who gets little or nothing even of his undoubted dues, and the traveller, who unless he had such a guard as I have had better sleep in a safe kin (*sin*) on the other side of the Ganges."[36]

The *zamindars* were able to multiply their armed retainers, forts, cannons and guns after the death of Sa'adat Ali Khan (1814). This became possible as the King was unable to check their activities, and British help too was not forthcoming to the king in his attempts if ever made to punish a rebellious *zamindar*. It should not be assumed that they were simply 'invincible' or the Awadh government was in any way less competent to control the situation. Sleeman describes how the Kanhpuria Rajput chiefs of Nain were suppressed by Raja Darshan Singh and Bakhtawar Singh during their term of *nizamat* of the district of Salon (in which lay the Nain estate). But when the affairs of this place were entrusted to a court favourite, Hamid Ali, the situation under went a change. Thereafter, "the Kanhpuria have recovered all the lands they had lost, restored all the *jungles* that had been cut down, and they are now more powerful than ever. They have strengthened their forts, and built some new and added greatly to the number of their armed followers, so that the governor of the district dares not do anything to coerce them into the payment of just demands of government or to check into their usurpation and outrages."[37] The Gaur *zamindar* of Banthar in Bainswara named Kesri Singh paid Rs. 1,50,000/- annually in revenue, but thought it expedient to maintain 1000 matchlockmen. With these forces he defeated and slew a *chakledar* Sobha Ram and *faujdar* Shaikh Karim Baksh.[38]

Such defences could have been broken very well, but the army employed to bring down these *zamindars* was never given adequate supplies as to carry any long siege of the *garhis*, most of which were situated in midst of thick bamboo jungle. On the other hand, the supply line of the besieged rebels could not be successfully broken, as the neighbouring *zamindars*, always entertained a strong sense of fellow-felling for them. Although the total strength of the Awadh forces was said to have been 54,000. It was "an ill-paid disorderly multitude employed in coercing the *zamindar* under the orders of the *chakledar*."[39] It was thought of it to be "useful only to the enemy, it is dangerous to the well being of the state, utterly useless for war, most mischievous during peace."[40] The number of the retainers kept by the *zamindars* was computed at 100,000 men and they were mostly drawn from the castes of the *zamindars*.[41]

The country was dotted with innumerable fortresses, surrounded with dense forests, carefully rendered inaccessible for state forces.[42] All the big *zamindars* invariably kept cannon and big guns for the defence of their forts. A combination of all these factors always proved more than a match for the "royal forces". Sleeman estimated that some 250 mud forts and about 500 pieces of cannon were deployed in their service.[43]

It seems that the British officials had no clear idea of the actual strength of the *zamindars*, and whatever they guessed was a gross underestimate. The actual position came to light only after the Rebellion of 1857 was over, and the British officials started combing operations in the province. As a result 1575 forts were destroyed and 720 pieces of cannon were seized.[44] In addition to these general statements, we possess a statement showing the armed strength of 149 landholders of the southern portions of Awadh. It was prepared by the deputy commissioner of Salon (then an administrative division of southern Awadh) in 1858 We find that every landholder invariably had a *kacha* or *pucca* fort and a number of armed retainers. Even small landholders having two villages maintained a fort. The statement gives us the following statistics.[45]

Table 2
The Forts, Guns and Retainers Belonging to the *Ta'alluqadārs* of Southern Awadh

	Strength			
Forts	*Infantry*	*Cavalry*	*Total*	*Guns*
150	78,211	3,313	81,524	308

Although details regarding the other parts of the kingdom are not available, still one can have an idea as to what the actual strength of the landholders was on the eve of the annexation.[46]

As a necessary corollary, the British Government carried out a systematic campaign to disband the retainers, confiscate the guns and destroy the forts of the landholders after the fall of Lucknow in 1858. We have an interesting lease-deed (*patta*) executed in 1265F/1858 in favour of a revenue grantee. It was stipulated that the lessee should have surrendered all pieces of cannon and guns to the government officials. All the forts situated in his area should have been destroyed, the forests cleared and the ditches filled. If any other landholder in his area had concealed any guns or cannon, the matter be immediately brought to the notice of the government. In case of failing to discharge these duties, stern action would be taken including the forfeiture of the lease itself.[47] Other confirmatory *sanads* issued to recognise the previously existing *allodial* rights of the *zamindar* and the revenue-grantees invariably carried a recitation to this effect.

Lalji laments the fact that, "among the Hindu inhabitants of the country (Awadh), the most numerous are the Rajputs. Most of the large *zamindaris* and the *ta'alluqadāris* of the kingdom belong to them. The fact that they possess large body of (armed) retainers and forts, had made them arrogant and hence they had become disrespectful towards the others. Some of these idiots show no consideration towards the priestly class of the Brahmans and openly defy religious customs.[48] The additional income so gained was again invested by the *zamindar* in raising the number of the retainers, forts and cannon.''[49]

In many ways the increase in the armed power of the *zamindar* was a direct consequence of the British interference in day-to-day affairs of the kingdom. No doubt the *zamindar* had always kept a number of retainers, maintained forts, rebelled or taken to banditry under Mughal rule. But by and large, they seem to have been kept in check till the reign of Shuja'ud Daulah. But after the battle of Buxar a sort of 'dyarchy' was introduced in Awadh and interference was attempted at all levels without any recognised system of action. The Awadh administration became a prey to changing policies of the British Governor-Generals ''Everything... mere guess work and experiment. One governor general, or one Residen had adopted one plan; next had tried some thing wholly different.''[50] On occasion, Company sepoys were deployed immediately to crush rebellions of *zamindars*, while on other such occasion, help was refused even on the requisition of the king himself. Such a situation could not but greatly encourage the *zamindars* to take up arms against the government as well as against the fellows *zamindar*.

References

1. See my paper, 'The Land Controlling Classes in Awadh — A Study of Changes in their Composition, 1600-1900', *U.P. Historical Review*, Vol. V., Allahabad, pp. 22-39. [Chapter XI of the book].
2. Irfan Habib, *Agrarian System of Mughal India*, p. 163.
3. Mufti Ghulam Hazrat, *Kwaif-i Zila-i Gorakhpur*, ff. 7a-b., Cf. Irfan Habib, *op. cit.*, p. 160.
4. Abul Fazl, *Ain-i Akbari*, ed. H. Blochman, Bib. Ind. Calcutta, 1866-77.
5. Documents in Regional Records Office, Allahabad, Accessioned in Register of Historical Documents Purchase Committee U.P. (hereafter Allahabad, followed by the accession number) Allahabad-1225 (Dec. 1689).
6. Allahabad - 786 (Jan. 1684).
7. Bhupat Rai, *Insha-i-Roshan Kalam*, MS. Maulana Azad Library, AMU, Aligarh, ff.2a-4a; 6a-8a.
8. *Ibid.*, *'arzdasht*, No.1.

9. *Ibid.*, *'arzdasht*, No. 2.
10. *Ibid.*
11. *Ibid.*
12 *Ibid.*, *'arzdasht*, No. 3.
13. *Ibid.*, Some fresh evidence has been examined to study the tensions between the *zamindar* and the *madad-i ma'āsh* grantees during this period in the same region. It has been shown that the grantees, holding ecclesiastical offices as well, could become an easy target of *zamindars*' wrath, rather than those who were simple grantees. See my paper, 'Tension and Conflict in the Agrarian Society of Awadh during the 17th Century — A Study of the Revenue Grantees' *PIHC* (1990), pp. 354-36. [Chapter IV of the book].
14. *Allahabad - 287* and *290* (4th Ry of Aurangzeb).
15. *Allahabad* - 1315.
16. *Firangi Mahal Document* No. 185 (35th Ry of Aurangzeb) Research Library, Centre of Advanced Study in History, AMU, Aligarh. This has been reproduced in Mufti Raza Ansari's *Bani-i Darse-Nizami* (Urdu) Aligarh, 1973.
17. This petition has many unique features, which are otherwise missing from contemporary historical literature. For further details see my paper, *PIHC* (1990), p. 356.
18. Ghutam Husain Khan, *'Imad-us Sa'adat*, Nawal Kishor Press, Lucknow, pp. 7-8.
19. Kamal-ud Din Haidar, *Swanihat-i Salatin-i Awadh*, pp. 7-8. Also see A.L. Srivastava, *The First Two Nawabs of Awadh*, Agra, 1933, pp. 33-35 (hereafter as *FTNA*).
20. *'Imad-us Sa adat*, pp. 7-8; *FTNA*, pp. 35-37.
21. *Mansur-ul Maktubat* ff. 6-7; f. 89;
22. *Ibid.*, ff.4-6; 38-40. It was asserted that these *zamindars* were "capable of creating disturbance in the twinkling of eyes" and were "more dangerous than the Marathas of Deccan, the hereditary enemies of the Mughal Empire". See also *FTNA*, pp. 39-40.
23. *Ibid.*, ff. 46-47.
24. *Ibid.*, ff. 7-8; 14-16; 17-18; 42.
25. *Ibid.*, ff. 30-31. In a letter addressed to Nawab Ishaf Khan (?) Safdarjung conveyed to him the news of his victory over the rebels of Tiloi. Their forts were captured and a number of Rajput chiefs were put to the sword. *Ibid.*, ff. 77-78. See also *FTNA*, pp. 92-94.
26. *Ibid.*, ff. 6-7.

27. *Foreign Department Secret Consultations*, 12 Jan., 1778, National Archives of India, New Delhi, (hereafter *FDSC* and *NAI*).

28. *FDSC*, 8 Jan. 1778, NAI.

29. *FDSC*, 8 Jan. 1778, NAI. For a later account of Almas Ali Khan, when he had become very old, see J.V. Valentia, *Voyages and Travels in India, Cyclone, The Red Sea, Abyssinia and Egypt*, 1802-6, 3 vols, London, 1809, see pt.1, pp.136-37.

30. *Foreign Secret Consultations*, 26 Feb. 1777 (c) and 21 April, 1777 (D), NAI.

31. Munshi In'amullah Raghib, *Ausaf-al Asaf*, MS. Aligarh 'Abdul Salam 480/1 *Farsi*, compiled in 1199 AH, transcribed in 1202 AH. The second section of the MS contains letters, despatches, petitions and *parwanas*: see ff. 69b-70a.

32. Bishop Heber, *A Narrative of a Journey Through the Upper Provinces, 1824-25*, London, 1828, pp. 84-85.

33. *Ibid*., p. 85.

34. *Ibid*., p. 86.

35. *Ibid*., p. 87. This was not the end of the matter as subsequently we find the situation deteriorating further. Henery Lawrence observed, "At Lucknow for years the Residents held public *darbar*, where the grantees attended, and pleaded against their own sovereign or his servants; thus were the monarch and his subjects arrayed against each other; thus was the sovereign degraded in his own capital, "*Calcutta Review*, (iii), 1845, pp. 414-45.

36. *Ibid*., p. 98.

37. W.H. Sleeman, *A Journey Through the Kingdom of Oudh*, Vol. I, London, pp.134-35.

38. Donald Butter, *Outlines of the Topography and Statistics of Southern Oudh and Cantonment of Sultanpur*, p.100.

39. Edward Thornton, *A Gazetteer of the Territories under the Government of the East India Company and the Native States on the Continent of India*, London, 1854, p.36.

40. Henery Lawrence, 'The Kingdom of Oudh', *Calcutta Review*, Pt. III, 1845, p. 388 (hereafter *CR*).

41. *Thornton*, p. 36.

42. *CR* (III), p. 421.

43. Sleeman, *op. cit*., Vol. II, pp. 210-11. In a different context we are told that in "midst of these forests, the landholders generally maintained one or more mud-forts, surrounded by a ditch and a dense fence of living bamboos, through which cannon shot cannot penetrate." *Ibid*., II, p. 279.

Bishop Heber also confirms this when he says that the stronger *zamindars* built mud forts; the poor *raiyat* planted bamboos, and thorny jungles round their villages. *(op. cit.*, p. 83)

44. *CR*, 1860, pp. 132-32.

45. This list provides exhaustive details which are seldom otherwise available. In the first column the locality of the fort is given, followed by the physical description of the fort and whether it is surrounded by a forest or not, then the name of the *ta'alluqadār*, what amount of revenue he paid, the actual strength of the retainers he maintained, the number of the guns he possessed. Although utmost care was taken to compile the information still it was mentioned, "that in addition to the above forts, every village in Oude almost, is more or less fortified — the houses being loopholed and often encircled by bamboo plantations." *Board of Revenue Records*, file number *395/1859*. [Oudh General].

46. The total number of the forts in Awadh belonging to the landholders were said to be around 633 immediately after annexation. *Foreign Consultations No. 136/53 dated 31 Oct., 1856. NAI*, New Delhi.

47. *Khairabad Documents No.* 10, Centre of Advance Study in History, Aligarh. For a calendar of these documents see Iqbal Husain, 'A Calendar of Khairabad Documents; 16th-19th Centuries', *Islamic Culture*, vol. LIII, Nos. (i) & (ii), Hyderabad, 1979.

48. *L'alji*, *Mirat-ul Auza*, Ms. Maulana Azad Library, AMU, Uny. Collec. (supply) *Farsi Akhbar* No. 60, ff.74a-76b.

49. *Ibid.*, f. 91.

50. *CR*, (III), 1845, p. 421.

8

Inheritance, Succession and the Customary Law in a *Sufi* Establishment of Awadh

The adaptation of customs and traditional laws from different regions and the evolution of the various institutions by juxtaposing 'mystical halos' and 'legal sanctity' had been an ongoing process in medieval *sufi* institutions. 'While motives cannot be denied behind such moves, only a sceptic will question the wisdom behind them. There is yet another perspective. In fact, the study of the twin processes indicated above, would indicate, that it was not only in the sphere of the rituals, customs and the externals that the interaction between the two traditions took place, but also in matters having a far-reaching impact on the fortunes of the institutions, the perceptions of the people and the growth of the composite culture in various regions.

A study of the evolution of the laws of the inheritance in the landed properties attached with the institution either by way of *waqf* or *madad-i ma'ash* is relevant here, as it will highlight the intrusion of the local customs in matters of succession.

The rules for the succession to the highest spiritual office the *sufi* institutions are examined separately. We find that a 'halo' was created around the person nominated to the office of the *sajjada-nashin*. Gradually, he was projected as a respository of the secretly infused mystic qualities. While the adherents of the *sufi* Shaikhs had every reason to acknowledge the 'superhuman' qualities of the nominee of their *pir* for their supposed 'prowess' and the 'knowledge of the secrets,. the phenomenon had become popular enough to stir the imagination of the masses and could mould the perceptions of the elite the study of the process through which a particular stage in this entire mental build has reached becomes additionally important. Attempt has been made here to delineate the processes of this phenomenon. These questions are examined mainly in the light of the evidence gleaned from the family papers of the *Khanqah-i Karimia,* Salon (District Rai Bareilly, U.P.).

Succession to the office of the *sajjada-nashin* had often been a matter of dispute among the heirs and the disciples of the departed holder of office. On occasions these disputes obliged the new incumbent (in case of his being an 'outsider') to move out from the place and to establish his own *khanqah* elsewhere. But such simple solutions were inapplicable where landed properties were also attached for the upkeep of the institution by way of *waqf* or other grants. In such establishments the new incumbent was entrusted with the manifold responsibilities, apart from spiritual matters.

Different sets of rules of succession were formulated by Aurangzeb in relation to the revenue grants, as it was asserted that, "since *madad-i ma'āsh* is an *'ariyat* (loan), therefore in such matters, the exalted order is sufficient".[1] By invoking this principle, the new regulations enforced rules different from the *shari'at* law of succession. The main features of the new legislation in relation to the grantees were follows:

(a) A grandson, whose father has predeceased his grandfather, is not entitled for a share in the ancestral property as technically he becomes *mahjub-al irth* (excluded from inheritance) under the *Hanafi* school of Muslim law, while under this legislation, in the *madad-i ma'āsh* holdings he was to get the same share as would have accrued to his father.

(b) In case, the deceased grantee has left a son and a married daughter, who has the means of subsistance from the side of her husband the whole property will be inherited by the son, but in case of the daughter being a widow or without the means of subsistance, she will get her share out of the proceeds of the property of the deceased grantee.

(c) If the deceased grantee has left only a daughter and not a son, the whole property will be inherited by her, and not by the other male relatives of the deceased. Similarly, the widow of the deceased was to inherit the whole property for her lifetime, but after her death, the property will go to her husband's relatives. In absences of these claimants, her relatives will get the share.[2]

The above changes in the law of inheritance were additional concession to the grantees, apart from making the revenue grants hereditary.

However, no separate provisions were provided for those grants, which were for the benefit of institutions. The general principle was, "by law (*shar'an)* the land of the *madad-i ma'āsh* is not alienable *(qabil-i tamlik nist)* and that the *ai'mma* land cannot be sold,"[3] it will be only a matter of conjecture it we presume that succession and inheritance in such grants were also regulated differently. During the later period only, the things became explicit and we can trace certain institutional features emerging from these grants. It is in this sphere that we notice the intrusion of local customs: hence the perceptions as well as the family traditions of the different *sufi* institutions vary from region to region.

The office of the *sajjada-nashin* signified the continuation of the *barakat* (charisma of the departed soul of the *sufi* Shaikh) for the people associated with a particular *khanqah*. He combined the 'hidden (*batin*) and the apparent *(zahir)* aspects of the spiritual legacy and prowess of his Shaikhs'. The 'hidden legacy' of the *silsilah* was also transferred to the successor designate along with the other paraphernalia.[4] It appears to have been a pleasant duty of the *sufi* Shaikh to choose the right person as his successor. In the deeds of nomination it was always asserted:

Hazārān durūdo wa hazārān sipās;
Ke gawhar sipurdah ba gawhar-shānās

(Thousands of blessings and thousands of thanks that a jewel is rendered unto one who knows its value)

Elements of mystification and the discourse of 'hidden and apparent' seem to have been a distinctive character of the institution. These concepts were stretched to accommodate a variety of interpretations. Thus, Shah Muhammad Naim 'Ata' while reiterating his nomination of Saiyid Shah Mohammad Husain Jafri, asserted that so far the institution *(khilafat-i karimi)* had been 'Faruqi in appearance', while 'Alavi in essence', but with this nomination after some times, it will have on 'Alavi appearance and Faruqi essence.'[5] Such visualizations were to place the institution at a 'hallowed pedestal.'

The deeds executed on the occasion of the nomination of a successor *(mithal-i khilafat wa janashini)* invariably has a recitation in favour of the 'hidden qualities of the new incumbent, besides his being a repository of knowledge (*'ilm-wa 'amal*) virtue and piety *(salah-wa taqwa)*. In 'spiritual hierarchy' of the *khanqah*, he was accorded a high status by the all concerned, as it was always asserted by the Shaikh that 'anyone who disputes with him, disputes me' *'(man naza faqad naza a'ini)'*.[6]

Once the successor was chosen, he was initiated into the higher aspects of gnosis *(m'arifat)* and truth *(haqiqat)* as he may be able to lead the *silsilah* in future. As a piece of final advice, the following couplets were always written after the bottom line of every nomination deed:

Nāmi goyam ke az 'ālam juda bash,
Bahar jāi ke bāshi ba khudā bāsh;
Hami khwāham ke ham chun khāk gardi,
Magar dar zer pāi pāk gardi.

(I don't say to keep away from this world, but wherever you stay keep on remembering Him; I only wish whenever you also turn into dust, let you remain under the feet of the pious ones only.)

Apart from the things in the 'realm of spirituality', we are fortunate in having a detailed description of the actual mechanism through which a successor was nominated at the Salon *khanqah*. It was during the First Regular Settlement of the Province of Oudh in 1860, that the British authorities carried out a detailed survey of the traditions and customs of each *pargana*, which had a bearing on land rights. Since at that time the *sajjada-nashin* of the *khanqah* possessed fifty-two villages either in *ma'afi* or *zamindari* rights, it became necessary to record the customs and the conventions governing succession and inheritance. For us, this is a valuable historical source of the *khanqah*.

At the very outset, it was asserted that adoption of a child *(mutabanna)* as a method of nomination of successor was not practised. Instead, the *sajjada-nashin* had full authority to choose and nominate anybody from amongst his sons or relatives, or a stranger to succeed him.[8]

Once he had decided to nominate someone, an auspicious date was fixed, when elaborate arrangements were made for the occasion. The ordinary people *(ri'aya)* from the *ma'afi* villages, notable persons of the area, the local chiefs and scholars were invited for the occasion. With a lot of pomp and show, gaiety and music, feasts and celebration, the future incumbent in the traditional attire was ushured by the *sajjada-nasheen* to his own prayer carpet. All the relics of the *khanqah* were handed over to him. On that very occasion itself the *sajjada-nashin* would dictate a document *(mithal-i khilāfat wa jānashini)*. He would put his own signature and a few notables present at the occasion would also put their signatures as witnesses. This way, whoever was declared as successor, would ultimately become the future *sajjada-nashin* and would take charge of all the villages, buildings, and everything connected with the *khanqah*.[9]

The incumbent to the office of the *sajjada-nashin*, apart from being the repository of the 'spiritual prowess' and 'hidden mystic qualities', had to be a scholar of the orthodox *(manqulat)* and rational *(m'āqū lāt)* sciences. This coupled with considerable landed properties and a substantial income through *futūh* (unsolicited gifts) raised his social status as well as the stature of the institution. High notions of his standing were entertained by the local people as well as by the officials which gave further legitimacy to such perceptions.

One of the popular notions was that the *sajjada-nashin* never goes out of the *khanqah,* although this was not the case as he went quite frequently to the shrines of his *shaikhs*. Yet the notion grew in such a way that Colonel Sleeman, who toured the kingdom of Oudh in AD 1849-50, approvingly says, "from the time that the heir is called to the throne, he never leaves his house, but stays at home to receive homage and distribute blessings and food to needy travellers of all religions." He further observes that "he is looked upon with great reverence by both Mohammadens and Hindus, for the sanctity of his character, and that of his ancestors who sat upon the same religious throne, for the throne his simple mattress is considered to be."[10]

Such notions had a wide acceptability in the area, and no body seems to have questioned them, and thus the legends kept on growing. Again we have the testimony of one Dost Muhammad Khan, *ta'alluqadār* of Paryanwan, *pargana* Salon who testified to the numerous qualities of the *sajjada-nashin* in an affidavit in AD 1880.[11] The evidence is important enough to merit detailed consideration:

(a) The family of the *sajjada-nashin* was established at the *qasba* Salon since last two hundred years. Due to the reverence people had for the ancestors of the family, the *qasba* itself was called *Hazrat-i Salon*.

(b) The 'spiritual prowess' *(kamālat)* of these saints was so widely known that large *ma'afi* grants were made over to them by the Mughal kings and Awadh *nawabs;* so they could continue with fulfilling the social obligations *(silsilah-i khair)* without worrying for the livelihood and so they should busy themselves in religious and mystic activities.

(c) Highest respect was always accorded to the family. During the periods when *nazims* and *chakledars* were appointed at Salon, they made courtesy calls the *sajjada-nasheen,* also while they entered the *qasba,* they use to stop the beating of the drum as a mark of respect for the institution.

(d) Three things made the *sajjada-nasheen* more distinguished; their 'spiritual prowess' attracted thousands of Muslim disciples and Hindu devotees, who made cash offerings; these included the Raja of Rewa, (M.P.) also; they were distinguished scholars of theology and the *ma'afi* grants have made them quite affluent.

(e) The *sajjada-nashin* never visited government officials and had never attended any court of law; instead most of the officials have visited him.[12]

At the initial stages, the land-owning classes of the area saw the grantees with suspicion, often resulting in armed clashes between them. As it has been argued elsewhere, the grantees with a position in the hierarchy of ecclesiastical offices were not immune from such clashes.[13] Although the evidence adduced for such analysis is basically from the Baiswara region, we can assume that the conditions in the Kanhpuria belt were not very different. The grantees with mystic predilections were comparatively safe from such assaults. This could be seen as a tribute to the 'far sightedness' and 'lying-low attitude' of the *sufis* and their institutions making it possible for them to exist in area dominated by *zamindars*, and to establish rapport with sections of the population.

References

1. The well-known *farman* of Aurangzeb issued in 34th RY/AD 1690. It was through this order that the *madad-i ma'ash* grants were made

hereditary and a set of rules was framed for deciding the share of an individual in the property of the deceased grantee. A copy of the *farman* is preserved at the Regional Records Office of UP State Archives, Allahabad accession no. 1880.

2. *Ibid.*

3. Cf. Irfan Habib, *Agrarian System of Mughal India,* p. 304 (notes).

4. Any discussion on the exoteric and esoteric nature of ***sufism*** will ultimately lead to the question of the inner relationship the system had with *shi'ism* and *Isma'ilism.* For a discussion on these aspects see Seyyad Hossein Nasr, *Sufi Essays,* Allen and Unwin, London, 1972, pp. 104-120.

5. Deed executed by Shah Muhammad Naim 'Ata in favour of Saiyid Shah Muhammad Husain Jafri dated 14th *Safar,* AH/ 1357AD 1938.

6. *Mithal-i khilafat wa Janashini* executed in favour of Saiyid Shah Muhammad Husain Jafri by Shah Muhammad Naim' Ata dated 10th *Jamad* 1 AH 1350/AD 1931.

7. The information used here is based on three actual specimens of the nomination deeds *(mithal-i khilafat wa janashini)* of the *khanqah-i karimia,* Salon. The text and the format of these deeds more or less conform to each other, besides having Persian couplets at the end, and signatures of the seven witnesses. The Shaikhs, who executed these deeds, put their signatures twice; one at the top of the left hand margin inside the world *saha* (certified), the other one at the bottom of the document with an endorsement in his own handwriting "I have given the dictation (of the text) and the (deed) has been written (by the scribe) accordingly." The following deeds have been used:

   (a) The deed executed by Shah Muhammad Naim' Ata in favour of Saiyid Shah Muhammad Husain Jafri, dated 10th *Jamad* I, 1350 AH/AD 1931.

   (b) The deed executed by Saiyid Shah Muhammad Husain Jafri in favour of Saiyid Shah Ahmad Husain Jafri, dated 9th *Jamad* I AH1389/AD 1969.

   (c) The deed executed by Saiyid Shah Ahmad Husain Jafri, the present *sajjada-nashin* of *khanqah* in favour of his successor-designate, Saiyid Shah Wali Husain Jafri, dated 10th *Jamad* I AH 1406/AD 1987.

8. *Rawaj-i-'aām ta'alluqadaran-malik-i a'ala wa adna', pargana* Parshade-pur *tehsil* Salon dated 4th December, AD 1869. This exposition was in response to the question sixteenth of the fourth chapter. The information is compiled in a tabular form, the last column was to record the customs of the,*'faqir sajjada-nashin* whose property

is inherited by the *sajjada-nashin.'* All the leading landholders, whose family customs were recorded promise to have put their signatures to abide by these rules of succession. On behalf of Shah Muhammad Husain' Ata, the then *sajjada-nashin,* his *karinda* Saiyid Kazim 'Ali put his signature.

9. *Ibid.* See also *Iqrar-i ma'afidar malik awwal,* village Barwalia included in the First Settlement Report of *pargana* Salon.

10. W.H. Sleeman, *A Journey Through the Kingdom of Oudh,* London, 2 Vols., 1858, Vol I, pp. 232-34.

11. The affidavit was filed by this leading *ta'alluqadār* in a court of law for the settlement of property disputes between Shah Muhammad Mehdi 'Ata, the then *sajjada-nashin* and his cousin Shah Muhammad 'Usman Ghani 'Ata.

12. *Ibid.*

13. See my paper, 'Tension and Conflict in the Agrarian Society of Awadh During the 17th Century — A Study of the Revenue Grantees; *PIHC,* Calcutta Session (1990), pp. 354-61.

9

A *Sufi* Institution of Awadh

Documents and letters belonging to the *sufi* establishment at Salon (district Rae Bareli, Uttar Pradesh) have been analysed to reconstruct an account of the growth of the landed properties of a seventeenth century mystic family and the multiplicity of land rights acquired by it through time.[1] But various gaps were left as a result of incomplete information on certain vital aspects. Since then, in the course of further explorations in the history of the establishment, I have come across a variety of evidence whose examination along with the records already studied not only strengthens the points made earlier, but also reveals some interesting aspects of the role of the *sufi* establishment.

The element of intrusion of local customs in matters of inheritance and succession, and even in respect of *waqf* properties is fully borne out by these documents. Some information also relate to the differences in the attitudes of the various social groups to the accommodations and adaptations made by the *sufi* institutions in evolving certain practices.

A calendar of the documents discussed here has been arranged in a chronological sequence at the end as Appendix B and each document is assigned a number for ready reference.[2]

The *khanqāh* established at Salon belongs to the Chishti-Nizami tradition coming through Shaikh 'Ataul Haq of Pandua (d. AD 1398) (West Bengal) and his son Shaikh Nur Qutb 'A lam (d. AD 1410) to Shaikh Husam-ul Haq of Manikpur (d. AD 1470) in Awadh. The seventh *sajjada-nashin* of Khanqāh-i Husāmiya Shaikh 'Abdul Karim (d. 1647), had selected Shaikh Pīr Muhammad to lead this *silsilah* in Awadh and nominated him as his successor. It is with this event that the shift took place from Manikpur to Salon. The newly established *Khanqāh-i Karīmiya* by Shaikh Pīr Muhammad (named after his preceptor) became the nerve centre of *Chishti-Nizamī* tradition in Awadh. According to the popular tradition in family, Shaikh Pīr

Muhammad was given some practical advices by his spiritual preceptor, *i.e.*, to 'avoid the path of confrontation' and try 'to become acceptable to all persons'. This *doha* in Awadhi language survives as the 'motto' of the institution for generations to come:[3]

پیرن رسنا تھام کے کر مسکینی بھیس

میٹھے بولو نئے چلو سبھی تمھارو دیس

O! Pīran, hold your tongue, become a recluse, utter the sweet words, follow the straight path, the whole world will be yours.

The family of Shaikh Pīr Muhammad claims to be Faruqi Shaikhs and says that while its original home was Medina, it had settled in Yemen; thereafter migrated to India and came to Nagor. The celebrated Qāzī 'Hamīd-ud-dīn Nagori (the teacher of Shaikh Qutb ud-dīn Bakhtiyār Kākī) belonged to this branch. From Nagor, the family came to Jaunpur during the period of the Sharqī Sultāns. Makhdum Shaikh Bahā'uddin Nathan and Shaikh Minallāh Addhan acquired much fame; the latter became famous as a *sufi* saint, and from him the family started using the title Addhani. One of his descendants Shaikh 'Abdul Nabi settled at Salon. We are in the dark about the 'exploits of the family' here till the time of Shaikh Pīr Muhammad, who was born in AH/994 AD 1585.[4]

After early education at Salon, he went to Manikpur (known at that time as *Dar al- 'Ilm*) for higher studies in rational and traditional sciences at *Kala Madarsa*. But after an 'incidental encounter' with Shaikh 'Abdul Karim, he got himself enrolled as his pupil. After being taught *Tafsīr-i Baizawi* (a Quranic commentary having *m'uatazalite* point of view as well) and *Hidaya*' (the digest of jurisprudence of the *Hanafī* school), he remained for quite some time under his spiritual guidance and instruction.[5] Shaikh Pīr Muhammad came back to Salon and as per instructions of his *Pīr*, undertook a *chilla*' (meditation for forty days in a prescribed manner) at the tomb of Saiyid 'Abdul Shakur and Saiyid 'Abdul Ghafur (said to be the companions of Saiyid Salar Mas'ud Ghazi, many of whose tombs are found in the region), popularly known as *Piran-i Paratha*. After the completion of this training, Shaikh 'Abdul Karim came from Manikpur to declare him his successor and asked him to take up his abode along with a *sanyāsī* (hermit). The family manuscripts record many anecdotes of his spiritual prowess *vis-a-vis* these *sanyāsīs* 'Quite expectedly' he defeated them spiritually and finally settled at the place where the *khanqāh*, mosque and the tomb (*maqbarā*) of the family stand presently.[6] The 'spiritual jurisdiction' of Mānikpūr shrine over Salon was there for all time to come. Thus Shaikh 'Abdul Karim has reportedly told his successor that.

آیو جایو پیرنا ہمرانگن ہوئے جایو (جار ؟)

ڈھلین مار جگایو ہم اٹھ لاگب سار

O! Pīran keep on coming to my place (whenever in trouble), wake me up (even if in a deep sleep) I will be on your side.

Shaikh Pīr Muhammad became a celebrity 'in the world of spirituality' during the lifetime of his Shaikh, and the latter was highly enamoured of his successor's popularity and made frequent visits to Salon to witness the esteem in which he was held by all. His sentiments are aptly expressed in one of his *dohās*:[7]

چاچر دیکھن ہم گئین پیرن کے دربار

دیکھت نینا جوبھ گیو بسر گیو گھر بار

Having gone to see the popularity of Pīran at his *darbār* (see the place); the eyes could not stand the glitter, I forgot even my own place.

Although he himself became a celebrity, his regard for his *pīr* lasted throughout. Therefore we find Saiyid 'Abdul Sattar of Alipur (now in District Sitapur, U.P.) one of the notable *khalifa* of Shaikh Pīr Muhammad expressing the following sentiments whenever the *pīr* of his *pīr* visited Salon[7a] :

مستی پیرم در و دیوار را مستانہ کرد   صد ہزاراں عالمِ علّامہ را رندانہ کرد

ابنِ آصف مست شد از دیدن پیرِ کریم   مستی عشقش ز سر تا پا وری دیوانہ کرد

> The charm of my *pir* is manifest all over, (due to this charm) scores of scholars and the men of learning have been spoiled; The son of Asif got intoxicated with the glimpse of *Pīr* Karim; intoxicated in his lore people have gone crazy.

The appreciative attitude of the *pīr* towards the *murīd*, when the latter had carved a niche for himself in social hierarchy, had been the hall-mark of *Chishti* tradition in India since the very beginning.

Soon, the Shaikh acquired considerable prominence as a mystic and theologian. Emperor Aurangzeb came to know about the man he was and invited him to Delhi 'to pay a visit to the shrines of his *pīr* so that the emperor could also meet him' [Document no. 1], but the invitation was politely refused [Document no. 2].

At the same time we find that the local officials had made over to him 'by way of an offering for the servants of one knowing the mystic truths' (*nazr -i khādimān-i haqāiq-wa m'aārif-i āgāh*), a grant of 200 *bīghā* land in village Mirzāpur Bakhtiyār, *pargana* Nasīrabād, *sarkār* Mānikpūr, *sūba* Allahabad. As the initial grant was made by the local officials, so it was temporary in nature (co-terminus with the tenure of the official concerned). Therefore an imperial *farmān* was issued on 5th *Shawwāl*, 19th RY/AD 1676 recognizing the rights of Shaikh Pīr Muhammad as the grantee [Document no. 3]. The Mughal chancery invariably designated such grants as *madad-i m'aāsh*, but probably this is the unique farmān where in stead of standard formula, a high sounding description has been given, in tune with the esteem in which the grantee was held by the local and imperial officials. The mystic died at an advanced age of 109 years in AH 1099 /AD 1687. It was through him that a branch of the *Chishti-Nizāmi* order was established in Patna by Shāh Mu'izuddin of Kurja. His *murīd* Shāh Mujibullah (d. AD 1777) established a *khanqāh* at Phulwāri, near

Patna, which still survives as an important centre of mystic activity in the present day Bihar.

In the lifetime of Shaikh Pīr Muhammad his son Shaikh Muhammad Ashraf, was assigned the revenues of a village Singhwal, renamed Ashrafabad, *pargana* Nasīrabād, by the *zamindārs* of the village. A perusal of the *hāsil* figures of the village from 4th RY to 17th RY, incidentally given in the *zimn*, shows that the revenue paying capacity of the village was greatly reduced. Hence the *zamindars* transferred their rights to the mystic, who sought tax exemption from the authorities in the form of *madad-i-ma'āsh*. This was made in absolute perpetuity on 18 *Jamād* 1 22nd RY/AD 1679 [Document no. 4]. He must have been a minor when he was named a beneficiary in the grant in lieu of his father, who already held a grant. His young age might explain why no spiritual titles are put before his name and the standard formula of *madad-i m'aāsh* is employed to describe the grant, in contrast with the respectful address and an unusual description of grant for his father. Shaikh Ashraf seems to have become quite a legend, and some sort of cult had developed around his personality. This has caught the imagination of an author like Mirzā Qatīl,[8] and the *sufi* poet of Awadhi language Shāh Qāsim Daryabādī.[9]

The rising graph of his popularity brought additional laurels for him. By the close of Aurangzeb's reign, he came to possess a vast area as *madad-i ma'āsh*, spread over eight *parganas* in *sūba* Allahabad and four *parganas* of *sūba* Akhtarnagar Awadh, either through imperial favours or through the local officials and the *zamindars*. All these were now conferred by Bahadur Shāh through the *farmān* dated 17th *Zilhij* 2nd RY/AD 1708 [Document no. 5]. In the *zimn*, a citation is made to the effect that "the grantee with a large number of mendicants is engaged in propagating the tenets of *shari'at* and *tarīqat* in the area" and that in "some of these villages he has established mosque, *musāfirkhānā*, and in the barren land has caused habitations to come up and has named them after his sons". These reinforced justification for his claim for an imperial *farmān* in respect of his urban property as well as the villages and *chaks* [Document no. 5]. Probably the same considerations led him to get another *farmān* from Emperor Muhammad Shāh on 19th *Rabi* 110th RY/AD 1729 [Document no. 6]. He died in AD 1754. The tomb with a very big egg-shaped dome was constructed in AH 1171/AD 1757 over his grave by an overseas merchant-disciple named Saiyid 'Abdullah, whose 'ship was saved from disaster due to the spiritual intercession of his Shaikh', so says the legend. The chronogram of the tomb has been reproduced in William Beale's *Miftāh-ut-Tawārīkh.*[10]

The *nawab-wazirs* during the first half of the eighteenth century had resumed a number of *madad-i ma'āsh* grants in Awadh and Allahabad provinces, though not from any sectarian motive, as has been suggested by Ghulam 'Alī Azād Bilgirāmi (c. AD 1761). A number of villages belonging to *Khanqāh-i Karīmia,* Salon, were also resumed and were included in the *jāgīr* of other nobles. It appears that it was a general order applicable in both the *sūbas* indiscriminately (*bar zabti-i-a' imma-i sūbājāt*). Shaikh Muhammad Ashraf petitioned to Nawāb Burhānul Mulk Sa'ādat 'Ali Khān seeking exemption to his grant from such order, as 'if this is not done, the maintenance of the *khanqāh* and the mendicants will become difficult'. The Nawāb acceded to his request and promised a separate *parwānā* to the officials for treating petitioner's grant differently.[11]

His eldest son Shāh Muhammad Pīr 'Atā acquired a fame unparalleled in the history of the institution. It was through him that the branches of this *khānqāh* were established at the far-off places, like Hyderabad Deccan, by Shah Shuja'ul Haq Badakhshāni. *Owāisiya* (Order of mysticism) was popularized by him at Salon.[12] As he predeceased his father, his younger brother, Shāh Muhammad Panāh was nominated to succeed as the future *sajjādānashin.* It is said that he was held in high esteem by the Emperor Shah Ālam II. When he held *darbār* at Allahabad in AD 1764 the mystic sent a request for a new *farmān* to be issued in the name of his son (the designated successor) Shāh Karīm 'Atā. The *farmān* was issued on 15th *Safar* 6th RY/1178 AH/AD 1764 [Document no. 7]. The significance of this act, i.e., seeking the imperial *farmān* in the name of the successor is hard to grasp, as we know that all the *madad-i ma'āsh* grants were made hereditary by Aurangzeb in 34th RY/AD 1690. Was it that the *nawab-wazirs* were reluctant to follow such an order indiscriminately, and hence care was taken to safeguard the property in the manner it was done by Shāh Muhammad Panāh?

The establishment seems to have been the largest of its kind in the southern parts of Awadh. Its annual income was estimated by Donald Butter (AD 1836) at Rs 30,000, which was utilized in entertaining the *bairāgīs* and *faqīrs* without any distinction of religion. The visitors used to flock to the *khanqāh* in large numbers and at a time there might happen to be about 100 mendicants. These were attended to and looked after by the *sajjāda-nashin* of the *khanqāh*, whose reputation was such that whenever any new *chakladār* was appointed in the *nizāmat* of Salon, he always paid a visit to him and offered him a few hundred rupees as *nazr*.[13]

W.H. Sleeman, while undertaking the tour in the kingdom of Oudh (AD 1849-50), refers to this establishment as the prime mystic institution of the kingdom. Shāh Panāh 'Atā the then *sajjādā-nashin* of the *khanqāh*, was looked upon with great reverence by both Muslims and Hindus for the sanctity of his ancestors and the institution. He did not go out of the *khanqāh* 'but remained there to receive the homage and distribute food to the needy and the travellers of all religions.' Sleeman estimated the annual income from the grant held by him in AD 1850 at about Rs. 25,000.[14]

In addition to the income from the revenue-free grants assigned by the Oudh rulers, the local officials as well as the princes in the distant places such as Bhopal, Sironj and Rewa made substantial offerings. This way, the actual income of the establishment was calculated to about Rs. 50,000 a year. Complimentary letters were sent to Shāh Panāh 'Atā by the Governor-General of India, and the Lieutenant Governors of NW Provinces. When Colonel Sleeman was passing through the district of Salon, Shāh Panāh 'Atā sent him "letters of compliments and welcome with a present of a tame antelope, some fruits and sugar". This goodwill gesture was reciprocated by Sleeman, who got the impression that "his character is held in high esteem by all classes of the people, of whatever creed, caste or grade".[15] However, in spite of this show of cordiality between the British authorities and the institution, it is worth recalling that immediately after the annexation of the kingdom of Awadh in AD 1856, Shāh Panāh 'Atā was in deep anguish, and thoroughly condemned their act. Thus, he expressed his feelings:[16]

ظلم واجد بہ ز عدل کمپنی

The 'oppression' by Wājid ('Alī Shāh) was better than the justice of the Company.

Between the annexation of Awadh (February 1856) and the events of 1857, there was a move to confiscate the properties of the *sajjādā-nashin*, but due to the strong social acceptability and the respect in which the institution was held by the Hindus and the Muslims both, the move to punish the institution for its alleged anti-British attitude was dropped. It is said that initially Major Barrow, the Chief Commissioner of Awadh after annexation, conducted an enquiry into the credentials of the grantee, but all the files and papers were destroyed during the events of 1857. The second enquiry could begin only during the first regular settlement of the province (AD 1860). The details of the enquiry conducted by W.C. Wood, the then Deputy Commissioner of Partapgarh, now forms a historical narrative giving the history of the landed properties accruing to the family since the period of Aurangzeb, the details of the buildings belonging to the institution and maintained out of the *waqf* fund, the income and heads on which the expenditure was incurred. A distinction was made between the personal expenses of the *sajjādā-nashin* and the charitable expenses of the institution, including the *madrasa*'.[17] On the basis of this report and on behalf of Lord Canning was a *sanad* on 26 September 1862, recognizing the allodial rights of S͟hāh Husain 'Atā, the then *sajjādā-nashin*, over 22 villages of his grant [Document no. 8]. It is pertinent to point out that now the grant was a conditional one; it was to continue so long as the income was devoted to the maintenance of the k͟hanqāh, buildings, tomb, mosques and running of a school of 'Muhammadan Education' and the continuance of the charities.

Till the promulgation of the UP Zamindari Abolition and Land Reforms Act of 1952, the family continued to have possession of these 22 villages, though with some vicissitudes, especially through litigation. After the abolition of the *zamindari* the annuity was given by the UP Government only for the *ma'āfi* villages and the amount fixed was Rs. 14,800 per annum. The net result of such a policy has been quite disastrous for the upkeep of the institution. The present *sajjādā-nashin* of the *k͟hānqāh* Shāh Saiyid Ahmad Husain Jafrī Islahi (himself a scholar) also feels, 'it is unthinkable to manage such an institution with the amount the government has fixed, but since the things have to be kept moving irrespective of the grant by the government, it shall be managed on our own'.[18]

The manner in which the *zamindars*, the local chieftains, and the provincial officials bestowed favours upon these mystics can be culled from the *wājib alarz* documents prepared during the course of the first regular settlement of the province of Awadh after the events of AD 1857. These papers recorded the 'past history of the village from the earlier period to which it can be conveniently traced'. On the basis of such village-wise information, the history of the families and clans of the various regions was arranged and incorporated in the settlement reports.

A few *wājib a larz* of the villages included in the *ma'āfī* of the grantees are available. A perusal of these records gives us some idea of the procedure adopted in bestowing these favours.

(a) Village Dhankesara, *pargana* Parshadepur, and village Barwaliya, *pargana* Salon, were in the estate of Raja Balbhadra Singh, the Kanhpuria chief of Tiloin. He had donated the revenues of these villages in favour of Shāh Pīr 'Atā, so that he may be able to meet the expenses incurred in feeding mendicants, destitutes and between visitors to his *Khanqāh*. Since then tile F 1174 /AD 1763 the grantees held the possession of the village on the strength of the *sanad* of the Raja, thereafter in F 1175/ AD 1764, the imperial *farman* of Shāh Ālam II included these villages also in the grant of the grantees [Document no. 7].

(b) The Raja of *ta'alluqa* Bhadri, *pargana* Behār, had allotted two tracts of forest land to Shāh Muhammad Panāh. The grantee got forest cleared and settled the area with the peasant castes especially *kurmīs*. One tract was named Panāh Nagar and another Hayāt Nagar (after his deceased brother, Shāh Muhammad Hayāt).

(c) A number of forest tracts were granted to Shāh Karīm 'Atā by Emperor Shāh Ālam II. The grantee undertook the clearance of the forest, settled the peasant caste of *Kurmīs* and named it after his father as Panāh Nagar.[19]

The existence of a large number of villages and *chaks* having the nomenclature similar to that of the family members of the mystic establishment in *pargana* Salon and *pargana* Kunda, suggest that many tracts of forest land were cleared by these grantees to settle the population and in turn raise their own income. Renaming of the well-known towns during the medieval period was an established practice, and the same done by the grantees at the local level, must have been in tune with the imperial policy. But a citation in a *farmān*, that "the grantee has caused habitation to come up in the barren land, and named them after his sons" is suggestive of the fact that it was not only the renaming of the old, but also establishing altogether new villages.

The traditions inherited and the practices adopted at the *khanqāh* Salon continued to survive in spite of the 'efforts of Saiyid Ahmad Shahid of Rae Bareli to purge Islam of the innovations (*bid'at*) and to wage a holy war against the Christians and the Sikhs'. In fact his 'religious zeal' prevented him from distinguishing between innovation in religion and an adaptation of the various practices in tune with the local customs adopted by the *sufi* establishments. This inability to differentiate the two and the failure to appreciate the spirit behind the ceremonies associated with the *Khānqāh* at Salon appear to have caused misunderstanding between him and Shāh Karīm'Atā, as the former's biographers indicate. He is said to have visited Salon at the time of *'urs* and found that during the audition (*sama'*) the *murīds* (disciples) indulged in *raqs* (dance) in the state of *wajd* (ecstasy) having earthen pots filled with water on their heads. Quite expectedly. Saiyid Ahmad objected to the ceremony on account of its being un-Islamic. If one is to believe his biographer again, Shāh Karīm 'Atā admitted his fault and abandoned the practice altogether.[20]

Leaving aside such claims, the practice actually referred to is that of *gāgar* (lit. a small earthen pot; taking out a procession from the *khānqāh* along with the disciples and musicians by the *sajjādā-nashin* and going to the shrine of *Pīran-i Parātha,* to fetch water in the pots after reciting *fātihā* there). The practice is said to have originated in the Chishti-Nizāmi Order in Awadh during the time of Shaikh Husāmul Haq of Mānikpūr. The practice continues at Salon irrespective of the assertion of the biographer. Similarly the association of *raqs* with *gāgar* is also a figment of his imagination. It appears that this time the gulf between the *sufis* and the 'zealots' among the *'ulema* was again widening, although a reconciliation was attempted between the two by Shāh Waliullah (d. 1761) and Shāh 'Abdul 'Aziz (d. 1827). Now, it was for the biographer of Saiyid Ahmad and persons like him to describe such practices as *bid'at.* Not only this, but even the well-known sufi concept of *tassawur-i shaikh* (perception of the perceptor) was said to have been compared with idolatry by Saiyid Ahmad when his own spiritual preceptor Shāh 'Abdul 'Azīz reportedly told him of it.[21]

On the other hand we find the practice of *gāgar* has caught the imagination of other contemporaries, who found in it, 'another chance of getting closer to *nūr* (lit. Light, Reality, Truth) and a way of attaining *ma'rifat* (gnosis)'. One of them, Shāh Kāzim (d. AD 1806) the founder of a *khānqāh* of *Qalandariya* Order at Kākori (UP) paid a number of visits to Salon 'for the blessings and guidance of Shāh Karim 'Atā. The practice of *gāgar* at Salon was well known to him and he refers to it in a respectful manner:[22]

اے ہو کریم عطا کرپا رکھ ہم پر ہم تجھ سے بڑی آس لگائی
نور سے بھر دو گاگر ہمری چھونچھی گاگر گھر جات لجائی
کاظم پائی کریم عطا میں رب کریم کی جوت سمائی

> O! Karīm Atā, have mercy on me, I have pinned my hopes in you; Fill my *gāgar* with *nur*, as I feel embarrassed at taking the empty one to my house; O! Kāzim I see the light of God in Karīm 'Atā.

Another poet of the later period has also expressed similar sentiments :[23]

> The bowl of Jamshed is envious of Husāmul Haq's gāgar, as the latter is filled with the wine of gnosis (*irfān*).

غیرت ساغر جمشید حسامی گاگر
مئے عرفاں سے ہے لبریز یہ نامی گاگر

It would be quite unhistoric to think that the perception of the *'ulemā* about the role of the *sufi* institutions and the customs they have adopted from region to region was in anyway monolithic in nature. On the contrary, we notice substantial differences among them.

This thing comes out clearly from the description given by another contemporary, Shāh 'Abdur Rahman, known as *mawahhid* (monotheist) of Lucknow, whose description of *tawhīd* is considered to be a very stringent indictment of *shirk* (polytheism).[24] In course of his sojourns in various parts of the country, he visited Salon and stayed with Shāh Karīm 'Atā for three months. He found in Salon, the tradition of '*darveshī* and *sultāni* going side by side, and found nowhere except in Salon the guest being looked after so well'. He had reasons to be impressed by Shāh Karīm 'Atā because of the way in which he 'looked after the welfare of the destitutes and mendicants at his *khānqāh*'. He entertained similar hopes for future also, due to the 'sophistication, erudition and scholarship of Maulavī Shāh Panāh 'Atā', the son and successor of Shāh Karim 'Atā[25]. It appears that unlike Saiyid 'Ahmad, Shāh 'Abdur Rahmān was looking for the things of *tāat-i mut'addi* (man's obligations towards man), a cordial principle in *Chishti* tradition. This is what Donald Butter also emphasizes when he says that Saiyid Ahmad could not gain much in Salon, as he was told by the *zamindars* and the *miyān* local title for *sajjādā-nashin* that for them relieving and aiding the poor, the lame and the blind was more pious than indulging in the holy war. They also told him clearly that they intended to follow the examples of the forefathers.[26]

The perceptions about the institution of the *sajjādā-nashin* (apart from the things in the 'world of spirituality' where he was bound to be supreme for the devotees and the disciples of the Order), and the rules relating to the succession to the office deserve some consideration. It was made out to be an exact replica (*fara'*) of *rāshidūn* Caliphate and according to the Sunnī belief, the *shari' at* laws of inheritance were not applicable to the institution of Caliphate. The methods in matters of succession were only two, i.e., the nomination in favour of the future successor during the lifetime of the Caliph, and the consensus (*ijma'*) among the prominent people (*ahl-i hal wa 'aqd*), the latter option was available in the absence of the former only. But after the nomination, *ijma'* was simply out of question. Exactly the same was applicable in matters of office of the *sajjāda-nashin*.[27] As will be seen, in the *khānqāh* of Salon, everything revolved around and was subjected to the person of *sajjāda-nashin* only. Hence the laws of succession and inheritance were kept in tune with the requirements of this spiritual office. This, ultimately, resulted in the intrusion of many local customs in the family laws of "*faqīr sajjāda-nashin* whose property can be inherited only by the *sajjāda-nashin*', as if they were a class in themselves.[28]

The customs and conventions peculiar to the family of the *sajjāda-nashin* got the legal sanctity when they were included in the *Rawāj-'Āam* of the pargana Parshadepur, tehsil Salon. In the preamble it is explicitly mentioned that as a result of the agreement between the superior land rights holders and the government that the "legal settlement of the villages belonging to us has been done for a period of thirty years, and the particulars peculiar to us and our clan (*qaum*) are described in details... We agree to abide by these rules". On behalf of Shāh Husain 'Atā, it was signed by Saiyid Kāzim 'Ali, *kārindā*. In fact, an analysis and comparison of the various clauses relating to the different *zamindar* clans-of the area on the subjects of enquiry with the ones relating to the *faqir sajjādā-nashin* makes an interesting study of the intrusions of the local customs, and the adjustments with the *shari'at* laws. However, the main features of the customary law relating to the *Khānqāh* Salon in relation to the succession and inheritance were as under: [29]

(a) The lawful heir and the legal representative of the *sajjāda-nashin* will only be the next *sajjāda nashin*. The latter was to be nominated by the previous incumbent to the office in his lifetime by observing certain customary ceremonies and rituals in a prescribed manner as detailed in the *Rawāj-i 'Āam* itself.

(b) The other heirs and the legal representatives of the *sajjāda-nashin*, including his widow were not entitled to any share in the properties left by the deceased. They could claim only a subsistence allowance the guests of the *khanqah* and all other obligations the previous incumbent had. The responsibility of looking after the widow and the unmarried daughters of the deceased, was of the future incumbent to the office of the *sajjādā-nashin*.

(c) The *sajjādā-nashin* himself was a custodian of the properties attached with the institution and thus he was not empowered to effect any change either by way of sale, mortgage or by oral gift.

We have noticed earlier that it was the office of the *sajjādā-nashin* around which the whole institution revolved, but finally we see him as a person, irrespective of 'his standing in the hierarchy of the world of spirituality', in the institution of *khānqāh* to safeguard the properties, customs, traditions and rituals, inherited and evolved in the course of time.[30]

Appendix A

Sajjāda -nashins of *Khānqāh-e Karīmiya* at Salon

1. Shaikh Pīr Muhammad (died 1687) nominated by Shaikh 'Abdul Karīm, the *sajjādā-nashin* of the *khānqāh* established by Shaikh Husāmul Haq at Mānikpūr (the *Nizami-Siraji* branch of the *Chishtis*).
2. Shaikh Pīr Muhammad Ashraf (died 1754) nominated by 1.
3. Shāikh Pīr Muhammad Panāh (died 1785) nominated by 2.
4. Shāh Muhammad Karīm 'Atā (died 1833) nominated by 3.
5. Shāh Muhamamd Panāh 'Atā (died 1860) nominated by 4.
6. Shāh Muhammad Husain 'Atā (died 1880) nominated by 5.
7. Shāh Muhammad Mehdi 'Atā (died 1900) nominated by 6.
8. Shāh Muhammad Na'īm 'Atā (died 1966) nominated by 7.
9. Saiyid Shāh Muhammad Husain Ja'frī (died 1979) nominated by 8.
10. Saiyid Shāh Ahmad Husain Ja'frī Islahi nominated by 9, the present *sajjādā-nashin* of the *Khānqāh*.

Appendix B

Document No. 1

Letter ascribed to Emperor Aurangzeb (undated).

Addressed to (Shaikh Pīr Muhammad) with high regards. After salutations— whereas this time I am preoccupied with the suppression of the turbulence at Deccan; hence it is not possible for me to pay a visit to you. If you are coming to Delhi to visit the shrines of your *pīrs*, I would welcome meeting you (*mulāqāt-i ān malakī -sifāt kardah āyad*).

Document No. 2

Letter ascribed to Shaikh Pīr Muhammad in reply to Aurangzeb (undated)

O! Emperor, the protector of the religion. This mendicant finds no courage (to attend the royal summons) what a rustic has to do at the imperial court *īn dahqāni rā bā bazm-i sultāni che kār*. If perchance some one happens to visit the *khānqāh* he is welcome; and *Karīm* (god) made me dependent upon none. He provides me when I feel hungry, if I am asleep, He cares, if (perchance) some sin is committed by me He helps me out. His favours are sufficient for me and to strive for more will be useless (ambition) (*Karīm-i mā bas bāqī hawas*).

Document No. 3

Farmān of Aurangzeb 5th *Shawwāl* 19th RY/AD 1676.

Whereas it has been submitted to the exalted court, that according to deeds (*asnād*) issued by the officials (*hukkām*) 200 *bīghās* of land from the village Mirzāpūr Bhakhtiyār, *pargana* Nasirabād, *sarkār* Mānikpūr, *sūba* Allahabad has been made over by way of offering to the servants of the one knowing mystic truths (*nazr-i khādimān-i haqāiq-o ma'ārif-agāh*), Shaikh Pīr Muhammad, and he is in actual possession of the land above mentioned and entertains the hope that in this regard an imperial *farmān* may be issued; therefore, the order is given over to him in *madad-i ma'āsh* in accordance with the particulars on the *zimn*, so that he may, appropriating revenues thereof for his own needs and engage himself in praying for the long life of the ever prosperous empire. Neither imperial officers nor those of the *jāgīrdārs* should allow any alteration: leaving the land in the hands of the grantee, they should not harass the grantee on account of land revenue or other taxes and cesses (details omitted), or by insisting upon cultivation, and all fiscal impositions and government dues whatsoever. Confirmatory orders should not be demanded every year by the grantees and if at some other place the grantee, has anything (land grants), it should not be taken into account (to reduce the present grant). Written on the 5th *Shawwāl*, 19th Regnal Year.

Zimn

Copy of (court) proceedings, dated thursday 14th Rajab, 18th R.Y. Corresponding to 1086 A.H. (1676-77 A.D.) corresponding to Ilahi month, written upon the note *(risala)* of the honoured Saiyid (titles omitted), the highly elevated *sadr*, Rizvi Khan, during the posting as recorder *(waqi'a nawis)*, Inayatullah, to wit; upon the recommendation of the governor (titles omitted), Himmat Khan, it has been conveyed to the exalted court that according to the deeds *(asnad)* issued by the *hukkam* (officials, or *jagirdars*), 200 bighas of land from the village Mirza Bakhtyarpur, *pargana* Nasirabad, *sarkar* Manikpur, *suba* Allahabad, has been made over as offering to the mystic Shaikh Pīr Muhammad, resident of *pargana* of Salon, and he entertains the hope that in this regard an Imperial *farman* may be issued; therefore the world-subduing order was issued that we confer the aforesaid land at the old site as per previous practice and upon the condition of (the grantee's) occupation and control thereof for their *mada-i imad-'sh* and if at some other place he (the grantee) has anything (i.e. land-grants), it should not be taken into account. *Waqia* dated 5th Rajab 18th R.Y. Transcribed according to the verification of the memorandum.

Document No. 4

Farmān of Aurangzeb 18th *Jamād* I 22nd RY/AD 1679.

Whereas, at this time the exalted *farman* has been issued that the village Singhwal in entirety, *pargana* Salon, *sarkār* Mānikpūr, *sūba* Allahabad, having of *jama*'of 32,000 *dām* should be assigned to Shaikh Muhammad Ashraf as *madad-i-m 'aāsh* according to the *Zimn*, from the half of *Rabi'* I, so that the assignee should spend all revenues for his own use, and should busy himself in praying for the welfare of the everlasting Empire. Therefore, it is incumbent upon the present and future officials to leave the said village in the possession of the grantee and should recognize it exempt from all the taxes and demands. Renewal orders should not be demanded by the grantee every year and if at some other place he has anything it should not be paid attention to, dated 18th *Jamād ul-Awwal* 22nd RY.

Zimn

Court proceeding dated 21 *Rabi* I, 22nd RY by the *sadr* Rizvi Khān during the posting of Daulatmand Khān *waqāi 'nawīs*; according to the letter of Mīr Muhammad Razā Karvi, the *waqāi 'nigār* of the province of Allahabad, it has been conveyed to the exalted court that Shaikh Muhammad Ashraf has settled with the consent of the *zamindar* in the village Singhwal under the aforesaid *pargana* and has named it Ashrafabad. Saiyid 'Abdul Rahīm *Sadr-i juzv* of Allahabad has also sent this recommendation. [They] entertain the hope that world subduing order will be issued that the aforesaid village has been conferred in its entirety as his *madad-i ma'āsh* for generations to come.

Hāsil figures of the said village:

4th RY	Rs. 50
5th RY	Rs. 31
6th to 9th RY	Rs. 91
10th RY	Rs. 21
11th RY	Rs. 26
12th to 16th RY	Rs. 66
17th RY	Rs. 61

Document No. 5

Farman of S͟hāh Ālam Bahādur S͟hāh Bāds͟hāh *Ghāzī*, 17th *Rajab* 2nd RY/AH/1119/AD 1708.

This *farman* is issued to the effect that villages, *c͟haks* and cultivable as well as the residential land, in the *pargana* of *sarkār* Mānikpūr and Lucknow *sūba* Allahabad and Awadh are conferred on the basis of the *asnād* of the *hukkām* and *zamindār*, in favour of the mystics S͟haik͟h Pīr Muhammad As͟hraf son of *sajjada-nashin* S͟haik͟h Pīr Muhammad of Salon, as revenue free (*ma'āf*) from the beginning of *kharīf tankūr*, the grantee should continue to hold his *madad-i ma'ash* and appropriate the revenue (*hāsilāt*) to himself and continue to keep him busy in praying for the longevity of the everlasting empire. Be it known to the '*āmils, jāgirdārs* and the present and future *karorī* to carry out this order in respect of the villages and *chukūk* as given in the *zimn* in favour of the grantee and after him, his progeny (*naslan ba'd naslan batnan ba'd batnan*). The grantees should not be harassed on account of taxes and cesses (details omitted) prohibited by the sublime court. Neither the grantees be asked to pay dues on account of *diwānī* or *sultānī*. Written on 17th *Zilhij* 2nd RY.

Zimn

Court proceeding dated 13th *Rajab* 2nd RY/AH 1119 prepared in the *risāla* of Amjad K͟hān, during the posting of Mir Muhammad as *waqā-i'nigār*. It was submitted to the sublime court by the *wazir* (titles omitted) *Khān-i Khānā* Zafargunj that the mystic Pīr Muhammad As͟haraf son of *sajjādā-nashin* S͟haik͟h Pir Muhammad Saloni is deserving of the (imperial favours) as he, with a large group of mendicants is engaged in propagating the tenets of *shari'at* and *tariqat* (mysticism). Also along with the *'ulemā* and mendicants he prays for the increase in the prosperity of the everlasting empire. He possesses, besides the *farmans*, the *sanads* issued by various *hukkām* and *zamindārs* for the continued possession, without any sharer of the cultivable and residential land (*ārāzi-i sakni wa-zara'i*) villages and hamlets chaks, *sarkār* Mānikpūr, *sūba* Allahabad, and *sarkār* Lucknow, *sūba* Akhtarnagar Awadh. In some of the villages he has established mosques, *musāfir-khāna'*, and in the barren land had caused habitations to come up, naming them after his sons. He now requests for the Imperial *farman*. It was, therefore, ordered that all the villages, hamlets, *chaks*, residential and cultivable land in the *pargana* of *sarkār* (above named) should continue to be as the *madad-i ma'āsh* of the grantee. If at some other place he has anything, it should not be paid attention to. Sheet of memorandum prepared according to the court proceedings.

The *wazīr* presented the matter for approval of the emperor a second time (*ba arz-i mukarrar*). After seeking the imperial consent, the *farman* was ordered to be written in accordance with *siyāha* of 21th *Rajab*, Ist RY.

List of the hamlets, *chaks*, gardens, dwellings and *havelīs* in possession of the grantee, and the Imperial land grants of which the grantees are in actual possession without any co-sharer according to the *zimn*.

A. *Pargana* of *sarkār* Mānikpūr, *sūba* Allahabad

1. *pargana* Salon

khās qasba' Salon *havelī*, tomb (*maqbarah*), houses and gardens	2 *bīghā* 10 *biswa'*
Village 'Atānagar with *sā'ir*	69 *bīghās*
takiya' Bahādur	10 *bīghā*
Gulābī *bāgh*	one plot
Musāfirkhāna'	one *bīghā*

Villages of *pargana* [Salon]

aslī	*dākhī*	*chak*
nine	one	one

(i) Village Pīrnagar Mohīuddīnpūr with *sā'ir bāzār* Usarī, (ii) village 'Atāgunj, (iii) village Khwājapūr, (iv) village Singhwal Ashrafabād known as Ashrafnagar with *sāir bāzār*, (v) village Barwaliya', (vi) village Rāmipūr, (vii) village Mādhopūr Ninaiyan, (viii) village Kenwalpūr, (ix) village Sindhiyāpūr.

chak: (i) chak Ramīpur

land in village Auna 7 *bīghā*

chaks in *pargana* Salon:

(i) Ashrufgunj Ratāson 55 *bīghā*

(ii) Panāhnagar Dharai 66 *bīghā*

(iii) Karīmnagar Rewli 45 *bīghā*

2. *Pargana* Guzarāh [Kadrah for Kunda?], three villages

(i) Muhammadābād, (ii) Pālhīpur, (iii) Bainti, also *sarāi La'l Beg, ghāt Bainti* and 'Azīzpur

3. *Pargana* Jāi's

(i) village Kesariya Salempur, (ii) village Mohan

4. *Pargana* Nasīrabād

(i) village Dhankesara, (ii) village Mirzāpur known as Pīrangunj.

5. *Pargana* Rae Bareli 5 villages and *chaks*.

(i) village Harchandpūr, (ii) village Rupāmau, (iii) village Malikpūrsarya, (iv) village Jiupūr, (v) village Narūka.

cuh : (i) *chak* Gokna', (ii) *chak* Sāhi

6. *Pargana* Dalmau one village (i) Amrudpūr.

7. *Pargana* Kara' : village Afzalpūr Sāton with cultivable land, 7 villages.

(i) Afzalpūr Sāton, (ii) Malīkpūr, (iii) *pūra* Muhammad Sa'eed, (iv) Mirzāpūr, (v) *kach* Sāton, (vi) *kach* Kantuwa', (vii) Konda Māran.

8. *Pargana* Mānikpūr Bihār, one village, 13 *chak*.

village (i) Kishandāspur

chaks : (i) Karimnagar, (ii) Pīrnagar, (iii) Panāhnagar, (iv) Panāhgunj, (v) Majhilgāon, (vi) Jhanka', (vii) 'Atānagar, (viii) Momi, (ix) Barai, (x) Bargadahā, (xi) Nihānu, (xii) Narsāhib, (xiii) *chak* 'Ayesha.'

B. *Pargana* in *sarkār* Lucknow, *sūba* Akhatrnagar Awadh.

3 villages, 21 hamlets and 140 *bīghā*, 8 *biswa*' '*arāzi*.

1. *Pargana* Bijnore, (i) village A<u>sh</u>rafnagar Dharwa' 2. *pargana* Amethī, (i) village Pīrjalālpūr, (ii) village Maurāmav Karīmnagar.

Document No. 6

Farman of Emperor Muhammad <u>Sh</u>āh 19th *Rabi* II 10th RY/AD 1729.

The plots of residential and agricultural land, *<u>ch</u>aks*, and villages in *sarkār* Mānikpur sūba Allahabad and villages in *sarkār* Lucknow, *sūba* A<u>kh</u>tarnagar Awa<u>dh</u> have been conferred upon <u>Sh</u>ai<u>kh</u> Muhammad A<u>sh</u>raf according to *farmans*, deeds of the officials and *zamindars*. This time, also, as per previous practice, the grant is confirmed in *madad-i-m'aāsh*. It is ordered that the grantee be allowed to appropriate the revenues thereof and engage himself in praying for the well-being of the empire. It is incumbent upon the present and future *'ummāl*, *jāgīrdār* and the *karorīs* to abide by the Imperial orders by allowing the grantees (to appropriate the revenue) from the villages, *dehāts* and *<u>ch</u>aks* as detailed in the *zimn*, generation after generations and for all times to come. The grantee should not be harassed on account of taxes and forbidden cesses (details omitted). *Sanads* of confirmation should not be demanded from the grantee every year and if at some other place the grantee has anything it should not be taken into account. Dated 19th *Rabi* II 10th RY.

Document No. 7

Farmān of <u>Sh</u>āh 'Alam II 15th *Safar* 6th RY/AD 1764.

Various villages, *<u>ch</u>aks*, gardens, and residential apartments in *sūba* Allahabad and A<u>kh</u>tarnagar Awa<u>dh</u> have been conferred upon Pīr Muhammad Panāh of Salon according to the *farmāns*, and deeds of officials and *zamindārs*. From the beginning of *kharif yichi Il*, all of the above are confirmed as *madad-i ma'āsh* to *Shāh* Pīr Karīm 'Atā, so that he may appropriate the revenues thereof for his own needs and engage himself in praying for the longevity of the empire.

It is incumbent upon the officials, revenue collectors, *mutassadīs*, *jāgirdārs* and present and future *karorīs* to abide by the orders of the sublime court. They should see to it that all these properties are held by the grantees generation after generations and for all times to come. The grantee should not be harassed on account of *māl o jihāt, sāir wa-ikhrājāt* (details omitted). Dated 15th *Safar* 6th RY/AD 1764.

Zimn

Details of the *yāddāsht-i wāqi'a,* list of the *dehāts*, *chaks*, gardens and residential *havelīs sūba* Allahabad, *sarkār* Mānikpūr.

Villages	44
chaks	21
'ārāzi	114 *bīghā*, 8 *biswa*'

(i) *Pargana* Salon : Havelī with *pā'inbāgh*, Karīmganj with old fort, Pīrnagar Mohīuddīnpūr, Muhammadābād, Pālhipūr, 'Atāgunj Usarī, Khwājāpūr, 'Atānagar, Ṭakiyā Bahādur, Gulābibāgh, Ashrafnagar Singhwal, Barwaliya, Rāmīpūr, *Musāfirkhāna' (7 bighās)* Madhopūr Ninaiyān.

(ii) *Pargana* Jā'is : K'esarya Saleempūr, Mahoba.

(iii) *Pargana* Nasīrabād : Dhankesra, Pīrangunj, Mirzāpūr.

(iv) *Pargana* Dalmau : Amrudpūr.

(v) *Pargana* Kara' : Afzalpūr Sāton (*zamīndāri* of the grantee), Mirzāpūr, Pūra Muhammad Sa'eed.

(vi) *Pargana* Mānikpūr : Bihār.

(vii) *Pargana* Rai Bareli :

chaks—Ashrafgunj, Panāhnagar Dharaī, Karīmnagar Rewlī, *chack* Atārthariya, 'Atānagar bāron (in *pargana* Dhaingwas).

Sūba AkhtarnagarAwadh, *sarkār* Lucknow 4 *pargana* (?)

(i) *Pargana* Bijnor : village Ashrafnagar, (ii) pargana : Amethi village Behta, (iii) Rasolī, Karīmnagar Sirāson.

Document No. 8

Sanad of Chief Commissioner of Oudh dated 26.9.1862.

It having been established after due inquiry that Shāh Husain 'Atā held the undermentioned land in *tehsīl* Salon, *zilā* Partapgarh in rent-free tenure under the former government, the Chief Commissioner, under the authority of Governor-General in Council, is pleased to maintain the tenure so long as the grantees perform their duties and keep up the buildings and the school according to the terms of the grant on the following conditions:

that he shall have surrendered all *sanads*, title deeds and the documents relating to the tenure in question;

that he and his successor shall strictly perform all the duties of landholder in matters of police and any military or political service that may be required of them by the authorities; and

that they shall never fall under the just suspicion of favouring, in anyway, the designs of enemies of the British Government. If any one of these conditions is broken by the present incumbent or any of his successors, the tenure will be immediately resumed.

(1) Village Mirzāpūr Bakhtiyar, (2) *Bazār* Karimganj, (3) Ashrafgunj Singhwal, (4) Palhipūr, (5) Khwajāpūr, (6) Kenwalpūr, (7) ʻAtāganj Usarī, (8) Mādhopūr Ninaīyān, (9) land *chak* Rāmīpūr 150 acres, (10) land in ʻAtānagar 7 acres, (11) Pīrnagar Mohīuddinpūr 35 acres, (12) Village Barwaliya, (13) Pirnagar Mohīuddīnpūr, (14) ʻAtānagar 27½ acres, (15) Ashrafgunj, (16) Panāhnagar Dhingwas, (17) *chak* Atārthariy 24 acres (18) Village Takiya Pura Baheliya appertaining to Madhopur Ninaiyan 117 acres, (19) Village Dhankesara 167 acres, (20) Muhammadābād, (21) Sindhyāpūr, (22) *chak* Karīmnagar.

Sd/-

Deposited in the Record

Room of the office of

Chief Commissioner, Oudh

26th September AD 1862

Details of the Documents Described in Appendix B

1. The text of the letter is reproduced in a late family text, *Ashraf-ul Inshā;* a collection of the letters exchanged between Shaikh Pīr Muhammad, Shaikh Pīr Muhammad Ashraf with his contemporary divines, princes and other notables, MS(1734), ff. 2a-3a (in the private collection of Shāh Muhammad Jalil ʻAtā, a *pīrzādah*, of Salon, now at Karachi, who kindly allowed me to have the photocopy of the manuscript).

2. *Ibid.*

3. An earlier copy of the *farman* was in possession of Shāh Saiyid Muhammad Husain Jaʻfrī, 9th *sajjādā-nashin* of *khānqāh* Salon (1966-79). The contents of this document have been described and translated by me in *'Two madad-i ma'āsh farmāns* of Aurangzeb from Awadh,' *PIHC*, 40th session, Waltair, 1979, pp. 302-14. The document was destroyed during the course of unfortunate incidents at

Aligarh Muslim University in May 1981. It was transcribed by Professor Irfan Habib also before its destruction.

4. The document has the same history as the document in the preceding note.

5. The *farman* is with Shāh Muhammad Amīn 'Atā, a *pirzādah* of Salon now in Khushāb, Pakistan. He has very kindly allowed me to have photocopy of the *farman*. [See plate no. 3]

6. Photographic reproduction (obverse side) of this *farmān* appears in Shāh Muhammad Hasan 'Atā *Harir-e Sang* Karachi, 1964, p. 119.

7. The transcript of this *farman* is with the present *sajjdā-nashin* of the *khānqāh* Saiyid Shāh Ahmad Husain J'afrī Islāhī.

8. This is a bilingual document and has been quoted in full by justice Sir Wazīr Hasan and Justice Gokaran Nath Misra in their judgement of a civil appeal in reference to Shāh Muhammad Na'im 'Atā (Defendant-appellant) vs. Muhammad Shamsuddīn (Plaintiff respondent). *Indian Law Reports* (Lucknow Series), Vol. II, 1927, Allahabad, pp. 109-32 (see pp. 111-12 for the *sanad*).

References

1. See my paper 'Landed Properties of a Sufi Establishment—A Study of 17th and 18th Century Documents from Salon in Awadh', *PIHC*, 47th session, Srinagar, 1986, pp. 417-31; also see 'Two *madad-i ma'āh farmans* of Aurangzeb from Awadh', *PIHC*, 40th session, Waltair, 1979, pp. 302-13.

2. Little information exists in the contemporary sources about *Khanqāh-i Husāmiya*, Mānikpūr. For biographical notices of Shaikh Husāmul Haq *see Shaikh 'Abdul Haq, Akhbārul Akhyār fi Asrārul Abrār*, Delhi, 1309, *AH*, pp. 171-73; K.A. Nizāmi, *Tārikh-i Mashāikh-i Chisht*, Delhi, 1953, pp. 203-4; John A. Subhan, *Sufism: Its Saints and Shrines*, Lucknow, 1960, p. 230. For a history of the *khānqāh* and the family tree of Shaikh Husāmul Haq see 'Abdullah Khān Qais, *Tārikh-i Kara' Mānikpūr*,. Allahabad, 1916, pp. 260-66.

3. These *dohās*, popular as *astuts*, survive with the musicians and the singers attached to the *khānqāh*. But some of them have been transcribed in the family papers and the manuscripts which are being used here.

4. Biographical notices of these ancestors of Shaikh Pīr Muhammad exist

in *Akhbarul Akhyar*, pp. 44 and 226-28. For him there are independent references in Muhammad Bakhtāwar Khān, *Miratul 'Alam*, Persian text, ed., Dr. Sajida Alavi, Lahore, 1979, II, p.417; Saiyid Shāh Ghulam 'Ali Shāh, *Mishkātun Nubuwah, mishkāt*-27, MS compiled in AH 1212. (I am grateful to Professor Sulaiman Siddiqi, Osmania University, Hyderabad for letting me use this manuscript). The author tells about the other name of Shaikh Pīr Muhammad as Shāh 'Abdul 'Ali, which could not be compared from the other sources; Mufti Ghulām Sarvar, *Khazinatal Asfiyā'*, Lucknow, AH 1280; Saiyid 'Abdul Hai', *Nuzhatul khawātir*, V, Hyderabad, 1911, pp. 97-98.

In other *tazkiras* his maternal grandson Saiyid S'adullah who got much prominence as a theologian, *sufi* and a scholar of comparative religions, is referred to as the grandson of Shaikh Pīr Muhammad, who in turn is called the great mystic and theologian of his times. See Khafi Khān, *Muntakha-bal-Lubāb*, Bib. Ind., Calcutta, 1860-74, II, pp. 559-60; Ghulām 'Ali Āzad Bilgirami, *Mathirual kiram*, Hyderabad, 1913, Vol .I, p. 217, Sher Thattavi, *Māqālāt-us- Shuarā, ed*, Pīr Husamuddin Rāshidī, Karachi, 1957, pp.122-23. For the history of the family, the institution, and the family tree see 'Abdullāh Qais, *Tār kh-i Kara' Mānikpūr*, pp. 261-69; *A Gazetteer of the Province of Oudh*, Vol.3., Lucknow, 1877, p. 290; H.R. Nevill, *District Gazetteer of United Provinces* (Rae Bareli), Allahabad, 1923, Vol. 39, pp. 101-103.

5. For the details of this incidental meeting see *wajibul 'arz* of village Panahnagar Barai', *pargana* Bihar, and of village *Barwalia*, *pargana* Salon, in the *First Settlement Report of 1860*; *Nuzhatal Khāwātir*, V, p. 97; *Tārīkh-i Kara Manikpūr*, p. 261. It is interesting that during the seventeenth century also a person before being initiated into mysticism, was supposed to do extensive courses in *Qurān*, *Fiqh* and *m'atazalite* thought.

6. Affidavit of Shāh Muhammad Mehdi 'Atā, the VII *sajjādā-nashin* of the *khanqāh*, dated 26th September AD 1881. This has been published in full by Shāh Muhammad Hādi 'Atā in *Musannif*, an Urdu Quarterly Journal, edited by Saiyid 'Ibārat Barelivi, Aligarh, 1945, III; no. 3, pp. 78-80.

7. *Ibid.*

7a. I am thankful to Shah Muhammad Shabbir 'Ata Nadwi of Salon, for saving me from the earlier slip, also he was kind enough to provide me the missing verses of this beautiful quatrain.

8. Qatil mentions Shaikh Muhammad Ashraf as an important saint of *Chishti* order with an anecdote. He says, his disciples buy parrots and make the birds recite the Shaikh's name (obviously without his consent)

and then leave the birds in the adjoining jungles of Salon. When the travellers and pilgrims listen to them, they are impressed with 'spiritual prowess' and the 'saintly qualities' of the Shaikh. Mirzā Muhammad Husain Qati, *Haft-i Tamasha,* Urdu trans. Dr. Muhammad 'Umar, Burhān, Delhi, 1968, pp. 168-69.

9. Shāh Qāsim Daryā bādi (AD 1731) *Hans Jawahir Bhākha*, Bombay, 1951, p. 4. There are three long *alhās* praising the 'saintly qualities' of Shaikh Muhammad Ashraf, his father, and his father's preceptor, Shaikh 'Abdul Karīm. The family tradition says that the poet was a disciple of Shaikh Muhammad Ashraf.

10. Besides giving the chronogram of the tomb, the chronograms inscribed at the main gate of the tomb (giving the death dates of the first five *sajjādā-nashins*) have also been reproduced in a chronological sequence. Similarly, the chronogram of the mosque of the *khānqāh* is also given. Thomos William Beale, *Miftāhut Tawārīkh*, Agra, 1849, passim. It was the general belief that the tomb was a replica (*naql*) of the tomb of Shaikh Baha' Uddin Zakariya of Multan. [See plate nos. 4 and 5]

11. Apart from the recipient of such favours, the family sources point out cordial relationship between the *nawābs* and the *sajjādā-nashins* of the *khānqāh.* It is said that Burhanul Mulk and Safdarjung visited Salon when Shaikh Muhammad Ashraf was the *sajjādā-nashin.* See Shāh Panāh 'Aṭa *Fakhrul Fuqara*' (MS). 1268 AH, of 95. A number of *parwānas* were issued by the *nawābs* granting exemption to these grantees from the resumption. See for the translations of some of these *parwānas in* my paper, *PIHC*, 47th session, Srinagar, 1986, pp. 428-29. [Ch. VI of the book.]

12. Little biographical details are available for him. But it is certain that He emerged as the most fascinating personality of the institution. He undertook a number of meditations for a considerable time span. He got a *havelī* constructed in village Pirāngar, *pargana* Mānikpur, *suba* Allahabad and one *chillagāh* (house for meditation) in the environs of *qasba*' Salon, called *musāfirkhāna*' also. The extensive ruins of these buildings and the surviving cult around the person of Shāh Mohammad Pīr'Atā stands as a testimony to his social standing and his stature in the world of spirituality' The *haveli* had its foundation in the river Ganges, with a mosque and *chillagāhs,* it is absolutely free from the sort of vandalism we usually notice in such ruins. The locals have that much respect for the *chillagāh* which is otherwise a hallmark of a shrine. Nawāb Safdarjang is said to have visited him at Pīrānagar where 'the saint reportedly performed a miracle at the behest of the *nawāb*'. See, *Fakhrul Fuqara'*, f. 96. Shāh Qāsim Daryābādi was full of praise for him and thus expressed" his admiration :

جیہہ پر عطا عطا کی ہوئی پاپ ہرا نرمل بھا سوئی
پیر دولارو کریم کے' اشرف پیر کے نند نرمل دوؤ جگت وہ ناکلنک جس چند

"The one who has the blessings of (Pīr) 'Atā, his sins are washed and he becomes pure. For, he is a favourite of Karīm (Mānikpūr) and son of Ashraf Pīr, these two could purify a world of their sins and blemishes."

13. Donald Butter, *Topography and Statistics of Southern Districts of Oudh*, pp. 139-40.
14. W.H. Sleeman, *A Journey Through the Kingdom of Oudh in 1849-50*, I, pp. 232-34. An abridgement of this celebrated travelogue has been prepared by P.D. Reeves. as, *Sleeman in Oudh*, Cambridge, 1971, pp. 128-29, 131-32.
15. *Ibid.*
16. On a different occasion he criticised Wājid ' Alī Shāh also, as he remained a mute witness when Maulavī Amīr of Amethī led a *jihād* against the alleged high-handedness of the *bairāgīs* in Hanumangarhi mosque. He castigated the *nawāb* as being directly responsible for the event by composing a highly suggestive chronogram for the tragedy :

بعد بارہ سو برس کے پھر ہوا پیدا یزید

"After twelve hundred years, Yazīd is born again, yielding AH 1272."

He described Maulavī Amīr 'Alī as *shahid* (martyr) also. These comments of Shāh Panāh'Atā are spread over in his diary (MS with the present *sajjada-nashin* of the *khānqāh*).

In fact, it would be quite unhistorical to define the behaviour and 'loyalty' of a *sufi* saint in any stereotype. Their 'responses and reactions' often came very close to the popular sentiments. In case of Shāh Panāh 'Atā we notice his many 'identities' overlapping each other in a small span of time, often defying logic.

17. Letter No. 504 of 13 July 1861 from Deputy Commissioner of Partapgarh to the Commissioner of Baiswara division resubmitting *m'aāfī* register Nos. 1 to 22 of Shāh Husain 'Atā with his docket No. 1936 of 20 November 1860.

18. Personal Interview.
19. This information is gleaned from the *wājibul arz* of each of these villages. The documents are the part of the *First Settlement Reports* of the *pargana* Salon and Parshadepur, now available at the Collectorate's Records Room, Rae Bareli.
20. The only authority for such story is Saiyid Muhammad Alī's, *Makhzani Ahmadī*, f. 56 (compiled in AD 1865). This story is repeated uncritically by Ghulām Rasul Mehr in his *Saiyid Ahmad Shahid*, Lahore, 1954, pp. 155-56. However, Saiyid Abul Hasan 'Alī Nadw in *Sirat-i Saiyid Ahmad Shahid*, 2 vols, Nadwatul 'Ulemā', Lucknow, 1939, has simply omitted the incident without any comment.
21. This is again from *Makhzan-ī Ahmadi*. However, Saiyid Abul Hasan 'Alī Nadwi has mentioned this thing in a diluted form with some sophistication.
22. Shāh Kāzim Qalandar (d. AD 1806), *Sānt Ras* or *Naghmatul Asrār*, Awadhi text edited with introduction, notes and translation in Urdu by Shāh Mujtabā Haidar, Lucknow, AH 1376, pp. 72-73; *dohā* nos. 484-89 [the numbering of the *dohās* is continuous]. The editor tells us in the notes things which are different from what Shāh Kāzim himself says, besides a factual error, i.e., Shāh Kāzim has alluded to the 'blessing of the four *pīrs* of Salon for overcoming his difficulties'. Hence they ought to be Shaikh Pīr Muhammad, Pīr Ashraf, Pīr 'Atā and Pīr Panāh, in stead of what we are told by the editor.
23. A lesser known poet of Salon, Ishtiyāq Ahmad Mushtāq, has composed a poem for the *gāgar* procession. This is included in his collection, *Bāgh-i-Naim*, MS compiled in AH 1350.
24. For the main arguments see his *Kāsiratual Asnān* and *Kalimatul Haq*. See also *Anwārul Rehmān Letanwīrul Jinān*, his *malfuzat* compiled by Maulavi Nūrullāh, Kali Prasad, Press, Lucknow, AH 1270 p. 33.
25. *Ibid*., p. 33.
26. Butter, *op. cit*., p. 165.
27. These perceptions are spelled out at a rather unusual place. A registered gift deed executed by Shāh Muhammad N'aim 'Atā, the 8th *sajjādā nashin* (1900-66) of the *khānqāh* in 1938 in favour of his successor Saiyid Shāh Muhammad Husain Jafri, *The 9th Sajjādā nashin of the Khānqāh* (1966-79). Gift deed executed on 23-12-1938 in the office of the Sub-Registrar, *tehsil* Salon, Rae Bareli.

    Since the nomination was made by Shāh Muhammad Na'īm 'Atā in favour of Saiyid Shāh Muhammad Husain Jafri (connected to Shāh Na'īm 'Atā's family through female line going up to Shāh Karīm 'Atā) ignoring the others of the male line, thus in order to pre-empt the others from making any claim to the office of the *sajjādā-nashin* (which in fact they did after 1966) Shāh Na'im 'Atā had made the position very clear. The custom of nomination was so firmly established that it could not be denied by others as such. After Shāh Na'īm 'Atā's death, the title dispute was one of the most hotly contested cases in the chequred history of the family's litigations. Finally, the court also accepted the action of Shāh Na'īm 'Atā in 1984 and the title was finally decided in favour of Saiyid Shāh Ahmad Husain Jafri Islahī, the present *sajjādā-nashin*. [Writ Petition no. 1682 of 1982 decided on 12 July 1984 by the Hon'ble High Court of Allahabad, Lucknow Bench, Lucknow. The ruling was reported in *Allahabad Weekly Cases*, X, Allahabad, 1984, pp. 928-32.

Shāh Muhammad Na'īm 'Atā' was a scholar, prolific writer on *Hadith*, *Fiqh*, *Tasawwuf* and grammar. A poet well known for his devotional poetry, anti-British feelings, and his role during in the Kisan Sahba Movement, he was a mystic with a high taste for *samā* and music. Although a *Hanafi*, he was in many respects very imaginative and even innovative by adopting well known principles from other schools of law, many of which were an anathema for the *Hanafīs*. An authoritative biography of such a person will be a venture worth undertaking. For his early life see, Saiyid Taqi Husain, *Nalae Anfas-i Gham* or *Gham-i Qiblae Alam*, Lucknow, AH 1318 ; for a list of his published and unpublished books (17 titles in Arabic and 6 titles in Urdu) and other biographical details, see 'Abdullah Qais, *Tārikh-i Kara' Mānikpūr*, pp. 267-69; Muhammad Usman Khan, *Yādgār-i-Naim*, Rai Bareli, 1966, it is in the form of an obituary by a disciple but gives some interesting details also. For his role in the peasant movement, though the analysis lacks sophistication, see M.H. Siddiqui, *The Agrarian Unrest in North India: The United Provinces (1918-1922)*, Delhi, 1978, pp. 155-56.

28. *Rawāj-i Aām* documents at the *pargana* level were compiled by the British authorities after the events of 1857. The leading land-owning classes were to record the customs and the traditions peculiar to their own caste in relation to six broad themes, which were sub-divided into twenty-two sections of specific nature. This 'customary law' had the sanction of the authorities as well. This was done for *pargana* Parshadepūr also, where the *sajjādā-nashin* had considerable landed property. This document has a separate column for recording the customary law of "*faqir sajjādā-nashin* whose property is inherited by the *sajjādā nashin*".

29. *Ibid*. See also *Iqrār Ma'āfidār Mālik Awwal*, village Barwalia, *pargana* Salon, included in the First Settlement of 1860.

30. Donald Butter, *op. cit.*, p. 139, especially when he says about the *sajjādā-nashins*, that they call themselves "a *fakir* though the *mālīk* (proprietor) of Salon".

شد بنا در سلون روضهٔ نور   که جهان را ازینست کسب شرف

داد هاتف بشارت از تاریخ   این بود آستانهٔ اشرف

Fig. 1. The dome and the upper view of *Rauza-i Ashrafi*, main building of the *Khanqah-i Karimia* Complex, Salon, The chronogram gives AH 1171/ AD 1757 as the date of construction.

Fig. 2.
Rauza-i Ashrafi, and the other Buildings of the *Khanqah-i Krimia* complex, Salon.

CHANGES UNDER BRITISH RULE

10

British Intervention and Agrarian Instability in the Kingdom of Awadh (1801-56)

The kingdom of Awadh was placed in a peculiar situation during the first half of the 19th century. The excessive interference of the British Resident in day to day administration had considerably diminished the authority of the king and his officials. The separate establishment of the Resident was practically an 'alternative seat of power'. According to an authoritative observer, Henry Lawrence (1845) :

> At Lucknow for years the Resident held public *darbar* where the grandees attended and pleaded against their own sovereign and his servants. Thus, were the monarch and his subjects pitted against each other, thus was the sovereign degraded in his own capital.[1]

Many of the evils besetting Awadh and the consequent disruption of local agrarian life during the first half of the 19th century arose as a result of British presence (and interference) in the administrative, military and economic spheres of the kingdom though this might not be only explanation for the distress and miseries to which the peasants in Awadh Kingdom were subjected to.

The administrative machinery of the Awadh kingdom was so thoroughly controlled by the British officials as to leave little discretion with its rulers. To quote Colonel Southland:

> There is no state in India with whose government we have interfered so systematically and so uselessly as with that of Oude... This interference has been more in favour of men than in favour of measures.[2]

Nawab S'aadat 'Ali, whom even English recognised as an extremely able and intelligent ruler, suffered from gross interference. The 'dirty hands' of the British were said to be employed against him in the disguise of reforms.[3] After such an 'active surveilance of the Resident and his constant advice' for the improvement of the administration things deteriorated to such an extent that by 1836 Donald Butter was speaking of a virtual collapse of the entire set-up.

Agrarian Instability

The basis of the political and economic structure of the kingdom was the land revenue. It was therefore natural for the British to suggest a number of reforms in this sphere from time to time. Such measures were tried by the successive rulers of the dynasty with little or no success. Surprisingly enough the experiments were always short lived and seldom lasted for more than a year or so.[5]

The resultant instability in agrarian conditions is well portrayed by Lalji, in a section of his work, *Mirat-ul-Auza.* He gives a vivid description for the reasons of the lawlessness and anarchy in the realm. The cruelty and arbitrary manners of the *'amil* and the *mustajir* and the neglect of their duties by the state officials, were said to be the twin causes of the evils. The chief fault is laid at the faulty nature of the revenue system. The settlement of the revenue upon those who pay it, was not made in accordance with their actual portions and shares. Even if it was distributed by the officials between the parties with their mutual consent, the *'amil* and the *mustajir* never respected the agreement. This naturally resulted in violent protests and reprisals. It so happened that one of the two brothers who was the *zamindar* of a *ta'alluqa* submitted the *qubuliyat* for the land-revenue before the *'amil* and the other brother was denied his legal share. The latter began to ravage the estate.[6] Peace would have come, "if the *'amil* had given the half share to the rebel brother---".[7]

The revenue officials such as the *'amil* and the *chakledar* had the tendency to demand a higher amount of revenue from the *zamindar* and the *ta'alluqadar.* The latter, unable or unwilling to pay the enhanced amount, used to make a summary levy and after collecting their retainers and adherents took flight to the neighbouring jungles and offered resistance to the forces commanded by the *'amil* or *chakledar.* Sleeman's diary of his tour is full of such instances. Such a policy brought havoc and misery to the rural people. In 1830 Maddlock observed:

> the *'amils* or his officers finding a yearly decrease of revenue are naturally urged to further exactions until, at length, the kingdom has arrived at such a crisis that hundreds of village have gone to ruin, the former cultivation is now a waste and the hamlets once occupied are now deserted.[8]

With *zamindars* or *ta'alluqadars* fleeing to the jungle with their retainers the wrath of the revenue officials generally fell on the unarmed peasantry. Butter comments:

> Whenever the *chakledar* pitches his tent, the work of plunder and devastation commences with the uprooting of the neighbouring villages to supply temporary huts for his troops; the *zamindars* and their immediate adherents at the same time flying to the jungles, when they ascertain an intention on the *chakledar's* part to increase their burden.[9]

Such a situation forced the *zamindar* to be always alert. They used to maintain substantial private armies and fire-arms.

It seems that by the time of the annexation the *chakledar* had greater liberty in using cannon and fire-arms against the defaulting villages. Donald Butter remarks :

> "During the reign of S'aadat 'Ali, a single cannon shot could not be fired by *chakledar* without being followed by immediate enquiry from Lucknow, as to its causes—now a *chakledar* may continue firing for a month without question.[10]

Henry Lawrence once personally witnessed an armed operation by the *chakledar* and speaks of , "the village being carried by storm; 7 or 8 of the inhabitants were killed and wounded, and all the rest were taken captive by the *'amils.*"[11] This should not be considered as an isolated case, as such occurrences were quite frequent as Lawrence goes on to remark :.

> We observe in the daily papers a detailed account of the death in battle of the *'amil* of Burailiha, and of the victorious *ta'alluqadar* having in consequence taken to the bush, to be a felon probably for life or atleast until he pays the blood money to the court. In this process several large landholders were temporarily declared outlaws.

Subversion of Law and its Repercussions

The rise of the banditry was an indirect result of the administrative system established with the help and advice of the British Resident. The main body of the bandits comprised peasants who had suffered because of the inequities of the *chakledars*, the unemployed soldiers, or those whose salaries were in arrears. Bishop Heber, while he was coming from Kanpur to Lucknow met with what had all the appearances of a state of siege at the very entrance of Lucknow, because a large sum of money, said to be 30,000 rupees, on its way to the treasury at Lucknow, had attracted a number of neighbouring peasants, who were assembled outside the walls with their weapons, waiting for the departure of the treasurer."[12] The sense of insecurity had developed so much among the people, that to Heber's surprise,

> all or nearly all the remaining population were as much loaded with arms as the inhabitants of the country but I should apprehend that Lucknow offered at this moment a more war like exterior than our own metropolis ever did during its most embroiled and troublesome period.[13]

Lalji similarly informs us that,

> because of the prevalence of the acts of depradations throughout the kingdom of Oudh, it was necessary for the inhabitants to keep themselves armed, hence every inhabitant carried arms with him even if he had to go outside the house to attend a call of nature.[14]

Some places had become quite notorious for the activities of these outlaws. For example, "Sarangpur, 10 miles south of Tanda, has a population of 9000 Hindu thieves, dacoits and thugs, whose depradations extended as far as Lucknow, Gorakhpur and Benaras."[15] Still Heber was not ready to think that the people of Oudh were 'habitually ferocious or bloodthirsty'.[16]

Apart from the political and military implications of the subversion of law and the consequent rise of the banditry, the entire range of economic activity was dislocated. When the *'amil* and *chakledar* failed to collect the stipulated amount of the land revenue from the defaulting *zamindar* and *ta'alluqadar*, they tried to squeeze the money from the rich merchants and bankers, the latter were forced to "make advances and take, as security for repayment, the receipt of the *zamindar* who was a ruined man, and at the moment a prisoner in the *chakledar's* camp."[17] Precisely for these reasons many bankers of Rae Bareli district having substantial capital worth up to four lakh rupees left the place and migrated to the neighbouring British districts such as Kanpur, Gorakhpur, Farrukhabad and Benares.[18] On the other hand, the *ta'alluqadar* and the *zamindar* when they fell into arrears in payment of land-revenue and apprehended an intention on the part of the *chakledar* or *'amil* to invade their estates, tried to extort money from the family bankers on easy rates to make the payment and thus to effect their escape from the wrath of the government revenue officials. C.A. Elliott has eloquently described the machination of the Rao of Dundeakhera against the family banker, Chundan Lal and the way in which the latter was forced to change his masters overnight.[19] The banker had carried on his business very well and prospered in such a way that while in 1810 he was the owner of only three villages in different parts of the district, in 1825, "his estate has risen to 2 1/2 lac and it continued to fluctuate between this amount and a minimum of 1.5 lac till 1850". [20] But his prosperity soon attracted the greedy eyes of the *chakledar*, who thought him to be a "squeezable man" and required him to pay more by 1/2 a lac than he had done last year (AD 1850).[21] The banker, foreseeing such an eventuality had thought it quite expedient to have "built a house and acquire good deal of landed property in Cownpoor district" so that he could claim protection as a British subject though residing in Oudh.[22] The general feeling of insecurity and mistrust prevailing among the bankers and merchants was aptly described by Lalji, who says

> The bankers and merchants of (Awadh Kingdom) do not keep their capital at one place due to the fear of the depredations of the *ta'alluqdar* and the *zamindar*..... and the illegal revenue demands of the *'amil* and the *tehsildar*. There are many who are the owners of property worth two lakh of rupees and have purchased *zamindaris* and villages in the British domains. (They) keep their cash and other valuable items at the houses built in (the British) dominions and on getting any idea of the disturbances send their families to these (houses).[23]

This flow of capital from Awadh to the adjacent British territories must surely have been a drain on the resources of Oudh.

The drain was not the only economic impact of the British presence, but a number of other spheres could be pointed out where the dictates of the Resident undermined the authority of the king in his own *kingdom*. The Awadh rulers in succession advanced lonas to or placed deposits with the East India Company. The interest occurring at the rate of 4% or 5% per annum was always earmarked for certain specific charitable purposes. This amount was remitted directly to the beneficiaries and spent on the specified purposes by the Resident himself, who was accountable to none. A number of deeds of such deposits and loans have survived to show who the beneficiaries actually were.[24]

The bond business carried out by the East India Company, too, implied similar objectives. These bonds carried 5% per annum interest. Sleeman estimated that the people of Awadh had approximately invested 3 crores of rupees in these bonds, and many middle class families entirely depended on the interest of these bonds.[25] The financial as well as the political implications of these transactions were manifold; a large sum of money was drained out of the kingdom, and the payment of annual interest by the Resident to the beneficiaries and to the religious as well as charitable institutions made large sections of people dependent on British favour.[26]

The merchants of Awadh kingdom who carried their businesses in the adjacent British districts as well, enjoyed the privilege of seeking the help of the Resident in redressal of their grievances, through the magistrates of the concerned districts. Chandan Lal, to whom we have referred above, was assessed for higher amount of revenue by Kasheeparsad Tewaree, the *chakledar* of Purwa. On his refusal the *chakledar* attacked and killed his brother and plundered property worth Rs. 25,000. The matter was brought to the Prime Minister 'Ali Naqi Khan, who did nothing to punish the culprits. Thereafter, Chundan Lal applied to the magistrate of Cownpore claiming "protection as a British subject though residing in Oudh."[27] The matter was referred to Sleeman who immediately took up the case and pleaded for justice. With this incident, the king got annoyed with Chandan Lal for defying his authority and ordered his banishment, but through the constant pressure of the Resident, Kasheeparsad Tewaree was dismissed from *chakledarship*, ordered to repay Rs. 25,000, banished from the kingdom for two years and declared incapable of entering the "government service again."[28] But it seems that such a course was insisted upon by Sleeman not with a view to seeking justice, but primarily for interfering with the affairs of king. Elliott says, that within eight years of the action, British officials had pardoned Kasheeparsad Tewaree and made him an honorary Commissioner.[29]

The Facade of 'Misrule'

The erosion of the king's authority during the second quarter of 19th century by a series of systematic acts of omission and commission by the Resident was an important factor for the decline of Awadh. It so happened that some of the notorious and proclaimed criminals found their way into the Residency or to the British cantonment. Similarly, the tenure of the appointment of many high officials of the king depended on the likes and dislikes of the Resident and on occasion the king was forced to dismiss and banish competent officials precisely for this reason. Masihuddin Ahmad, the plenipotentiary of the deposed king (Wajid 'Ali Shah) to the Queen, cited the instances in some detail--Raja Hunwunt Singh, the *ta'alluqadar* of Dharwapoor and Kalakankar, constantly evaded payment of the Government dues and put to defiance the authority of the king. But he found his way to the Residency on invitation by the Resident.[30] The remonstrances made by the king were of no avail. His helplessness is depicted when he speaks of "offenders being allowed to find protection in my dominions, without my having the power to bring them to justice"[31] It was also pleaded that if such landholders got protection from the English, others would get encouragement and they too would evade the payment of the revenues. Such a courses would ultimately, set forth misgovernment, give rise to innumerable evils, and lead to confusion and anarchy.[32] But inspite of such pleas being made, nothing was done by the Residents to rectify the course they had adopted.

Another incident, cited by Masihuddin Ahmad, shows that Sleeman constantly meddled with the authority of the king, disregarded the decisions of the highest native courts of law as well as of the king himself. One Wusee Ully Khan, under secretary to the prime minister, was supposed to be a very competent and efficient official of the Awadh kingdom. Unfortunately Sleeman had developed a prejudice against him. He asked the king to order his banishment from Lucknow as a seditious person. The king declined to act without getting any proof of his 'alleged seditions', as this was likely to "cause considerable disorder in my kingdom".[33] Sleeman insisted and blatantly declared, "there is no necessity to prove his guilt as the appointment imposed upon him is not his *jageer* or hereditary property." Wussy Ully Khan continued to be harassed by Sleeman on one pretext or another, even after he had proved his fidelity and devotion to the *nawab's* government. Sleeman's disrespect towards the established norms of the period and his contemptuous disregard of the authority of the king and his highest officials showed them that the "king...(was) a mere cipher, the Resident accounted all in all ..a real mayor of the palace and the kingly authority fell into utter contempt".[34]

Undoubtedly, the agrarian and economic life of the kingdom of Awadh before the annexation displayed a stagnant form of the Mughal system subjected to heavy external pressures and widening internal fissures. Although, we have seen how such a situation had arisen, still it was in the interest of the British officials and the Resident at the court of Lucknow to present a picture of 'misrule' and thus, to justify further interference in the affairs of the kingdom. It is difficult to separate facts from the fiction or at any rate, to evolve a balanced picture from the mass of biased evidence. It may readily be acknowledged that 'misrule' was present, but in a subsidiary state it was quite inevitable.[35]

It is difficult to find much to commend in the kingdom. Yet, despite the manifold evils by which it was beset, the Awadh system was not one of the total spoliation or anarchy as has been described by its critics. Its very ineptitude protected the peasants and the *zamindars* of Awadh from the extreme distress which the *mahalwari* system of the colonial rule imposed contemporaneously on the adjoining ceded and conquered provinces.

References

1. Henry Lawrence, 'The Kingdom of Oudh', *Calcutta Review*, III, 1845, pp. 414-15.
2. *Ibid.*, p. 377.
3. *Ibid.*, pp. 385-78.
4. Donald Butter, *Outlines of the Topography and Statistics of Southern Districts of Oudh and Contonment of Sultanpur*, p. 96.
5. Jagdish Roy, 'The Revenue System of the Nawabs of Oudh', *JESHO*, II, 1958, pp. 92-104.
6. Lalji, *Mirat-ul Auza ff.* 11b-12b.
7. *Ibid.*, 13a.
8. Henry Lawrence, *op. cit.*, p. 388.
9. Donald Butter, *op. cit*, pp. 50-51.
10. *Ibid.*, p. 101.
11. Henry Lawrence, *op. cit.*, p. 388.
12. Bishop Heber, *Narrative of a Journey Through the Upper Provinces of Hindustan*, 1824-25, London, 1828, p. 46.
13. *Ibid.*
14. Lalji, *op. cit.*, p. 75a.
15. Donald Butter, *op. cit.*, p. 52.
16. *Ibid.*

17. Bishop Heber, *op. cit.*, p. 52.
18. Donald Butter, *op. cit.*, p. 86.
19. *Ibid.*
20. C.A. Elliott, *The Chronicles of Onnao,* pp. 135-37.
21. *Ibid.*, p. 139.
22. *Ibid.*
23. C.A. Elliott, *op. cit.*, pp. 141-43.
24. Lalji, *op. cit.*, 80b-81a.
25. C.U. Aitchinson, *A Collection of Treaties Engagements and Sunnuds Relating to India and Neighbouring Countries,* 6 vols., Calcutta, 1876, II, Treaty numbers XLIV, XLVII, XLIX and L.
26. R.D. Reeves, *Sleeman in Oudh* (being Sleeman's Diary of his tour on Awadh during 1849-50, ed and abridged with introduction and notes) 1971, pp. X-XI.
27. *Ibid.*
28. C.A. Elliott, *op. cit.*, p.....
29. The passengers travelling in such carriages could not be detained by the officials of the state. This privilege was often misused, hence the king strongly protested and also threatened that such carriages would be subjected to check. See Masihud Din Ahmad, *Oude Its Princes and Its Government Vindicated,* London, 1857, Reprinted as *British Aggression in Awadh* with an introduction and notes by Dr. Safi Ahmad, Meerut 1968, pp.140-41.
30. *Ibid.*
31. *Ibid.*
32. *Ibid.*, p. 81.
33. *Ibid.*
34. *Ibid.*, p. 84.
35. By the first quarter of the 19th century, the British interference had become a reality. Captain Mundy visited the Court of Lucknow in 1827 and his observations are worth mentioning. "Ostensibly his nawabship has been promoted with rank of servant to that of Lord. Virtually, he has only changed masters like all other potentiates...he is so strictly supervised, that he can scarcely... enact any state measure without the interference of his superattentive allies." *Pen and Pencil Sketches*, London, 1833, p.13.

11

The Land Controlling Classes in Awadh—A Study of Changes in their Composition, 1600-1900

Superior rights in land have been linked in Awadh, as elsewhere, with the domination of a particular clan, or caste, over an area. These rights could originate quite independently of any royal action. The association of caste with more or less well defined tracts of country was so conspicuous in Awadh that C.A. Elliott was led to conclude that *pargana* boundaries were fixed on the basis of the 'possession of an undivided clan.'[1] However in so far as these superior or *zamindari* rights were fully alienable, the territorial hegemony of a clan or caste was open to the dissolving effects of money. It could also be disturbed by the deliberate policy of Government to dislodge a clan from an area and install some other group in its place.

A study of the position of various land-holding clans, their share in the agricultural surplus and the changes which came in their fortunes during the period 1595-1900 can be extremely fascinating. One such study had been attempted by Bernard S. cohn for the Banaras region. After comparing the data for circa 1595 with those for circa 1900 he concluded that, "the rise of one group or class did not necessarily mean the concommitant fall of another."[2] A similar study has been attempted by K.K. Trivedi for western Uttar Pradesh. His conclusions are quite different from Cohn's. He has shown that changes in land holding classes were quite substantial and that a large number of castes recorded in the *A'in* had been largely eliminated from various localities, being supplanted by others. In most cases the money-lending castes which replaced them are not even recorded as *zamindar* in the *A'in*; but they appear with sizeable holding by 1900.[3]

The study of the *zamindar* clans of Awadh must obviously begin with the rich information in *A'in-i Akbari*. Abul Fazl has given us a detailed census of the dominant castes in each *pargana* along with the *naqdi* (*jama*') figures assessed upon it. Very often more than one caste are recorded for a *pargana*. We have therefore divided the amount of *naqdi* proportionately in order to determine the share payable by one caste from the *pargana* in question.

A cursory glance at Table I (prepared with the help of the data provided by *A'in*)[4] will show that more than 75% of total *jama*' of the *pargana* recorded in the *A'in* was from land under the various Rajput clans : Bais 18.50%; Bachhils 5.22%; Ghelots 5.11%; Bachgotis 4.73% Bisins 4.13%; others 3.42%; undifferentiated, 25.64%. The Brahmans and Muslims trailed far behind, accounting for only 6.42% and 1.86% shares in the total *jama*' of the *suba*. The remainder was controlled by other minor clans and some of which are unidentifiable.

The Bais Rajputs are recorded as *zamindar* of 27 *parganas* in Awadh by Abul Fazl. In the *sarkar* of Awadh, they are co-sharers in three *parganas* holding 6% of the total *naqdi* of the *sarkar* and one *pargana* each in *sarkar* Bahraich, Khairabad and Gorakhpur, while in *sarkar* Lucknow they possessed 15 *parganas* singly and six *parganas* as co-sharers, in all they controlled 18.22% of the total *naqdi* of the *suba*. These *mahals* formed a contiguous block. The tract acquired the name of Baiswara in the 17th century, the first occurrence of the name appears to be in Shahjahan's time, when the recalcitrance of the Bais *zamindar* caused the creation of a special *faujdari* jurisdiction of Baiswara,[5] "consisting of many *mahals*, that are the native place of the seditious *zamindar* of the caste of Bais".[6] They supported the rebellion of Bahadur, the Bachgoti chief in Aurangzeb's first R.Y.[7] and apparently lent aid to the Chauhans of *pargana* Shahpur in or about AD 1700 . The disturbances were suppressed with some difficulties and Rad Andaz Khan, the *faujdar* of Baiswara reported his successes with much satisfaction.[8] C.A. Elliott provides us with detailed information on the settlement of the Bais Rajputs in the Baiswara region from their traditional settlement till about 1860.[9] We are told that there were 22 *parganas* in all, under the dominance of this clan:-

District (according to present distribution)	*Pargana*
1. Rae Bareli	1. Dundiakhera
	2. Unchgaon
	3. Kombhi
	4. Bar
	5. Kehengur
	6. Ghatampur
	7. Serhapur
	8. Mukrid
	9. Dalmau
	10. Bihar
	11. Pattan
	12. Punhan
	13. Rae Bareli
	14. Hurha
2. Unnao	15. Satanpur
	16. Purwa
	17. Maurawan
	18. Serwan
	19. Asoha
	20. Gorinda
	21. Pursundan
3. Lucknow	22. Bijnor

"The Baiswara *Nizamat* included very little more than the *pargana* in the above list."[10]

The Bais *zamindar* seem to have extended their possessions in *pargana* Dalmau and Bijnor, since Abul Fazl has recorded the former under 'Turkmans', and the latter under the 'Chauhan Rajputs'.[11] On the other hand, after the suppression of the revolt of 1857 some Bais proprietors lost their possessions. The most notable loser was Raja Beni Madho Singh of Shankarpur whose large estate was confiscated for his involvement during the years 1857-59. The final picture with regard to the land holdings of the Bais clan suggests that by and large all the *mahals* recorded in the *A'in* were kept in fact by them, but only a few new additions were made to the land holding of this clan by c. 1900. It appears then that the possessions of Bais Rajputs at least did not, on the balance, suffer any contraction over the three hundred years spanning 1600 and AD 1900.

The Bachgoti Rajputs are recorded as exclusive *zamindars* of six *parganas* and jointly of one in *sarkar* Awadh where they thus seem to have accounted for 18.85% of the total *jama.*' In *sarkar* Lucknow they held only a share in a *pargana* and 2.6% of the total *jama*' of the *suba* Awadh their *parganas* were assigned 4.87%. All the *parganas* except one, formed a contiguous block of territory in the south-eastern portion of Awadh in 1595. The Bachgoti *zamindar* raised considerable disturbance in AH 1070/AD 1660. Their leader Bahadur recruited a large number of followers from amongst the local '*ganwars*, the turbulent Bais' and other bad characters of the area. The banner of revolt was raised in the Baiswara division. He devastated a considerable area. Such were the dimensions of the revolt that an imperial force was deputed under the command of Bahadur Khan.[12] The rebellion was suppressed and peace restored in the area.[13] Subsequently we hear little of this clan. But they largely retained their *zamindar* and held on to almost all the *pargana* against which they are entered in the *A'in*. The famous Khanazad house of Hasanpur (Muslim Bachgotis) and their latter branches of Maniarpur and Gangoso and their large *ta'alluqadari* possessions in the present district of Sultanpur and Fyzabad.[14] We know that five of the Bachgoti *parganas* of the *A'in* lay in Sultanpur district, while one each lay in the districts Fyzabad and Barabanki, the *parganas* Baktha is yet to be identified.[15] Other notable possessions of the Bachgotis lay in the *ta'alluqa* of Kurwar, Samrautha and Khajurahat, the Rajkumars had the estates of Dera, Pirpur, Meopur Dharua and Nanemau.[16] We find that in addition to their old possession some new 'estates' were also acquired by them. The *ta'alluqa* of Khajurahat was established during the time of Shujauddaula and the house of Bhiti came into existence during the first half of the 19th century. Most of the villages of these *ta'alluqa* lay in the *Ain*'s *pargana* of Pachhimarath and *haveli* Awadh, where the Bachgotis are not recorded as *zamindar*.

The Chauhan Rajputs held one *pargana* each in the *sarkar* of Khairabad, Awadh and Lucknow. In two *parganas* of Awadh they are recorded as the co-sharers, and so they controlled areas yielding 4.33% of the total *jama*' of the *suba*. These *zamindars* had grown strong enough, subsequently, to cause trouble and harassment to the imperial authority at the close of the Aurangzeb's reign. It was reported by the deputy *faujdar* of the Baiswara division, Sher Andaz Khan, that these troublesome people had collected a force of their kinsmen consisting of about 8,000 or 9,000 persons and gone into rebellion. The usual allegations, namely, refusal to pay the land revenue was also levelled against them. As a result of the successful operation carried out by the imperial forces against the rebels, 12 strong fortresses and about 1500 captives were captured by the army. Also we come across the recommendation of the *faujdar* to confer the *zamindari* rights of the area over one Saiyid Muzaffar who helped imperial forces with all possible means.[17]

Comparing the relative position of the Chauhan possessions between 1595 and 1900, it appears that some of their old possessions had been lost to their powerful neighbours while they had themselves established their sway in areas where they are not recorded in the *Ain*. The *pargana* of Daryabad and Sara had almost completely passed out of their hands. *Pargana* Inhauna was kept intact by Chauhan *Khanazads* (Muslims). In *pargana* Rudauli and Bijnor they are only recorded as inhabitants, but not as the proprietors of the land; they might have been under proprietors for which unfortunately we possess no information.[18] Their new acquisitions lay in the District of Kheri. The large *ta'lluqa* of Oel, Mahewa and Kaimahra consisted of 326 villages and 28 *pattis*, assessed at Rs. 1,89,744. Originally, it was a Janwar possession; the Chauhans, got it as a 'dowry, gifts, since their predecessors had no one to succeed them. The Jangre Rajputs, a branch of the Chauhans, also possessed the large estate of Bhur, Isanagar and Ramnagar in Kheri District. Their total possessions consisted of 161 villages and 14 *pattis* and were assessed at Rs. 1,54,745[19]. It appears that on balance the Chauhans did not suffer, though there were some territorial changes.

The *zamindari* possession of Raikwar and Janwar Rajputs display striking similarity with that of Chauhans in 1595. Their most numerous possessions lay in *sarkar* Bahraich, where they held six *parganas* and paid 24.67% of the total assessed *jama*'. In *sarkar* Awadh, the Raikwar held 3 *parganas* as co-sharers with 19.34% in the total *jama*'. One *pargana* belonging to the Janwars lay in *sarkar* Khairabad. In the *jama*' of the *suba* their share amounted to 7.10%. A comparison with the relative size of their land-holdings in 1900 suggests that the Raikwars had lost a good deal of their possessions while some of the Janwar houses had acquired very large estates in those areas where they are mentioned as *zamindar* caste by Abul Fazl.[20]

The Raikwars lost hold of the *pargana* Guwarich and Daryabad; the *pargana* of Siluk was kept in tact by them. In *parganas* Fakharpur and Hisampur they retained at least some landed possession. The

Janwars also lost their old possessions. First of all, the entire *pargana* of Rajhat and large tracts in *pargana* Sujauli and Sultanpur were transferred to Nepal in 1860. From the *pargana* Sadarpur they were expelled during the Nawabi period. *Pargana* Dangoi was included in the *ta'alluqa* of Ayodhya and Nanpara. As against these losses, the new estates acquired by them are of some interest. The estate of Balrampur and Payagpur were now owned by Janwars while Mallanpur and Ramnagar constituted the possessions of the Raikwars. By taking into account their *ta'alluqadari* possessions and revenue obligations, some idea can be formed of their position about 1900. In 1900, the Janwar possessions in Gonda and Bahraich districts consisted of 1189 villages and 52 *pattis*, assessed at Rs. 8,47,388, while the Raikwar possessions in these districts consisted of 413 villages and 126 *pattis*, assessed at Rs. 3,37,089.[21]

The Bisin Rajputs were the most dominant clan in the Gorakhpur *sarkar*. They were *zamindar* in nine *parganas* farming a contiguous block of the territory in the south-western portion of the *sarkar*, and these *parganas* accounted for 45.66% of the total *jama'*. In *sarkar* Khairabad they were co-sharers in two *parganas* while one *pargana* each of their *zamindari* lay in *sarkars* of Bahraich and Lucknow. In the total *jama'* of the *suba* their share amounted to about 4.13%. Comparing these data with 1900, it appears that there had been quite drastic changes in the fortunes of this clan. With the close of the tenure of Qazi Khalilur Rahman (1680-1707),[22] there was a spontaneous rise in the power of the local chieftains. There were constant conflicts among local *zamindar*. During the 18th century the *banjaras* acquired considerable power in the north-eastern regions in the *sarkar* of Gorakhpur. In course of time, they became a scourge to almost the entire area. No individual chieftain was able to withstand their onslaught. These conditions came to an end with cession of this territory to the domains of the English East India Company in 1801.

It seems that during the 18th century owing to these conditions the position of Bisin land holding in this *sarkar* underwent complete change. Not only this, in the other four *pargana* of *sarkar* Bahraich, Khiarabad and Lucknow, they are not even mentioned as the superior right holders of land. In the Gorakhpur *sarkar* there were only a few Bisin estates with considerable land holdings. The prime family was of the Raja of Majhauli. In 1900, it held 152 villages, assessed at Rs. 67,756. Their possessions were quite large, but in order to meet the threat posed by Banjara depredators, they abandoned a large portion of his estate to newly established estates to Tamkuhi and Padrauna. This created a powerful buffer zone between Majhauli and eastern portions of the *sarkar*, notorious for Banjara depradations.

The estates of Sarnet Rajputs may also be dealt with here. The great Sarnet houses of Bansi Raj was established as a result of a dowry gift received from the Bisins of Majhauli. In AD 1900, the Bansi Raj was extensive enough to merit assessment of Rs. 1,21,685.

A precise comparison of the individual *pargana* held by Bisins in 1595, with their possessions in 1900 cannot be attempted, but they seem on the whole to have declined. Muslim Pindari chiefs and Europeans also received estates during the British period which reduced the Bisins' relative position.

The *Ain* places most of the possessions of the Surajbansi and Sombansi Rajputs in *sarkar* Gorakhpur. Their share in the total *jama*' of the *sarkar* amounted to about 22.03%. The Sombansis held one *pargana* each in *sarkar* of Awadh and Khairabad. These two clans jointly controlled barely 3.49% of the total *jama*' of the *suba*. For the same reasons as for the Bisin, their position declined in *sarkar* Gorakhpur. However in some adjacent areas, where they are not recorded as *zamindar* in the *Ain*, they came to possess large *ta'alluqadari* estates. In AD 1900 the Sombansi estates contained 80 villages and 8 *pattis* assessed at Rs. 41,766, while the estates of Surajbansis consisted of 206 villages *pattis*[23], and accounted for Rs. 1,84,282. In most of their *paraganas* in Gorakhpur *sarkar* Europeans received large grants in the British period. However in these areas as well as in many other places the Kalhans Rajputs are mentioned quite frequently, the Surajbansi as well as Sombansis had matrimonial ties with the Kalhans Rajput.[24] In *pargana* Sandi *sarkar* Khairabad, the Sombansis held 55 villages out of 140 in AD 1900.[25]

In the *A'in's* tables, the Gehlot Rajputs held jointly with Bachgoti Rajputs the *pargana* of Sandila and Pachhimarath while they held the exclusive *zamindari* of *pargana* of *sarkar* Lucknow. Their share in the total *jama'* of the *suba* amounted to 5.22%. Similarly the Bachhils, apart from the *pargana* where they were co-sharers with the Gehlots, had *zamindari* rights in four *parganas* of *sarkar* Khairabad. Their revenue obligations in the total *jama'* of the *suba* amounted to 5.11%. They appear to have lost their position subsequently and have been elegated to the position of under proprietors. Their most conspicuous loss was in *pargana* Sandila where Muslim *zamindars* were able to establish their large *ta'alluqadari* estates. In modern times we get little or no information about the fortunes of either of the two clans in the localities where they were holding in 1595.

The Bandalghoti Rajputs are recorded in the *A'in* as co-sharers in *pargana* Garh Amethi (*sarkar* Lucknow) and accounted for barely 1.11% of the total *jama'* of the *suba*. They have however succeeded in maintaining their position in this area. The Bandalghoti *ta'alluqa* of Ameti and Shahgarh in the present district of Sultanpur passed through quite fluctuating fortunes; still in 1900, the Bandalghoti possessions, here consisted of 334 villages and 5 *pattis*, while the total assessment on them amounted to Rs. 2,38,590.[26] The other Rajput clans of Gaurs and Tomars are shown in the *A'in* as jointly holding two separate *parganas* in *sarkar* Khairabad and Bahraich respectively. Together they accounted for 2.33% of the *jama'* of *suba*. They were no more prominent around 1900.

Apart from the above major *zamindar* clans, there are many other castes recorded in the *A'in* with small shares in the total revenue of the *suba*. Such are the Chendels (1.5%), Amins or Ahmins (1.97%), Ahirs (1.77%), Kumbi (0.49%), Jats (0.08%) and the Kuhnas (0.23%). The presence of Jats in the province of Awadh seems quite curious. In the 19th century there were only some scattered Jats settlement in the districts of Gonda, Bahraich and Kheri, but by and large they were tenants or sub-proprietors.[27] Similar was the status of the Ahirs and the Kumbis.

'Undifferentiated' Rajputs clans held the largest *zamindari* possessions in Awadh. Abul Fazl recorded them in almost every *sarkar*. In *sarkar* Awadh they were only next to the Bais Rajputs with a shrae of 23.43% in the total *jama'*, in *sarkar* Gorakhpur they followed the Bisin and had 16.87% of the total *jama'* as their share. In *sarkar* of Bahraich and Khairabad they formed the most dominant group of *zamindar* with 47.07% and 43.05% of the total assessment. In *sarkar* of Lucknow the position was different. Here they trailed behind the large *zamindari* of the Bais Rajputs and the Muslims of various clans. In the total *jama'* of the *suba* their share amounted to a quarter (25.64%).

A study of the *zamindari* possession in the modern sub-divisions of Awadh belonging to Rajputs other than the clans specifically recorded in the *A'in* presents some difficulties. In the *District Gazetteers* the *ta'alluqa* possessions are often recorded under ownership of a clan which does not appear in the *A'in'*. It is quite possible that in the reign of Akbar their sub-divisions might not have acquired such importance as to merit separate mention. But even if some individual Rajput clans escaped the *Ain's* record, the large *zamindari* it assigns to unspecified Rajputs when combined with the *zamindari* possessions of Rajputs clans give us a very impressive size of the aggregate Rajputs possessions in Awadh. This position is largely confirmed by the *District Gazetteers*. Hence there is no reason to believe that Rajput *zamindari* possessions as a whole declined in the province, except perhaps for marginal decline affected by the post-Mutiny confiscations. Lalji in his *Mirat-ul Auza* (1850) tells us that, "among all the castes of the Hindu inhabitants (of the kingdom of Awadh) the Rajputs are most numerous and a number of *zamindaris* and *ta'alluqadaris* are possessed by them (the Rajputs). Next to them were the Muslim owners—this fact, says Lalji, "had made them so arrogant that they had grown quite contemptuous toward the (priestly class) of Brahmans."[28]

The Brahmans are recorded as co-sharers in two *parganas* of *sarkar* Awadh and they controlled 3.80% of the total *jama* of that *sarkar*. In *sarkar* Khairabad their presence is recorded in four *pargana*, but they controlled as much as 17.73% of the total *jama* of that *sarkar*. In *sarkar* Lucknow they are entered in eight *parganas* and held 4.73% in *jama*.' Of the total revenue of the *suba*, the Brahmans as a whole paid 6.42%. Comparing this data with those of circa 1900, it appears that they made considerable inroads in other areas. While the *mahals* recorded in the *Ain*' continued to be held by them in fact they seem to have established their hold over an extensive area in *sarkar* Gorakhpur, where the *Ain*' does not enter them at all. Ghulam Hazrat [c. 1810] informs us that "most of the villages (in *sarkar* Gorakhpur) were in the *zamindari* possessions of the Rajputs and Brahmans, while the Muslims and other (castes) had only a quarter share (in *zamindari*')[29]. Most of these changes, it appears, were affected during the period of 17th century, for, "since the introduction of British rule (AD 1810) there had been no great change in the relative position of the different castes in this respect (proprietory tenures), with the exception of the alterations affected by the confiscations of estates for rebellion during the Mutiny."[30] In the modern districts of Gorakhpur and Basti, the Brahmans were the leading landholding caste having 26% and 34% of the entire area respectively.[31] In *sarkar* of Bahraich, they are not recorded as *zamindar* but by the lose of 19th century, they had acquired quite considerable landed possessions. The *ta'alluqadars* of Singha Raja of Ayodhya[33] owned large possessions in the district of Gonda, because of the favours from the Nawab-Wazirs.

The former held 325 villages and 78 *pattis* assessed at Rs. 2,09,760,[34] while the later had 669 villages and 124 *pattis* and assessed at Rs. 4,79,348 in land revenue.[35] The estate of Sisandi falling under the limits of the modern districts of Unao and Lucknow (and falling within *sarkar* Lucknow in Akbar's time) was actually obtained in *theka* or revenue farm in 1226 *Fasli* (AD 1817), but was subsequently converted into a hereditary possession.[36] Since a comparison of their revenue paying capacity is not possible on the basis of the data provided for c. 1900, no exact impression can be formed to show changes in their position between 1595 and 1900. But it can be observed from the total number of the Brahman *ta'alluqadars* and their vast possessions in various districts by 1900, that they had become much more important an element among the landed proprietors of Awadh than they were in 1595.

The Muslim *zamindars* accounted for roughly 10.86% of the total revenue of the *suba* of Awadh in about 1595. The Afghans are recorded as the exclusive *zamindars* of the *pargana* Utraula, *sarkar* Gorakhpur, while in *pargana* Sidhaur, *sarkar* Lucknow, they are recorded as co-sharers, Ansaris were in possession of the contiguous *paraganas* of Ibrahimabad and Satrikh in *sarkar* Awadh and the *pargana* of Amethi in *sarkar* Lucknow. Saiyids only held the *pargana* Bilgram and Unam, while the Shaikhzadas were the co-sharers with them in *parganas* Fatehpur and Haveli Lucknow in *sarkar* Lucknow. The *zamindars* of the *pargana* Inhauna and Satinpur in *sarkar* Awadh, were converted Rajputs of Chauhan and Bachgoti clan. It appears that by 1900 the position of Muslim land holdings had undergone a drastic change. For one thing, deliberate attempts seem to have been made by the Government from time to time to create Muslim *zamindars* in the midst of recalcitrant Rajput chiefs. Sher Andaz Khan, the deputy *faujdar* of Baiswara at the close of Aurangzeb's reign specially recommended the creation of Muslim *zamindars* in *pargana* Shahpur and Harha after the revolt of the Rajput *zamindars* of these *parganas*. The recommendations were made in favour of those officials who had led successful operation against the rebels.[37]

The Afghans have acquired large estates in many parts of the *suba* in addition to their continued hold over the *pargana* in which they are recorded as the *zamindars* in 1595. In *sarkar* Gorakhpur they held *pargana* Utraula and they retained this in their house till 1903 with a brief interruption caused due to seizure by the Janwar Rajputs of Balrampur in 1830. Soon afterward they were restored to their lost possessions and by 1903 they held 73 villages and 5 *pattis* assessed at Rs. 44.977.[38] The estate of Nanpara was a creation of later times. The founder of this house is said to have been appointed as *qiledar* of *sarkar* Bahraich by Emperor Shahjahan in *Fasli* 1193. During the *Nizamat* period Shujauddaulah in *Fasli* 1260 bestowed upon this house the title of Raja' and granted *jagir* comprising Sangha, Bahraich and Kaluapara. In 1903, the *ta'alluqa* had grown considerably and it included 333 villages and 9 *pattis*. The revenue paid by them amounted to Rs. 2,48,500.[39]

In the district of Lucknow one Faqir Muhammad Khan, an Afridi Afghan was granted a piece of land by Nawab Shujauddaulah. In 1827 he obtained the land of the *pargana* (Malihabad) and held it till 1843, in the meantime acquired several villages by default. He also obtained a lien of several other lands and thus founded an estate known as Fatehnagar.[40] Later on the estate was divided between his two sons, becoming known as Shalmau and Kasmandi Khurd. As a whole it consisted of 26 villages and 12 *pattis* assessed at Rs. 39,342.[41] Another noticeable possession of the Afghans lay in the district of Hardoi, this being the estate of Basitnagar. It was bestowed upon Dildar Khan, the son of Diler Khan (founder of Shahabad). as *jagir* by Emperor Aurangzeb. The grant was resumed by Nawab, Sa'adat 'Ali Khan but the successors of Dildar Khan managed "by means of purchase, and other well-known means to acquire about 40 villages."[42] About 1903 the family possessions consisted of 29 villages and 6 *pattis,* and the total revenue demand was Rs. 22,270.[43]

The Shaikhzadas (or Shaikhs) seem to have lost only their small possession of *pargana* Lucknow Haveli to Burhan-ul Mulk Sadat Khan in AD 1722[44] while their other possessions remained in tact with many more additions during the subsequent period. The holders of the large *ta'alluqadari* estates of Mahmudabad, Bithara and Bhatwamau were actually the descendants of the Shaikhzadas of *pargana* Fatehpur. Their original possessions were enlarged as a result of the post-Mutiny confiscations of some Rajput estates; they obtained the large *ta'alluqa* of the Bisin Raja of Mithauli consisting of 68 villages and assessed at Rs. 46,600. As a whole they now possessed 306 villages and 43 *pattis* for Rs. 2,67,024 in 1903.[45] The estate of the Qidwai Shaikhs, Jahangirabad, dates back to the days of emperor Jahangir, in whose name it was founded. They purchased the Bisin estate of Somranwan, a portion of Usmanpur *ta'alluqa* and some other village.[46] The more significant additions were made in this estate only during the last quarter of the 19th century. In 1873 they held just 65 villages and 30 *pattis,* while in 1903 this *ta'alluqa* comprised 94 villages and 67 *pattis.* The Government demand was fixed at Rs. 1,32,547.[45] A branch of the Jahangirabad family was settled at Ambhapur in Bahraich district. Their possession comprised villages and 25 *pattis,* all of them situated in *pargana* Hisampur.[48] It was through matrimonial alliances that the Qidwais was able to acquire possession of this *ta'alluqa* from the *qanungos* of Hisampur.The Tipraha *ta'alluqa* of Khairati Shaikhs originated in quite a peculiar manner. It was established by local *tahsildar* and flourished under his successors. But as a result of the post- Mutiny confiscations it dwindled to only 15 villages and 4 *pattis,* the total assessment being Rs. 9,200.[49]

There were many Shaikh families possessing large estates in the districts of Barabanki and Hardoi. Their traditional accounts suggest that they had settled at an early date, but they came into prominence only during the 17th century and in the *nizamat* period with their appointments as petty revenue officials. In the subsequent period they acquired superior rights over large tracts of land by using methods 'too well known' in Awadh. The ancestors of Bhilwal *ta'alluqa* are said to have been appointed *chaudhari* by Shahjahan in 1616 in *pargana* Subeha. In course of time they enlarged their possessions to the extent that in 1903 they were the owners of 30 villages and 13 *pattis* assessed at Rs. 32,569.[50] The *ta'alluqa* of Kakrauli owes its origin to Shaikh Firoz, who was appointed *Chaudhuri* by Akbar. The family held this title during the *Nizamat* period, when their rights and privileges were assessed for Rs. 10,000 with the absolute gift of certain villages as *nankar* in the later period many members of this family worked as *chakledars* in the Awadh administration. About 1900, this estate comprised 91 villages and 7 *pattis* assessed at Rs. 89,140, including the confiscated property of Unao *zamindar.*[51] The Shaikhs of Gopamau are said to have been appointed *chaudharis* by Humayun and had retained the title till the Annexation. Subsequently, they acquired two rent free villages and a cash *nankar* of Rs. 1700. Many other villages were obtained by purchase. Around 1900 their possessions were large enough to be assessed at Rs. 17,798.[52]

The Ansaris and Saiyids are recorded as the *zamindars* of *pargana* Ibrahimabad and Satrikh in *sarkar* Awadh and *pargana* Amethi in *sarkar* Lucknow in the *Ain.* They seems to have retained their possessions of Ibrahimabad and Satrikh in tact for the succeeding three centuries. By 1900, 60% of the *pargana* was held by these proprietors in *ta'alluqadari* tenures.[53] In *pargana* Amethi, they seem to have continued their hold till 1900. The large estate of Salempur and Adampur Bhatpur consisting of 30 villages and 2 *pattis* assessed at Rs. 48,566, was held by the scions of the old family.[54]

The Saiyids are recorded as the exclusive *zamindars* of the *pargana* Bilgram and Unam in *sarkar* Lucknow by Abul Fazl. During the subsequent period of the *nizamat* they acquired landed possessions in other parts of *suba* Awadh as well. In district of Fyzabad the *ta'alluqa* of Pirpur was established by one Mirza Muhammad Ali Beg during the reign of Shujauddaulah. Subsequently the neighbouring *ta'alluqa* of Saidanwan was also amalgamated in it. About 1900, it comprised 130 villages and 108 *pattis* assessed at Rs. 1,26,898.[55]

There was a spectacular rise similarly in the fortunes of the *ta'alluqa* of Samanpur. The family had originally three revenue-free villages, but between 1759-63, one Malik Nurullah rose to influence and obtained engagements for 50 villages. Subsequent additions were made in the *ta'alluqa* in course of time and about 1900 the estate consisted of 165 villages and 23 *pattis*, the revenue standing at Rs. 1,05,284.[56] The traditional account of the Saiyid of Bilgram connects them with the celebrated house of the Barha Saiyids of Muzaffarnagar. During the Mughal period the place had attained a great name for the learning and prowess of its inhabitants, a tradition which continued during the later period as well. Many persons of this place obtained high posts in Mughal service, a fact which might explain their continued ownership of land in *pargana* Bilgram and its vicinity from the time of *Ain* till 1900. The old Saiyid families had two *ta'alluqas* namely Bhogetapur and Asafpur, jointly consisting of 52 villages and 3 *pattis* and assessed at Rs. 49,940[57]. In *pargana* Unao the old Saiyid family retained their landed possession, and about 1900, they were the chief *ta'alluqadar* of the *pargana* and held 9 out of a total 36 villages assessed at Rs. 10,628 in addition to their position of *chaudhuri* and *zamindar*[58].

The holders of revenue-free grant also enlarged their possessions with full fledged proprietary rights in land with the connivance of the Government. There are instances when the old hereditary owners of land were dispossessed, on the pretext of rebellion coupled with the allegation of their refusal to pay land-revenue, in order to settle Muslim divines. On occasions these grants were made in hitherto barren land, expressly with the purpose of extension of cultivation and settlement. Such grants could have had but little effect on the overall position of land holdings of various clans. But some individual cases might be mentioned. The ancestors of the family of mystics established at Salon were granted 200 *bighas* of waste land by Aurangzeb in his 19th RY/AD 1676. Subsequently a son of Shah Pir Muhammad was bestowed the revenue-free grant of the village Ashrafnagar Singhol. In AD 1679 subsequent additions were made by later Mughal Emperors, such as Bahadur Shah and Shah Alam II. During the *Nizamat* period a number of villages were added to the already existing grant. Asafuddaulah who is said to have paid a visit to the shrine at Salon and to had granted 12 revenue-free villages in perpetuity by expelling the old clan of proprietors who were Kanhpuria Rajputs for their alleged contumacy or rebellion. These villages yielded annually Rs. 25,000[60].

Grants of similar nature existed in Gorakhpur. The Sabzposh family is said to have received some *madad-e ma'ash* grant from Babur, but in the course of time their possessions were enlarged to such an extent that in the time of Asafuddaulah it consisted of about 49 villages and in 1900, the whole grant was assessed at Rs. 14,778.[61] The house of Miyan Saheb Gorakhpur traces its origins to the later days of Muhammad Shah. Their *Shi'i'te* learnings brought them a revenue-free grant of 15 villages during the period of Asafuddaulah. Their loyal conduct during the revolt of 1857 proved still more beneficial to them; they were rewarded with the grant of more villages. By 1900 the family possessions consisted of 61 villages at a light assessment of Rs. 8,889.[62] Here it is not possible exactly to determine as to which clans of land-holders suffered due to these new allotments. Large Muslim Pindari estates were created in the present district of Gorakhpur by officials of the East India Company in order to avert the possibility of further disturbances by settling some of the Pindari leaders in remote parts of the country. Their large possessions included the confiscated property of the Raja of Barhiapor in satisfaction of arears of revenue. It consisted of no less than 145 villages but the assessment was purposely fixed at the low figure of Rs.7,105.[63]

In the *Ain-i Akbari*, there is no entry under the *zamindari* column for the money lending classes such as Banyas, and Khatris, in *suba* Awadh. The extension of the landed possessions of these classes particularly the *Kayasths* and the *Khatris* in Awadh during the 19th century was not as substantial as in the Doab.[64] Awadh did not undergo the same turmoil in land possession as the areas subjected to the notorious *mahalwari* system. During the time that this system was in operations at its highest pressure Awadh was not annexed until 1856, and remained immune from its inequities. Since fewer estates were put on sale there was smaller opportunity for mercantile and bureaucratic inroads into land-ownership. The total landed possessions of Kayasths in Awadh (excluding Gorakhpur division) consisted of 156 villages and *pattis* 188 assessed at Rs. 208,361, while the Khatri estates contained 103 villages and 72 *pattis* assessed at Rs. 1,00,665.[65] In Gorakhpur division ceded to the British as early as 1801 the position of these classes was much better. The Agarwals and Kayasths together held 136 villages assessed at Rs. 24,693 in Gorakhpur district alone, while in Basti district the Kayasths possessed 71 villages of the total area. It is possible that insecurity too had some role to play in the absence of land-purchases by financiers in pre-1856 Awadh. Lalji says that "the bankers and the merchants of (the Awadh Kingdom) do not keep their capital at one place due to the fear of the depredations of the *ta'alluqadars* and *zamindars* .... illegal revenue demands of the *amil* and *tahsildar* .... there are many who are the owners of the property worth two lacs of rupees and have purchased *zamindari* and villages in British dominions."[67]

The establishment and the subsequent rise of the Sikh'estates'in Awadh was purely a post-Mutiny phenomena. The large estate of Kapurthala came into existence by a deliberate act of Government in order to reward the 'loyalists' for their role in the Mutiny. As a result many old hereditary land owners were dispossessed of their *zamindaris*. The estate of Kapurthala consisted of 504 villages and 49 *pattis*, assessed at Rs. 2,73,567.[68]

In Awadh, then superior land-holders appear to have maintained their composition broadly unchanged between the end of the 16th and 19th centuries. The *ta'alluqadari* tenures introduced some new elements, but even here the clans already possessing *zamindaris* seem to have dominated. The big *zamindars* appear to have had the earliest access to *ta'alluqa* engagements in the Awadh kingdom and this remained so under the British. On the other hand when some *zamindars* castes recorded in the *Ain-i-Akbari* escape notice in the *District Gazetteers*, this may entirely be due their conversion into underproprietors under the *ta'alluqadari* system. It may well be, as we have urged in the case of the money-lenders and bureaucrats, that the stability of composition of the *zamindar* class was due essentially to the late date at which Awadh was annexed. Otherwise the story of its *zamindars* might have been the same as those of Western Uttar Pradesh.

TABLE 1

Zamindar Castes in Awadh in c. 1595

Zamindar castes	*AWADH*		*KHAIRABAD*	
(A) Rajputs :	*Revenue*	*Percentage*	*Revenue*	*Percentage*
Bais	36,35,070	8,87	4,57,332	1.04
Gaur	—	—	36,93,053	8.29
Bachgoti	77,21,766	8,85	—	—
Surajbansi	—	—	—	—
Bisin	—	—	20.82,593	4.74
Sombansi	13,60,753	3.32	30,55,339	6.96
Gehlots	14,15,701	3.45	—	—
Janwars	—	—	4,15,587	0.9
Bachhils	14,15701	3.45	39,77,894	9.07
Raikwars	—	—	—	—
Chandel	—	—	—	—
Chauhans	41,41,078	10.11	20,91,908	4.77
Rajwars	79,24,908	19.34	—	—
Tomars	—	—	—	
Undifferentiated	96,98,537	23.68	1,03,09,841	23.51
Total Rajputs	73,13,514	91.07	2,60,83,622	59.28
(B) Other Castes :				
Brahmans	15,57,763	3.80	76.33,331	17.4
Syeds	—	—	—	—
Afghans	—	—	—	—
Ansari	15.71.712	3.83	—	—
Kumbis	10.04.183	2.45	—	—
Amins	—	—	39,67,684	9.04
Ahirs	—	—	35,66,055	8.13
Misc.	3.08,75	—	12,21,733	2.78
Others	—	—	4,57,332	1.04
Total Others	44.42,446	9.93	1,68,46,135	38,39

Source : *Ain-i-Akbari* : The figures are the result of a comparison of the texts of Mss. Br. Museum Add. 5645 and Add. 6552.

LUCKNOW		*BAHRAICH*		*GORAKHPUR*	
Revenue	*Percentage*	*Revenue*	*Percentage*	*Revenue*	*Percentage*
2,29,96,750	28.49	13,16,051	5.45	6,76,792	567
—	—	—	—	—	—
21,04,023	2.60	—	—	—	—
—	—	—	—	10,67,385	8.94
—	—	15,82,345	6,56	51,61,321	43.27
—	—	—	—	15,60,294	13.08
91,13,997	11.28	—	—	—	—
—	—	12,11,843	5.01	—	—
53,11,950	6.57	—	—	—	—
—	—	47,40221	19.65	—	—
43,56,254	5.39	—	—	—	—
25.05,047	3.10	—	—	—	—
—	—	—	—	—	—
—	—	9,66,539	4.00	—	—
1,67,72,057	20.77	1,05,64,180	43,79	20,12,533	16.87
6,31,60,078	80.00	2,03,80,179	84.46	1,04,77,825	87.83
38,27,339	473	—	—	—	—
45,74,428	5,66	—	—	—	—
8,46,240	1.04	—	—	13,97,367	11.7
52,39,457	6.48	—	—	—	—
—	—	—	—	—	—
—	—	—	—	—	—
—	—	—	—	—	—
—	—	21,40,858	8.87	—	—
		16,19,480	6.71	51,100	.42
1,44,87,464	19.91	37,60,338	15.58	14,48,467	12.13

References

1. C. A. Elliot, *Chronicles of Onao,* p. 149. He argues that since the boundaries of the *mahals* were not fixed in accordance with the physical or geographical features of the country, the only reason "for their irregular tracing seems to be proprietory rights".

2. Bernard S. Cohn, 'Structural Changes in Rural Society' *Land Control and Social Structure in Indian History* (ed). R.E. Frykinberg, London, 1969.

3. K.K. Trivedi, 'Changes in Caste Composition of the *Zamindari* Clans in Western Uttar Pradesh, C. 1595-1900'. *Indian Historical Review,* Vol. II no. 1, Delhi, 1975, pp. 47-67.

4. Abul Fazl *Ain-i Akbari,* Persian Text edited by W.H. Blochmann (Bib, Ind.Series) Vol. I, pp.71-84.

5. Abdul Hameed Lahori, *Badshahnamah,* Bib. Indica (i) pp. 243, 278. The *sarkar* of Lucknow and district of Basiwara were under one *faujdari;* subsequently Baiswara become a separate *faujdari;* Also see Zahiruddin Malik, "Problems of *faujdari* Jurisdictions in Baiswara" *PIHC* 1973 (Chandigarh Session). For a note on Bais *zamindars,* see my paper in the cyclostyled papers of the members of the Department of History, AMU presented at 42nd sessions of *Indian History Congress* Bodh-Gaya, 1981.

6. *Insha-i-Roshan Kalam,* MS Azad Library, AMU Aligarh, f.7a.

7. Muhammad Kazim, *Alamgirnamah,* Bib. Ind., Calcutta, 1873, vol I, p. 450.

8. *Insha-i Roshan Kalama, f.3a.*

9. C.A. Elliott, *op.cit.,* pp. 67-68.

10. *Ibid.*

11. Abul Fazl, *op. cit.,* pp. 71-84. However, the *Insha-i-Roshan Kalam* records the *mahal* of Bijnor under the Bais zamindars (f.7). They have been called as *zamindaran-i zor talab.* Nevill informs us that the *pargana* of Dalmau was possessed by Bais Rajputs. See H.R. Nevill, *District Gazetteers of the United Provinces of Agra & Oudh,* (hereafter *DG*), Vol. 39, pp. 168-69.

12. Lahori, *op.cit.* Vol. I (i), pp. 243 and 278.

13. Muhammad Kazim, *Alamgirnamah,* Vol. I, p. 450.

14. *DG,* vol. 46, pp. 88-93.

15. Irfan Habib, *An Atlas of the Mughal Empire,* Sheet No. 8A, p. 29 (notes).

16. For a detailed description of the rise of these *ta'alluqas* see DG, vols. 39, 43 and 46.

17. For a detailed description of the nature and the dimension of this revolt see *Insha-i-Roshan Kalam,* f. 3.

18. *DG*, vol. 48, p. 37.
19. *DG*, vol. 42, pp. 85-7.
20. *DG*, vol. 44, pp. 81-85; vol. 45, pp. 81-83.
21. *DG*, vols. 44-45.
22. This information is from the *Gorakhpur Gazetteer*, pp. 180-82. There is no contemporary documentary confirmation of this. Qazi Khalilur Rahman was probably the *amil* or revenue-collector.
23. *DG*, vols. XXXI-XXXII.
24. W. Crooke *'The Tribes and Castes of the North Western India*, Calcutta, 1896. See s.v. Surajbansis and Sombansis in vol. IV.
25. *DG*, vol. 41, pp. 245-49.
26. *DG*, vol. 46, pp. 95-97.
27. *DG*, vol. 48, p. 159.
28. Lalji, *op. cit., ff.* 74b-76a.
29. Ghulam Hazrat, *Kwaif-i Gorakhpur* MS. (*Farsiya Akbar*) Azad Library, AMU, ff. 6a-b.
30. *DG*, vol. 32, pp. 87-88.
31. *DG*, vol. 32, pp. 87-88 and vol. 31, p.108.
32. For the spectacular rise of this family see Derogha Haji Abbas Ali, *An Illustrated Historical Album of Rajas and Ta'alluqadars of Oudh* hereafter referred to as *Album*) Allahabad 1880, p. 22 and *DG*, vol. 44, p. 102.
33. See *Album*, p. 4 and *DG*, vol. 43, pp. 79-80.
34. *Album*, p. 22.
35. *Ibid.*, p. 4.
36. *Ibid.*, p. 22.
37. *Insha-i Roshan Kalam* describes the rebellion of the Chauhan Rajputs of village Khanjura, *pargana* Shahpur and its suppression by one Saiyid Muzaffar Mohni, who was recommended *zamindari* rights of these villages. The creation of the *zamindari* right of the *pargana* Harha is recommended for one Saiyid Mohiuddin, who mights prove useful in suppression of the revolt of the Rajputs. See ff. 3a and 7b.
38. *DG*, vol. 44, pp. 263-65.
39. *DG*, vol. 45, pp. 75-76; see also *DG*, vol. *Album*, p. 15.
40. *Album*, pp. 59-60 and 65; see also *DG*, vol. 37, pp. 92-93.
41. *Ibid.*
42. *DG*, vol. 41, pp. 88-89; see also *Album*, p. 25.
43. *Ibid.*

44. Kamaluddin Haider *Sawanihat-i Salatin-Awadh*, pp. 7-8, Lucknow, 1879.
45. *DG*, vol. 40, pp. 62-65, *Album*, pp. 8-10.
46. *DG*, vol. 48, pp. 101-2; *Album*, pp. 14-15.
47. *Ibid.*, Appendix, pp. 39-41.
48. *DG*, vol. 45, p. 85.
49. *Ibid.*
50. *DG*, vol. 48, pp. 106-7.
51. *DG*, vol. 41, pp. 86-87.
52. *DG*, vol. 41, p. 81.
53. *DG*, vol. 48, p. 270.
54. *Ibid.*, p. 113.
55. *DG*, vol. 43, pp. 97-100.
56. *Ibid.*, pp. 100-102.
57. *DG*, vol. 41, pp. 90-92; 179-83.
58. *DG*, vol. 38, pp. 247-48.
59. For the translation and annotation of the *farman* issued by Aurangzeb in 1676 see chapter III of the book.
60. *DG*, vol. 39, pp. 101-3.
61. W. H. Sleeman,' *A Journey Through the Kingdom of Awadh*, vol. I, pp. 234-35, see also Donald Butter, *Topography Statistics of the Southern Districts of Awadh*, Calcutta, 1939, pp. 139-40.
62. *DG*, vol. 31, pp. 119-20.
63. *Ibid.*
64. *DG*, vol. 31, pp. 120-21.
65. The total of the *ta'alluqadari* possession of these castes is obtained from the list given in the end of the volume of the *District Gazetteers* of Awadh. In the post-1856 Awadh Districts, their most numerous possessions lay in Sitapur,Kheri, Rae-Bareili, Unao and Barabanki Districts.
66. *DG.*, vol. 31-32.
67. Lalji, *op. cit.*, ff. 80b-81a.
68. *Album*, pp. 3-5 and also *DG*, vols. 42, 45 and 48.

RESISTANCE

12

The Profile of a Saintly Rebel—Maulavi Ahmadullah Shah

Maulavi Ahmadullah Shah happens to be a well-known figure of the rebellion of 1857. British officers who had performed the task of crushing the uprising in the province of Awadh speak in respectful terms of his personal qualities, and organising capacity. Apart from these memoirs the despatches of British officials on the day to day occurrences bear out the exceptional courage and valour displayed by him during the years 1857-58.[1] Most modern studies of this period in English tend to rely heavily on these accounts.[2] Little attempt had been made to utilize his versified biography and to have a substantive idea of his career during these years. Similarly, the reports in the contemporary newspapers and the short notices in the lesser known works of the contemporaries has also escaped notice of historians.[3]

From documentary and literary evidence in Arabic and Urdu one can reconstruct an account of Ahmadullah Shah's life, which at any rate remains obscure in English accounts, and obtain many details, not otherwise known, of his role during the 1857 Revolt[4]. This will help us in assessing his role in the course of events during 1857-59, and to understand the character of the popular uprising.

Saiyid Ahmad Ali Khan *alias* Ziauddin, titled Dilawar Jang, was a son of Nawab Muhammad Ali Khan of Chinapattan (Madras). Born in the second decade of the 19th century, he received, as a prince, the best education of the time. We are told that during his childhood he won warm commendations of his teachers for his exceptional memory, intelligence and industry. After the completion of studies in classical languages and traditional Islamic sciences (*Tafsir*, *Hadith*, *Fiqh* and logic) he received extensive training in the art of warfare.[5] He seems to have acquired some knowledge of English. As an enterprising young prince his fame reached far and wide. He visited Hyderabad as a guest of the Nizam in connection with some marriage proposal, and though the proposed marriage did not come off, he stayed in the city for quite some time. His biographer tells us that he undertook an expedition on behalf of the Nizam to coerce some rebellious Raja into submission. The details of the expeditions are revealing enough as indicating his preference for deceptive methods of warfare. [6] But such spectacular success earned a number of enemies for him. In a surprise move the jealous courtiers planned an attack on his person, but fortunately he escaped unhurt.[7] The British officers at Hyderabad formally requested his father to allow him to visit England. Thereafter, he proceeded to London, and had an opportunity of meeting the King as well as the notables of that kingdom. His biographer, Fath Muhammad Taib had not provided the details of his stay at England, except the fact that he was allowed to display his skill in the use of arms at his own request.[8] On his return visit to India, he stopped at Mecca,[9] and Medina, then passing through Iraq, reached Iran, where the king wanted him to join his service, but he declined the offer and proceeded to India.[10]

By the time he was back in India, he became inclined towards mysticism and after an intense search for a *sufi* guide, became a disciple of Saiyid Furqan 'Ali Shah, a saint of the *Qadri* order at Sambhar (Rajasthan).[11] He remained with his *pir* for some time to get initiated into the doctrines of the order. From here he was directed by his spiritual guide to proceed to Gwalior. Now, he was called as Ahmadullah Shah by his Shaikh, a title by which he became known afterwards.

At that time Gwalior happened to be in the 'jurisdiction' (*wilayat*) of another *sufi* saint of the *Qadri* order, Mehrab Shah Qadri. After some initial hesitation, Ahmadullah Shah was initiated by him in the creed second time. In the company of the new *pir* he spent atleast 4-1/2 years, roaming in the vicinity of Gwalior since the new initiation entailed practical training and propagation of *jehad*, or 'Holy War'. As part of new strategy, he was directed to go to Agra. Mehrab Shah is said to have given him a new name, Waliullah, but this did not gain currency.[11]

Probably as a part of new strategy, audition, parties were arranged in a big way as to attract crowds and preach the call for *jehad*.

Although the *Qadris,* are averse to the very idea of audition parties, we find sermons were delivered calling upon people to be ready for *jehad* after these parties were over.

Another contemporary testimonry about his activities in Agra is worth reproducing:

> (Ahmadullah Shah) arrived at Agra with a large number of *murids.* He took a palatial house at rent, kept *naqqaras* at the gate, the drums were beaten five times a day. As his popularity grew, many more became his *murids.* Audition parties *(majlis-i qawwali)* were arranged. I also became a frequent visitor at his place....[12]

It was generally believed that 'neither fire can burn his disciples, nor sword can do any harm to them'. During the course of these audition sessions, the Shah was fond of practising meditation for long durations by way of holding his breath *(habs-i dam).* It was on one such occasions that Shah told the author of *Khawariq-e Mastan* that "from this date after six months, there will be great disturbance in the territories of the government".[13]

From Agra, Shah left for Aligarh to meet Raja Mursan. He stayed in the '*sarai* of Ratan Lal and was offered *(nazr)* rupees two hundred and fifty in cash, one high prized horse and two hunting dogs by the Raja'. The author (of these lines) "too had the occasion to visit Aligarh and meet Shah there". Shah told him about his intention to go to Lucknow, "where he will sit on the throne and issue his own coins, the whole army will obey him and the treasure will also be under his control".[14]

It seems that at Agra he was very vocal in pleading for *jehad;* hence complaints were lodged with the British authorities to the effect that, "he is a *derwesh* only in name, actually he is a prince and is preparing the masses to wage a war against the government. No action was initiated against him, instead the complainants themselves were made to suffer".[15]

Sometimes afterwards he again went to Gwalior to discuss further course of action. Probably by this time the incidents at Hanuman Garhi and the death of Maulavi Amir 'Ali in course of his *jehad* had became widely known and this might have influenced Ahmadullah Shah. In any case he decided to proceed to Lucknow, the capital city of the recently annexed kingdom of Awadh, where he arrived in November 1856. His arrival in the city was reported in the weekly Newspaper of Lucknow, namely *Tilism,* on 21th Nov. 1856 in the following manner:

> These days a person called Ahmadullah Shah in disguise of a *faqir* but having all paraphernalia of royalty has arrived in the town and stayed in the *sarai* of Motamad-ud daulah, but has now shifted to Ghasiyarimandi........People of the town visit him in a large number on Mondays and Thursdays to take part in mystic gatherings *(majlis-i hal-o-qal).* A number of feats are performed in midst of these gatherings... Such display takes place every morning and evening for viewing of the masses...[16]

The impact of these gatherings on the population of Lucknow can be gauged by the next report of *Tilism* which appeared two months later. On 30th January 1857 it was reported that "Ahmadullah Shah in Ghasiyarimandi is very fearless in saying whatever he wishes to say and a large crowd is always there, often Maulavi Amiruddin Ali is remembered. Although he is unable to do anything, orally he always pleads for *jehad*".[17] Certainly, his call for *jehad* bore fruits. Along with a group of chosen followers he decided to make a surprise attack on the 'Christians' when all of them gather together on a Sunday (in a church ?). But his followers could not adhere to the time schedule. The plan failed and the news was leaked to the British.[18] The *kotwal* was sent asking him to give up the call of *jehad* and to surrender his arms and ammunitions. But Shah replied :

> since you (i.e. the *kotwal*) are also a Muslim and if you follow *shari'at,* and all the necessities (to wage the war) are available, then *jehad* will be obligatory even on you. Likewise I also consider *jehad* obligatory for me, but for want of means (to carry on the struggle) I have not been able to undertake it. Otherwise I am quite ready for it.[19]

The *kotwal* was not convinced, and the English thought it necessary, to post some sepoys to check the inflow of the visitors and even to record their names.[20] At the some time orders were issued to the *thanedar* of Chinibazar for putting curbs on his activities. Finally, Shah was forced to leave the town and go wherever he wanted along with his arms.[21] Such an order was not resisted by him, although we are told by Taib that "thousands of *telingas* (sepoys) used to come there (in the audition parties) and they discussed with him and went away."[22]

Ahmadullah Shah now left Lucknow apparently for Bahraich, with 10 or 12 men (in other reports only with five or seven men). A halt was made of Fyzabad, where he stayed in the Chawk *sarai*. Here again he started preaching *jehad.*[23] Hardly two or three days were passed in delivering the sermons that the authorities got alarmed as 'chuprases informed the magistrate of the really dangerous tendency of this man's doings, and accordingly the officer incharge of the city issued the necessary orders for his arrest. The principal terms demanded from this Maulavi were, that he and his armed followers numbering about seven, should give up their arms, which should be kept in safe custody; further, that all this preachings, distribution of money, so conducive to be disturbance of peace, should be entirely put an end to. A deliberate refusal was given to every attempt of coercion, early next morning an infantry company .... attached them..... these fanatics fought fiercely." Ultimately, the Shah was arrested and placed under guards in the cantonment as,"he seemed too dangerous a character to be kept in the city jail".[24] After a brief trial he was imprisoned in the district Jail at Fyzabad.[25]

With the outbreak of Mutiny at Fyzabad on 8th June 1857, the gates of prison were broken open and Ahmadullah Shah was chosen by the mutineers as their leader, and the notables of town presented themselves before him and offered *nazar*. On assuming the leadership, he issued orders for the destruction of the temples of Hanumangarhi, reportedly built at the site of a destroyed mosque. Although he was well aware of its consequences, he still thought it necessary to redress the grievances of the Muslims. Now, it was natural for the Hindus to feel alienated, therefore they thought of withdrawing their support to him as, "just now he is planning for the destruction of *garhi,* nothing can be predicted for the future." The difference of opinion among the officers of the sepoys over the question of leadership was also made known to Shah. Therefore, he left for Lucknow thinking "the victory will be bestowed by the favours of God, rather than by the support of these people (the dissatisfied soldiers)". But, Taib syas, soon the sepoys realized their folly, and they joined Shah's forces. Consequently at the time of the battle of Chinhat, he commanded both the Hindu and Muslim sepoys of Fyzabad.[26]

With the battle of Chinhat began the second phase of the Shah's career. Now, he was a busy commander of forces, planning the attacks on the British positions and strengthening the defences. Since most of these details are quite well known and, moreover Syed Moinul Haq has fully utilized the information of Taib's *mathnavi*, there is little need to repeat all those facts again; still there are quite a few aspects which can be highlighted in order to understand his mission.

The first engagement of the Shah with the British forces took place at Chinhat when the British made a surprise attack in the early morning of 30th June 1857. The columns were hurriedly organised and Ahmadullah Shah and his contingent distinguished themselves in hand to hand fight: they even captured many assault guns. In inflicting a crushing defeat on the British, the Shah had a very significant role. He wanted to take full advantage of confusion in the British camp, but other leaders failed to realize the importance of such a strategic move. The Shah's contingent was left alone to pursue the enemy. Taib bitterly complains that for want of joint action at the decisive movement, the English could consolidate their position. Anyway, the Shah led an assault on English fortifications (Residency) and suffered a bullet injury. But he remained undeterred, yet "there was need for the cannons and the arrows, not of the lances, swords; therefore, the Shah had to beat the retreat and fixed his quarters at Tara Kothi. This continued to be his headquarters for quite some time."[27]

Taib also pointed out the reasons for the early estrangement between Shah and Prince Birjis Qadar. He recalls that as a result of the military victory against the British, the sepoys as well as the army commanders had become very arrogant, causing much hardship to the inhabitants of the city, and even the people of means were being plundered indiscriminately. This lawlessness on the part of the sepoys was objected to by the *'mujahedin'* who brought the matter before the Shah. Thereupon it was decided that a leader should be chosen to check the indiscipline and disorderly conduct of the sepoys. Quite contrary to the expectations, the army leaders decided in favour of prince Birjis Qadar. The Shah sharply reacted to this. His plea was that since *jehad* could be conducted only under the leadership of an *imam*, it was necessary that the creed of the *imam* should be the same as that of *mujahidins;* moreover, *jehad* is not obligatory for the *Shias;* in declaring Birjis Qadar as the leader, the most important ingredient of *jehad* was missing. Therefore, the fight against the British could no more remain a battle for religion. Hence, the *mujahidins* could fight only for self-defence. Further, since the *mujahidins* had offered the stiffest resistance to the British, they had an inflated sense of importance. Also, the Shah had arrived to fight at the behest of his *pir*, and the leadership should have been conferred upon him.[28] This seems to be only a theoretical position taken by Shah. In practice he did lend full support in attacking the Residency. At the request of Barkat Ahmad, his disciple and the commander of the Fyzabad contingent, he personally participated in an assault on Baily Guard. Again in this attack a bullet pierced his right hand.[29]

Taib broadly confirms the general impression that at Lucknow the British position was threatened by the two separate factions having conflicting and even contradictory interests, and hence the military leaders frequently changed sides, and quite often shifted their loyalties from one camp to another. But after the British capture of Lucknow, the Shah became the main rallying point of anti-British forces, so a joint venture to fight the British was proposed by prince Birjis Qadar. The Shah readily agreed. In the ensuing fight, half way the forces of the prince withdrew, leaving the *ghazis* to face the cannon fire of the English. Ultimately, the Shah was forced to retire to the palace at Gaughat. In this battle also he was severely wounded, and one of his disciples Nur Ahmad particularly excelled in the fight.[30]

Probably, the occupation of Gaughat gave some strategic edge to Shah over the rival camp. Consequently siege was laid on his position by the prince's forces, but he refused to fight these "new adversaries as he never wanted to fight Indians, since he thought of himself as their leader and guardian. The siege went on for ten days, without affecting the morale of the *mujahidins* ; the prince's army commander made another plea that since treasure was buried in the palace and its vacation will help the distribution of the salaries of the soldiers. The request was readily conceded though it is needless to point out that the treasure story was a hoax."[31]

The common soldiers had utmost respect and consideration for the Shah, and whenever he thought of going somewhere else, they prevailed over him to change his mind. The entire responsibility for opposition to him lay with the sepoy leaders.

At the same time, it must be conceded, that the unruly mob of the sepoys was hardly under any one's control. Sharaf ud-daulah, one time prime minister of Awadh kingdom, was suspected of treachery, so sepoys arrested him and wanted to execute him. The Shah did not approve of this, so far the time being he was put into prison, but he was killed there. Taib absolves the Shah from any responsibility of his murder and says that had this been his intention, none of the conspirators would have escaped.[32]

A murderous assault was made on the Shah during his morning walks. However the target was missed. In spite of the Shah's wish the assassin was killed by his bodyguards.[33]

Unable to hold the ground at Lucknow, Ahmadullah Shah decided to withdraw with his small following towards Sitapur and establish his quarters at Bari. Hazrat Mahal (the mother of Birjis Qadar) also thought it expedient to join him. Although the initial response of Shah was cautious, yet ultimately he agreed. Taib is very explicit that after reaching Bari, Prince Birjis Qadar had the honour of offering *bay'at* (spiritual allegiance) to Shah. The arrangement put the entire management in the Shah's hands, and he forced the officers of Begum to part with their wealth. This would have certainly caused resentment. Therefore, when the Shah decided to make a surprise attack on the Gorkha army of Nepal returning after much plunder, his new allies ditched him. As a result, the *mujahidins* were left alone in the assault. One Sa'adullah distinguished himself during this assault. Many acts of valour and chivalry were performed by his supporters.[34]

After suffering considerable losses at Bari, the Shah was forced to retire to Muhammadi. Here a last bid was made to take a firm stand against the British. Although his health was deteriorating very fast, he was the guiding spirit behind all the planning and execution of the designs of the army. But Taib says that here he demanded the total support of the sepoys and the army commanders before deciding upon any course of action. He sought to arrange the supply of the ammunition for his forces. Accordingly an envoy was sent to Nawab Bahadur Khan of Barelly for the supply of lances. Although, we are told, the envoy was received courteously, lances were not supplied, as they were needed by the Barelly army itself.[35]

It was at Muhammadi that the Shah had declared himself to be the independent ruler. The coronation was said to have taken place on 15th March 1858, and coins were also struck with the following legend:

> The slave of Mehrab Shah struck his coins in the seven countries; A supporter of the faith of Muhammad is king Ahmadullah.[36]

No such coins have apparently survived. Probably the measure was announced to boost the sinking morals of the fighting forces. We hear that at Muhammadi he received many rebel leaders like Azeemullah Khan, Prince Firoz Shah, Nawab Bahadur Khan of Barelly, and one Ismail Khan under the banners of the Shah. Besides these generals some sixteen thousand sepoys also gathered there.[37]

Many details of the military campaigns of Ahmadullah Shah in Rohilkhand region have been given by Taib. In view of Syed Moinul Haq's excellent summary of these events, there is no need for a repetition.[38] Finally, we have a first hand account of the death of Shah at Pawayan by Maulana Fazle Haq Khairabadi, who was an eye witness on the occasion:

> With the innocent *amil*.[39] (Ahmadullah Shah) a most treacherous game was played by an infidel (*kafir*) rustic *zamindar*. On oath he had promised that when both the armies came face to face (Shah's army and the British forces) he would support the Shah along with a contingent of four thousand brave soldiers. As a result, the guns and the cannons sprayed the fire from the front, while stabbing was done at the back by this treacherous, hypocritical *zamindar* and his contingent. In fact, they were acting at the behest of the Christians. They had become friends of the Devil. Consequently that God. worshipping *'amil* attained martyrdom in the battle field itself, and many of his supporters followed suit. After the martyrdom of these (brave men), the cowardly supporters fled from the battle field only to be slaughtered by their Christian pursuers. Hence, all the inhabitantd became obedient to Christian rule. Two faithful commanders gave a very tough battle in spite of the fact that they did not possess sufficient war material, still the enemy was killed in thousands.... This was the last of the saddest incidents, and heralded the end of the war....[40]

A large number of documents have been reproduced by Abrar Husain Faruqi relating to the assassination of Shah by Raja of Pawayan. From the reports of the British officers, one gains an impression of the sense of relief they obtained after receiving the news. The Raja received a cash reward of Rupees fifty thousand.[41]

Before the outbreak of mutiny, Maulavi Ahamadullah Shah carried systematic propaganda to emphasise the need for *jehad* in the present area of Uttar Pradesh. This call of waging a religious war had considerable impact upon the popular mind. At least we know for certain about Agra, Aligarh, Lucknow and Fyzabad. At the same time he should not be considered a lone preacher. Certainly, a significant role must have been played by people like Saiyid Furqan 'Ali Shah and Mehrab Shah Qadiri in this direction, but unfortunately very little is known about these figures. Their intense propaganda bore the desired result as all the English officers are unanimous in saying that the most 'fierce fight was given by the fanatics or the *jehadees,* who entered the battle field crying *din! din!*'.[42]

References

1. See, for example, G.B. Melleson, *A History of Indian Mutiny,* Vol. III, pp. 541-44, London, 1878-80; J.W Kaye, *History of the Sepoy War in India 1857-8,* London, 1880; Innes, *Lucknow and Oude in the Mutiny,* London, 1896; G. Hutchinson, *Narratives of the Mutinies in Oude,* Calcutta, 1859.
2. S.N. Sen, *Eighteen Fiftyseven,* Publication Division, New Delhi, 1957; Rudrangshu Mukherjee, *Awadh in Revolt, 1857-1858, A Study of Popular Resistance,* OUP, 1984, However, a biographical sketch has been attemped by Gautam Bhadra, 'Four Rebels of Eighteen Fiftyseven, *Subaltern Studies,* Vol. IV, (ed.) Ranjit Guha, OUP, 1985, pp. 263-275, but like R. Mukherjee he too was not aware of versified biography of Shah.
3. By way of exception, Syed Moinul Haq, *The Great Revolution of 1857,* Pakistan Historical Society, Karachi, 1968, had made full use of Taib's account but unfortunately he had no access to the Weekly Newspapers in Indian Archives and Libraries. Similar is the case with a number of important Urdu works for example Intizamullah Shahabi, *East India Company aur Baghi Ulema,* Delhi (no date), Ghulam Rasul Mehr, *Atharah Sau Sattawan ke Mujahid,* Lahore, 1957, Mufti Intizamullah Shahabi, *Ghadr ki Chand Ulema,* Delhi, (n.d.). Abrar Husain Faruqi, *Mathir-i Dilawari,* Lucknow, 1965, utilizes all the evidences about Maulavi Ahmadullah Shah with a number of photoplates of the rare documents. See also Muhammad Ayub Qadri, *Jang-i Azadi 1857 Waqi'at aur Shakhsiyat* (in Urdu), Karachi, 1976, pp. 525-40 for a fairly comprehensive account of Shah's activities.
4. Fath Muhammad Taib, *Tawarikh-i Ahmadi,* Lucknow, Tegh Bahadur Press, 1925. The author of this *mathnavi* (composed in A.H. 1280/A.D. 1863) was a landed aristocrat of Lucknow and had become a disciple of Ahmadullah Shah in 1856. On the instructions of Mehrab Shah Qadri of Gwalior, the spiritual guide of the author's *pir,* he set out to compose this *mathnavi,* but at the same time he seems to be very cautious about

the authenticity of the facts The work is divided into 40 sub-sections, and the main discussion on the activities of Ahmadullah Shah is confined to sections 11 to 35, but the verses are numbered in continuation. For the purpose of precise reference, the numbers of the verses has been cited. This edition had been reprinted with copious notes and a useful introduction by Abrar Husain Faruqi, as *Mirat-i Ahmadi*, Hardoi, 1973. Although in English works he is invariably referred to as 'Maulavi' or 'Maulavi of Fyzabad', to be in tune with Taib the epithet 'Shah' has been retained here.

5. *Ibid.*, 7: 551-567.

6. *Ibid.*, 8: 580-596. It is said that on reaching near the territory of the defiant chieftain (the name of the Raja and area could not be ascertained) he left the soldiers in the neighbouring forest across the river and entered the territory of the Raja in disguise of a wondering ascetic. Soon the fame of the 'holy man' reached the Raja who paid a number of visits to him. Thus, he was able to persuade him to go for outing in the neighbouring forest, where the army was camping. The Raja was made captive and could secure his release only after submission.

7. *Ibid.*, 8: 597-632.

8. *Ibid.*, 9: 644-666.

9. *Ibid.*, 9: 674-690.

10. Saiyid Furqan 'Ali Shah belonged to a family of *madad-i ma'ash* holders established at Sambhar since the Mughal period. For sometime, he was in the service of Maharaja Ram Singh of Jaipur. He was initiated into the mystic order of the *Qadris* by one Shah Hafizullah of Khatav, district Nagaur, who in turn was a disciple of Shah Habibullah Qadri of Lahore. (This information was obtained by one Mirza Abdul Hafeez Beg, Superintendent, Rajasthan *Waqf* Board, Jaipur during the course of a field survey conducted in November 1969). Cf. Abrar Husain Faruqi, *Mirat-i Ahmadi*, pp. 323-27.

11. Mehrab Shah Qadri was a soldier in the contingent of some Maratha *sardar*. But due to strong mystic tendencies he resigned after sometime and, we are told, went for meditation and contemplation. It is also said that he preached *jehad* against the British to all his disciples. The special favours shown to Ahmadullah Shah were due to the fact that the latter too had extensive training in the art of warfare, hence he was thought quite capable of leading the *jehad* movement in practical form. Hewever, it is not known whose disciple Mehrab Shah Qadiri was. The *Shajra-i Manzuoma* of Ahmadullah Shah reproduced in Faruqi lends no support in this matter due to its rather incoherent nuture. The *dargah* of Mehrab Shah Qadri still exist in good condition and is situated at Jiwajiganj, Laskar, Gwalior. See Abrar Husain Faruqi, *Mathir-i Dilawari*, pp. 284-92.

12. Maulana Mohammad Akram Faiq, *Khwariq-i Mastan*, Mufeed-i 'Aam Press, Agra, A.H.1317, p. 29. The author's ultimate sympathies are with the 'victors' as he praises the British for, 'providing stability' and having'established the tenants of justice for high and low', also they were unmatched as 'they possessed an excellent army'. To please the new masters further he says that at Aligarh Shah had made an offer to him also to join at Lucknow where he will be made the *imam* of the army' but realizing 'the futility of the cause,' (the Shah was going for), he had refused the offer. *Ibid.*, p. 32.

13. *Ibid.*, p. 32.

14. *Ibid.*, pp. 32-33. The author further says that thereafter Shah left for Lucknow and the author went to Moradabad. The mutiny reports confirmed all the predictions Shah had made. Although he showers all praise on the bravery and valour displayed by the Shah, he hastens to point out the futility of the whole venture. During the course of events, 'our author had moved away further to Bachrayun where things were peaceful and no harm was done to him' (p. 33).

15. *Taib*, 14: 1016-1029.

16. *Tilism*, No.18, dated 21st November 1856. This paper was edited by Maulavi Muhammad Yaqub Ansari of *Firangi Mahal*, Lucknow, during 1856-57. The last issue of this paper was published on 10th May, 1857. For a discussion on the importance of this newspaper see Iqbal Husain, 'Lucknow Between the Annexation and the Mutiny', *UP Historical Review*, Allahabad, Vol.II, No. I, pp. 40-51. R. Mukherji and G. Bhadra, both have used this article to give the early career of Ahmadullah Shah

17. *Tilism*, No. 28, dated 30th Jan. 1857, p. 1, while at Fyzabad, he used to create some sort of awareness among the people by telling about the 'martyrdom of Maulavi Amir Ali and his companions, they use to visit the graves of the men killed in the religious quarrel of Hanumangarhi mosque. See SAA Rizvi, (ed.) *Freedom Struggle in Uttar Pradesh*, (hereafter as *FSUP*) Vol. I, pp. 381-83.

18. *Taib*: 14: 1034-1047. 'In fact one verse is very clear where Taib says, as he had been ordered (by his *pir*) to fight the Christians, he preached it (*jehad*) to every one'. Cf. Syed Moinul Haq, *op. cit.*, p. 592.

19. *Tilism*, No. 28, dated 30th January 1857, p.1; also in *Taib*: 14: 1047-1057.

20. *Tilism*, No. 29, dated 30th January 1857, p.1.

21. *Tilism*, No. 32, dated 27th February 1857, pp.1-2.

22. Syed Moinul Haq, *op. cit.*, p. 60.

23. *Tilism*, No. 32 explicitly asserts that while proceeding from Lucknow, he made it known to all the visitors that he was leaving for Bahraich,

and he stayed at Fyzabad simply as a passenger. For details of Fyzabad happenings, see *Taib*: 15: 1065-1097.

24. Hutchinson, *op. cit.*; cf. Syed Moinul Haq. *op. cit.*, p. 61. The incident of Fyzabad became widely known and all the leading newspapers reported in detail. *Tilism*, No. 33, dated 4th March, 1857 reported the matter a second time; *Delhi Urdu Akhbar,* No.10, dated 8th March, p. 3, also reported the incident briefly; *Sahr-i Samiri*, No.17, dated March 1857, took a note of the happenings of Fyzabad in rather satirical manner. The editor, Raghubar Narayan 'Aysh says that "he is the same person who had established himself at Ghasiyarimandi, but considering him a dangerous person, the *kotwal* had expelled him.....earlier Maulavi Amir 'Ali also led a *jehad*, in spite of the opposition of the king he was able to enrol many, but in the end everybody met destruction, they were beheaded when they came face to face with the soldiers."

25. *Taib*: 15: 1065-1097. Shah was not just roaming from place to place aimlessly, but in fact his preachings and sermons had considerable impact upon his disciples. The testimony of Hutchinson is worth noticing: "This man (Ahmadullah Shah) after passing through a vast number of cities and stations under our rule, in all parts of India, and establishing his disciples therein, reached Fyzabad in February 1857. Subsequent investigations elicited that everywhere he had preached a *jehad*, or religious war against the *kafirs* of infidels, as the Europeans were politely designated. From some places he had been summarily ejected, but in others evaded expulsion, meeting with no real check until he came to Fyzabad" *(op. cit.*, p. 292).

26. *Ibid.*, 16: 1135-1155. The sentences with inverted commas are verse nos. 1139 and 1144 respectively.

27. *Ibid.*, 1170-1236.

28. *Ibid.*, 18: 1243-1288. The arguments set out by Taib over the question of *imamat*, on the role of *mujahidin* and on the necessity of *jehad* find strange corroboration from the arguments of these issues in a pamphlet called *Risala-i Fath-i Islam*. Although the authorship of the pamphlet is yet to be determined, one can fairly conclude that it is the most representative piece of writing on the ideology and organisation of the *mujahidin*. It is divided into two portions. The first portion contains a discussion of highly academic nature about the necessity of *jehad*, the role of *mujahidin* and the *ghazi* were to play, the difference between plunder and distribution of *ghanimah* (war booty), the appointment of an *amir* and the necessity of offering him *ba'yat* on the specific issue of *jehad*, the wisdom of the sages behind the theory of *Quraish* descent of the *imam* and its impracticability in the then prevailing circumstances, and last but not least, an appeal to Hindus for joining the struggle against the common enemy. Apart from this, certain practical measures were

also suggested to continue the fight and to carry on the struggle. While the second portion of the pamphlet was in the form of an *ishtihar* "meant for the Hindus and the Muslims of India, so that they should think over, and should prepare themselves for the slaughter of the English in order to protect their *din* and *dharam*." This call was to be popularised among the masses by the *maulavis* and the *pundits*. By its very nature the *ishtihar* was meant for publilc consumption in the form of propaganda literature for the rural people.

In fact when one compares the British describing the'rebels and their leaders as scoundrels, *badmash*, *shuhada*, riffraff, and the *mujahidins* as a debased class of the people and fanatics, and also employ the most abusive language (which they never do for the Irish rebels or for Australian convicts, or during the American war of Independence) in their dispatches and reports throughout the course of events of 1857-59, one can understand why this pamphlet uses,'the most insulting language to describe the British especially Queen Victoria' which has injured the sensitivity of modern scholars. R. Mukherjee, *Ibid.*, p. 148. G. Bhadra' is not very happy with such 'abusive condemnation of the 'whole chain of British colonial authority from the crown to the common soldiers and administrators'. For him the image of the 'good Queen Victoria appears to have been ideal. *Ibid.*, p. 271. The lack of any 'sensitivity' among these 'subalterns'about the way British wrote and behaved during this phase is held to be really unfortunate.

In fact the *mujahideens* and their leaders have offered such stiff resistance to the British and had shown such deathless valour that after the suppression of the events of 1857 that the entire class of the *ma'āfidar* had become a suspect in the eyes of the British. As during the course of first regular settlement each confirmation of the *ma'afi* was subject to their *ma'afidar* having displayed 'loyalty during 1857'. Those who were hostile to the British or those who supported the rebels or even those who remained neutral, their grants were summarily confiscated or drastically reduced. For the role of *mujahidin* in 1857, see K.M. Ashraf,'Muslim Revivalists and the Revolt' in P.C. Joshi's (ed.) *Rebellion, 1857*, pp.71-102. An English translation of *Risala-i Fath Islam* can be found in *FSUP*, vol. II, pp.150-62. However, here the original *Risala* has been used.

29. *Ibid.*, 19: 1293-1311.
30. *Ibid.*, 21: 177-1418.
31. *Ibid.*, 23: 1553-1570.
32. *Ibid.*, 25: 1737-1749.
33. *Ibid.*, 25: 1724-1727.
34. *Ibid.*, 26: 1766-1812.

35. *Ibid.*, 28: 1883-1909 for the versified account of the *farman* despatched to Nawab of Bareilly and verse nos. 1910-1940 for the versified version of the *'arzdasht* of the Nawab in reply to the *farman;* see also Faruqi, *op. cit.*, pp. 133-36.

36. *Ibid.*, 30: 2024-2065, for coins and the despatch and of *farman* to various rulers, See Syed Moinul Haq, *op. cit.*, p. 544 and n.

37. For his activities in Rohilkhand region see *Taib*, 29: 1941-2023; and 31: 2066-2145. The British officers were also equally concerned about his movements; they too kept themselves informed about everything Shah was doing. In this connection letter from the Chief Commissioner of Oudh to the Secretary Govt. of India is worth mentioning. "the defeat of the rebels at Bareilly and Shahjahanpur drove the Moulvi Ahmadullah Shah with his followers back into Oudh, where he was joined by Nurput Singh of Rohia. After reconnoitering Palee with a strong body of sowars, the Moulvi with nine guns and seven thousand men made a movement on the Thane of Palee, which he entered on the 22nd instant. From hence he marched on to Sandee, and immediately threatened the position of the Commissioned Colonel Clarke at Dhurmpur.

    The circumstances in which Colonel Clarke found himself "fully justified him in withdrawing all his civil officers to Futch Gurh at once before their retreat was cut-off." Letter No., 373 (1858), 29th May 1858, *Foreign Secret Consultations*, Nos. 56-57, 25th June 1858, National Archives of India, New Delhi.

38. The best account has been provided by Syed Moinul Haq, who has utilized the account to Taib fully. See *op. cit.*, pp. 544-50.

39. It is quite interesting that Shah has been designated simply an *'amil* by one of his chief supporters. Does it mean that the claim of independence by Shah posed no challenge to the authority of Birjis Qadar?

40. Fazle Haq Khairabadi. *Al Thauratal-Hindiya* (Arabic) edited with comprehensive notes and a useful introduction by Abdul Shahid Khan Sharwani as *Baghi Hindustan*, Bijnore, 1947. Urdu translation of the text has also been provided in parallel columns, at the end. See pp. 409-413; also compare Syed Moinul Haq, 'The Story of the War of Independence, 1857-58', *Journal of Pakistan Historical Society*, Vol. V, Pt. I, (Jan. 1957), pp. 21-57, especially, pp. 48-49.

    Maulana Fazle Haq of Khairabad (1797-1862) happens to be one of the most fascinating and a multifaceted persons of his times. Belonging to the well-known family of the scholars of Khairabad (Awadh), after perfecting in traditional and rational sciences at his father's *madarsa*, he came to Delhi, where during this period some of the bitterest theological controversies were taking place resulting into a vertical division within the *sunnis* on purely hypothetical issues, such as the question of the intercession of the Prophet (*shifa 'at*) and the finality of the Prophethood (*imtina 'un-nazir*). A man of his genius could not remain a mute witness to such debates even if it involves some polemics. He proved to be one of the most bitter critics of Maulavi Shah Ismai'l of Balakot fame over the question of *jehad*. But strangely enough during 1857, he changed his position and caused the leading theologians and the divines to issue the *fatwa* for *jehad*. A detailed study of his intellectual environment is worth analysing in order to understand the ideological trends of this period in a better way. For his role during 1857 see Iqbal Husain, 'Fazle Haq of Khairabad — A Scholarly Rebel of 1857', PIHC, 48th session (1987), pp. 355-65

41. Abrar Husain Faruqi, *op. cit.*, for the photographic reproductions of various applications, reports and orders along with their transcripts, see pp. 192-243.

42. It is strange that the scholars working on this period have seldom touched upon this important aspect; this is in spite of the fact that there is no dearth of material giving the point of view of the 'vanquished'. These proclamations, letters and intelligence reports give a peep into the 'rebels' point of view. Apart from Syed Moinul Haq and K.M. Ashraf in the recent years Iqbal Husain has taken up this subject seriously. For his important contributions (so far), see *PIHC*, 46th session (1985), pp.371-86; *PIHC*, 48th session (1987), pp. 355-65.

Bibliography

All sources including documents, manuscripts, published books and the articles actually cited in the main body of the book are listed in the Bibliography. There are some other works, including books of reference that I have used, which are also included. The Bibliography is classified into Persian Manuscripts, Persian printed works and the English sources, and modern works and records, all listed alphabetically. The records belonging to the *Khanqah-i Karimia*, the *Sufi* establishment at Salon, Rae Bareli are listed separately with sub-classification made on the basis of the nature of the documents.

A— Sources :

(i) *Persian Manuscripts, Documents and family Papers*:

1. *Collection of Acquired Documents* in the *National Archives of India*, New Delhi (Accessioned till 1985). These have been cited as National Archives of India (NAI) with Accession Number immediately following.

2. *Bilgram Documents* belonging to 16th-18th centuries, Research Library, Department of History, AMU.

3. *Documents in the Central Records Office*, Allahabad. The documents used by me are those accessioned in the first series, cited as *Allahabad Documents* with accession number following. Recently most of the documents have been renumbered, these have been cited as *Regional Archives*, Allahabad (RAA) followed by accession number.

4. *Firangi Mahal Documents* belonging to 16th-19th centuries including one of the Akbar's earliest known *farman*, Research Library, Department of History, AMU.

5. *Jais Documents* belonging to the 16th-19th centuries, Research Library, Department of History, AMU.

6. *Khairabad Documents*, Research Library, Department of History, AMU, useful for an understanding of *zamindari* and *madad-i ma'ash* rights.

7. Mufti Ghulam Hazrat, *Kwaif-i Zila-i Gorakhpur*, MS. AD 1810, Aligarh Muslim University, Subhanullah Collection (954/12, *Farsi Akhbar*).
8. Lalji, *Miratul-Auza*, MS. in Maulana Azad Library, AMU, University Collection (Supplementary), *Farsi, Tarikh*- 60.
9. *Akhbarat-i Darbar-i Mu'alla,* Newsletters from the Imperial Court, Aurangzeb's Reign. Nine Volumes in box no. 47 at the Royal Asiatic Society, London, (Microfilm in Research Library, Department of History, AMU).
10. Bhupat Rai, *Insha-i Roshan Kalan,* letters on behalf of R'ad Andaz Khan, *Faujdar* of Baiswara, 1698-1702 and of his son and Deputy Sher Andaz Khan, MS. AMU, Maulana Azad Library, Abdus Salam Collection, 109/339.
11. Santokh Rai, *Insha-i Mansur* or *Mansur-ul Maktubat*, letters on behalf of Nawab Safdarjung to Emperor Mohammad Shah and his *wazir* Qamaruddin Khan. These letters were compiled by one Awadhi Lal, AH 1212 (the date of compilation); the only copy of this manuscript survives in Tagore Library, Lucknow University, Lucknow.
12. Munshi Inamullah Raghib, *Ausaf-ul Asaf*, MS. Abdus Salam 480/1 *Farsi*; University Collection (Supplementary) 25 *Farsi, Tarikh*, Maulana Azad Library, AMU. The year of transcription is AH 1202. The second chapter of section 2 contains letters despatches and *parwanas* issued on behalf of the Nawab.
13. Rai Chaturman Saxena, *Chahar Gulshan*, MS, AMU, Aligarh Habibganj Collection 23/157. The information pertains to the early years of the reign of Muhammad Shah.
14. Shah Ghulam 'Ali Shah, *Mishkatun Nubuwah*, MS, Private collection (with Professor M. Sulaiman Siddiqui, Osmania University, Hyderabad). AH 1212, the date of transcription.
15. Khwaja Yaseen, *Glossary of Revenue and Administrative Terms*. (late 18th Century, Persian Manuscript, British Museum. Additional 6603. Also in Private Collection, Patna, (Rotograph in Research Library, Department of History, AMU, Aligarh) The latter has been cited in the book.

16. Salon Papers:

(i) Aurangzeb's *farman* of 19th RY (AH 1086/AD 1676) granting two hundred *bighas* of land in village Mirzapur Bakhtiyar, *pargana* Manikpur to Shaikh Pir Muhammad Salani. Photo copy of the document survives with the present *sajjadanashin* of the *Khanqah* and the transcript (made from the original) with Professor Irfan Habib. [see plate no. I]

(ii) Aurangzeb's *farman* of 22nd RY (AH 1090/AD 1679) granting the revenues of village Ashrafganj Singhwal, *pargana* Manikpur to Shaikh Pir Muhammad Ashraf. Only a transcript of this document survives with Professor Irfan Habib. [see plate no. II]

(iii) Bahadur Shah I's *farman* of 2nd RY (AH 1119/AD 1708) confirming the possessions of Shaikh Pir Muhammad Ashraf in eight *parganas* of *suba* Allahabad and four *parganas* in *suba* Akhtarnagar Awadh. It has exceptionally rich details in the *zimn*. The original is with Shah Muhammad Amin 'Ata, a *pirzada* of Salon, now at Khushab, Panjab, Pakistan. [see plate no. III]

(iv) Muhammad Shah's *farman* of 10th RY/AD 1729 granting the confirmation to the *madad-i-ma'ash* grants of Shaikh Pir Muhammad Ashraf over all his landed possessions. Photographic reproduction (only obverse side) included in Shah Hasan Ata's *Harir-i Sang*, Karachi, 1964 (see page 127 for the plate).

(v) Shah Alam II's *farman* of 6th RY(AH 1178/AD 1764) granting a confirmation to the *madad-i ma'ash* holdings of Shah Muhammad Karim 'Ata in the various *parganas* of *suba* Allahabad and Awadh. Transcript of the document survives in the case file of Regular Suit No. 5 of 1945 in the Court of Sub-Judge, Pratapgarh (Shah Muhammad Naim 'Ata vs. UP Sunni Central Board of Waqfs), the suit ended in a compromise between the parties on 2.5.1946.

(vi) Nasiruddin Haider's *farman* of AH 1250, granting confirmation to the *madad-i-ma'ash* grants held by Shah Muhammad Panah 'Ata and thereafter his son and successor Shah Muhammad Husain 'Ata in *parganas* Salon, Pershadepur, Jais, Manikpur and Behar. Copy with Shah Muhammad

Hameed 'Ata, a *pirzada* of Salon now at Karachi.

(vii) *Parwana* of Nawab Safdarjung dated 15th *Ramzan* 1st RY/AH 1167 addressed to Raja Ram Narain, the *wazir*, directing him to ensure that no interference is made in respect of village Barwaria, *pargana* Salon as the village in entirety was in the *madad-i-ma'ash* of Shaikh Pir Muhammad Ashraf. Copy with Shah Muhammad Hameed 'Ata.

(viii) *Sanad* issued on 26th September, 1862 by the Chief Commission of Oudh under the authority of Governor-General in Council addressed to Shah Muhammad Husain 'Ata confirming the *muafi* grants of 22 villages and *chaks* of *tehsil* Salon *zila* Pratapgarh, copy with the present *sajjadanashin* of the *khanqah* Saiyid Shah Ahmad Husain Jafri Islahi (also reproduced in full in *Indian Law Reports*, Lucknow Series), vol. II, 1927, Allahabad, pp. 111-12.

(ix) Letter of Shaikh Muhammad Ashraf to Burhanul Mulk alongwith the *Nawab's* endorsement on the same sheet at the right hand margin on the letter, undated. Copy with Shah Muhammad Hameed 'Ata.

(x) Letter of Shuja'uddaulah to Shaikh Pir Muhammad Panah, undated, intimating, that no orders have been issued for the resumption of the *ai'mma* villages of the grantee. Copy with Shah Muhammad Hameed 'Ata.

(xi) *Rawaj-i 'aam ta' aluqadaran-i Malik-i a'ala wa adna, pargana* Parshadepur. Compiled during the course of First Regular Settlement recording the customs and the traditions peculiar to the leading land owning castes of the area which had a bearing on the question of future inheritance and succession of their landed possession. Files in the District Collectorate Office, Rae Bareili. Copy with the present *sajjadanashin* of the *Khanqah*

(xii) *Wajib-ul arz* of villages Barwalia, Dhankesara, Hayatnagar, Karimnagar, Panahanagar, *pargana* Salon district Rae Bareili. These documents were compiled in the course of First Regular Settlement in Oudh after 1857, giving the information about the nature of the proprietory rights in the village and the early history of its settlement. Files in the District Collectorate Office, Rae Bareili. Copy with the present *sajjadanashin* of the *Khanqah*.

(xiii) *Iqrarnama* executed by Shah Muhammad Karim 'Ata in favour of his eldest son Shah Muhammad Ashraf 'Ata dated 11th *zilhij* AH 1238/1822 affecting a transfer of the *madad-i ma'ash* holdings in full proprietary rights. Copy with the present *sajjadanashin* of the *khanqah*.

(xiv) *Iqrarnamah*, executed by Shah Muhammad Karim 'Ata in favour of his second son Shah Muhammad Panah 'Ata dated 6th *Jamad* I AH 1248/1832. This deed was executed to maintain the *waqf* character of the *madad-i ma'ash* properties attached with the *khanqah*. Copy with the present *sajjadanashin* of the *khanqah*.

(xv) *Misal-i Khilafat wa Janashini*, deeds of nomination in favour of the successors-designate by the *sajjadanashins* of the *khanqah-i karimia*. The following deeds have been used:

(a) The deed executed by Shah Muhammad Naim 'Ata in favour of Saiyid Shah Muhammad Husain Jafri, dated 10th *Jamad* I AH 1350/AD 1931.

(b) The deed executed by Saiyid Shah Muhammad Husain Jafri in favour of Saiyid Shah Ahmad Husain Jafri Islahi, dated 9th *Jamad* I A.H. 1389/AD 1969.

(c) The deed executed by Saiyid Shah Ahmad Husain Jafri Islahi, the present *sajjadanashin* of the *khanqah* in favour of his successor-designate Saiyid Shah Wali Husain Jafri, dated 10th *Jamad* I AH 1406/AD 1987.

(xvi) *Ashraful Insha*, a collection of the letters exchanged between Shaikh Pir Muhammad and Shaikh Pir Muhammad Ashraf with the contemporary divines princes and other notables. MS. in the private collection of Shah Muhammad Khalil 'Ata, a *pirzada* of Salon, now at Karachi/Muscat.

(xvii) Shah Muhammad Ashraf 'Ata, *Bayaz*, MS. AH 1212 (the date on the seal) At the end of the MS a list is appended giving the details of the landed properties and other buildings in possession of Shah Muhammad Karim 'Ata. MS. with the present' *sajjadanashin* of the *khanqah*.

(xviii) Shah Muhammad Panah 'Ata, *Fakhrul Fuqara*' MS. AH 1268, with the present *sajjadanashin* of the *khanqah-i karimia*.

(xix) Shah Muhammad Panah 'Ata, *Bayaz*, MS, AH 1272 (the date on the seal), His Comments on the Hanumangarhi episode and the death of Maulavi Amir 'Ali; on the Annexation of Awadh are recorded at the beginning (MS. with the present *sajjadanashin* of the *khanqah*).

(xx) Shah Muhammad Mehdi Ata, *Lam' atul Anwar* or *Hadya-i Hamidya*, Nawalkishor, Lucknow, AH 1316.

(xxi) Shah Muhammad Naim 'Ata *Al-Hajjul Najidah'ala an al Talaqat al Salasul Wahida*, (Arabic) Ms. with the present *sajjadanashin* of the *Khanqah*, Urdu version appeared in *Islam aur 'Asr-i Jadid*, vol. XVIII, special issue pt II, pp. 139-49. Delhi, 1986, with a prefatory note by Saiyid Naqi Husain Jafri, pp. 141-43

(xxii) Saiyid Taqi Husain, *Nala'i Anfas Gham* or *Gham-i-Qiblae 'Alam*, Lucknow, AH 1318.

(xxiii) Saiyid Taqi Husain, *Naghma-i Iram*, a collection of his poetry, edited by Shah Muhamad Naim 'Ata, introduction by Saiyid Shah Ahmad Husain Jafri Islahi, Rae-Bareli, AH 1380.

(xxiv) Saiyid Shah Ahmad Husain Naeemi Saloni, 'Hazrat Shah Pir Muhammad Saloni ke *Malfuzat* wa *Maktubat*' (in Urdu), *Khuda Bakhsh Library Journal*, No. 69-74, Patna, 1992, pp. 248-55.

(xxv) Saiyid Abul Hasan 'Ali Nadwi', 'Maulana Shah Halim 'Ata Saloni', in *Purāne-Chirāgh*, (in Urdu), Vol. I, 2nd ed. Lucknow, 1980, pp. 259-72.

(xxvi) Shah Hadi 'Ata,'Qasba Salon ka Khandan-i Karimi' (in Urdu), *Musannif Quarterly*, Vol. XII Aligarh, 1945 (iii) pp. 78-80. The author reproduces the statement of Shah Mehdi 'Ata given before a Law Court in 1880.

(xxvii) Shah Hadi 'Ata,'Muntakhabat-i Sa'adi ka bab-i doem', (in Urdu), *Musannif Quarterly*, Vol. XIII Aligarh, 1946 (i). The author reproduces Persian Texts of the letters addressed to the *sufis* of Salon by the Mughal Princes alongwith a short summary in Urdu.

(xxviii) Shah Hasan 'Ata, 'Al-Mautul 'Alim Mautul 'Alam', in *Ma'arif*, (in Urdu), No. 3 March 1956, pp. 228-35.

(xxix) Shah Hasan 'Ata, *Harir-i Sang*, (in Urdu), Karachi, 1964. A collection of his poetry, but contains a brief (though superficial) note on the family history, also contains photographic reproductions of the *farman* of Muhammad Shah and some other documents.

(xxx) Saiyid Naqi Husain Jafri, 'Hazrat Shah Muhammad Husain Saloni', in Munadi, (in Urdu), Vol. 54, No. 5-8, Delhi, 1979, pp. 18-20.

(xxxi) Saiyid Naqi Husain Jafri, 'Shah Hasan 'Ata' in *Namwaran-i Aligarh*, (in Urdu), Vol. 3, pt. II, pp. 285-95 [being special number of quarterly *Fikr-o-Nazar* Aligarh.

(xxxii) Saiyid Naqi Husain Jafri, *Kuch Mashriq se Kuch Maghrib se*, (in Urdu) a collection of essays on literary criticism of which one (pp 38-48) gives an idea of the literary attainments of the family, Delhi, 1993.

(xxxiii) Ishtiq Ahmad Mushtaq, *Bagh-i Naim*, author's poetic collection dedicated to Shah Muhammad Naim 'Ata, compiled in AH 1350 (MS with the present *sajjadanashin*).

(xxxiv) *Salik*, began as a monthly organ of *khanqah-i karimia* Salon of which only two issues were published (Sept-Oct 1963). The first issue has a leading article on the history of the establishment. It was edited by Saiyid Shah Ahmad Husain Jafri Islahi and Rafiq Shah Saheba Naimi.

(xxxv) Khwaja Hasan Sani Nizami, 'Bargah-i Salon', in *Munadi*, (in Urdu) Vol. 50, Delhi, 1976 pp. 22-24.

(xxxvi) Muhammad Yasin Khan Naimi, *Tazkirah* (in Urdu), Lucknow, 1966. Although it is in the form of an obituary by a disciple for his *pir* Shah Muhammad Naim 'Ata, but it provides a peep into the ensuing succession dispute for the office of the *sajjadanashin*.

(xxxvii) Muhammad Usman Khan Naimi, *Yadgar-i Naim*, (in Urdu), Rae Bareli, Basically it is also in the form of an obituary but provides some interesting information as well.

Printed Persian and Other Sources

1. *Delhi Urdu Akhbar*, edited by Saiyid Abdullah and published from Delhi during 1856-57, only few issues of this paper are available at the National Archives of India.

2. *Akhbarat* in the Central Record Office, Hyderabad. Some of these have been published alongwith English translations by

Yusuf Husain Khan, *Newsletters, 1767-1799*, Hyderabad, 1955.

3. Zahiruddin Muhammad Babar, *Baburnamah*, English translation by A.S. Beveridge, London, 1921.
4. Saiyid Ghulam 'Ali Azad Bilgrami, *Maasir-ul Kiram*, 2 vols. Hyderabad, 1913.
5. Saiyid Ghulam 'Ali Azad Bilgrami, *Subhat-ul Marjan fi Asar-i Hindustan*, ed, Muhammad Fazlur Rehman Nadavi, Aligarh, 1986.
6. Sujan Rai Bhandari, *Khulasatul Tawarikh*, ed. Maulavi Zafar Hasan, Delhi, 1918.
7. Shah Qasim Daryabadi, (d. AD 1731), *Hans Jawahir Bhakha*, Bombay, 1951.
8. K.K. Dutta, *Some Farmans, Sanads and Parwanas*, Patna, 1962.
9. Abul Fazl, *Ain-i Akbari*, ed. H. Blochmann, 2 vols. Bib. Ind. Calcutta, 1867-77. I have collated the statistical Information with Br. Mus Add. 6552 and 7632 (Microfilms in the Research Library, Department of History, AMU.)
10. Abul Fazl, *Akbarnamah*, ed. Agha Ahmad 'Ali and 'Abdur Rahim, 3 vols. Bib. Ind. Calcutta 1873-87.
11. Maulana Muhammad Akram Faiq, *Khawariq-i Mastan*, Agra, AH 1317.
12. Revenue Grants and other Persian Documents, Texts, edited and translated by B.N. Goswami and J.S. Grewal, *The Mughals and the Jogis of Jakhbar*, Simla, 1967.
13. Shaikh Abdul Haq *Akbar-ul Akhyar fi Asrar-ul Abrar*, Delhi, AH 1309.
14. Fazle Haq Khairabadi, *Tahqiq Alfatwa fi Abtal at Taghwa*, Urdu translation with detailed introduction by Muhammad Abdul Hakim Qadiri, Mubarakpur, 1988.
15. Fazle Haq Khairabadi, *Al Sauratul Hindiya*, (Arabic), ed. with comprehensive notes and a useful introduction by Abdul Shahid Khan Sharwani as, *Baghi Hindustan*, Bijnore, 1947. Urdu translation of the text has been provided into parallel columns at the end.

16. Saiyid Ahmad Khan, *Risalah Asbab-i Baghawat-i Hind* (in Urdu), ed. Mahmud Hussain, Karachi, 1955.

17. Muhammad Bakhtawar Khan, *Mirat ul 'Alam*, ed. Dr. Sajida Alavi, 4 Vols., Lahore, 1979.

18. Muhammad Hashim Khafi Khan, *Muntakhabul Lubab*, 2 vols. ed. K.D. Ahmad and Haiq, Bib. Ind. Calcutta, 1860-74.

19. Saqi Mustaid Khan, *Maasir-i Alamgiri*, ed. Agha Ahmad Ali, Bib. Ind. Calcutta, 1870-74.

20. Shah Nawaz Khan, *Maasirul Umara*, tr. H. Beveridge, Calcutta, 1941.

21. Muhammad Kazim, *'Alamgirnamah*, ed. Khadim Husain and 'Abdul Hay, Bib. Ind. Calcutta, 1865-73.

22. Muzaffar Husain Khan, *Nama-i Muzaffari*, 2 vols. Lucknow, 1917, An Urdu History of the family of Diler Khan with a large number of the texts of Persian Documents together with some photo reproductions.

23. Muhammd Saleh Kumbo, *Amal-i Saleh*, ed. G. Yazdani, 4 Vols. Bib. Ind. Calcutta, 1912-46.

24. Abdul Hameed Lahori, *Badshahnama*, ed. Kabiruddin Ahmad and Abdur Rahim, two vols. Bib. Ind. Calcutta 1867-72. The vol. I is divided into two parts (i) and (ii).

25. Abdul Latif, *1857 ka Tarikhi Roznamcha*, (in Urdu) ed. and translated with detailed notes by Professor Khaliq Ahmad Nizami, Delhi, 1958.

26. Saiyid Ghulam 'Ali Naqvi, *'Imadus Saadat*, Lucknow, 1897.

27. Raja Durga Prasad, *Tarikh-i Sandila*, (in Urdu), Lucknow, 1915.

28. Saiyid Abdullah Qais, *Tarikh-i Kara Manikpur*, Allahabad, 1916.

29. Shah Kazim Qalandar (d. AD 1806), *Sant Ras* or *Naghmatul Asrar*, Awadhi text edited with introduction, notes and translation in Urdu by Shah Mujtaba Haider, Lucknow, AH 1376.

30. Mirza Muhammad Husain Qatil, *Haft-i Tamasha*, Urdu translation by Dr. Muhammd 'Umar, Delhi, 1968.

31. Saiyid Muhammad Abul Hasan Qutbi, *Aina-i Awadh*, (in Urdu) AH 1303, Nizami Press, Kanpur.

32. Shah 'Abdur Rehman, *Anwarul Rehman Letanwirul Jinah*, (*malfuzat*) compiled by Maulavi Nurullah, Lucknow, AH 1270.

33. *Sahr Samiri*, a Weekly Newspaper edited by Raghubar Narain 'Aysh, and published from Lucknow during 1856-57.

34. Mufti Ghulam Sarwar, *Khazinat-ul Asfiya*, Lucknow, AH 1280.

35. Fath Muhammad Taib, *Tawairikh-i Ahmadi*, Lucknow, 1925. (compiled in AH 1280/ AD 1863). This has been reprinted with detailed notes and a useful introduction by Abrar Husain Faruqi, as *Mirat-i Ahmadi*, Hardoi, 1973.

36. Mir Ali Sher Thattawi, *Maqalat-us Shuara*, ed, Pir Husamuddin Rashidi, Karachi, 1957.

37. *Tilism*, a Weekly Newspaper edited by Maulavi Muhammad Yaqub Ansari and Published from Firangi Mahal, Lucknow during 1856-57, Research Library, Department of History, AMU, Aligarh.

38. Saiyid Abdul Wali 'Uzlat, *Diwan-i 'Uzlat*, ed. Abdul Razzaq Qureshi, Bombay, 1962. The poet was a great grandson of Shaikh Pir Mohammad Saloni, hence the editor in his introduction has provided a brief account of Salon establishment also, pp. 1-12.

English Sources

1. C.U. Aitchinson, *Collection of Treaties Engagements and Sunnuds relating to India and Neighbouring Countries*, 6 vols., Calcutta, 1876, (vol. II has been used).

2. Maulavi Masihuddin Ahmad, *Oude: Its Princes and its Government Vindicated*, London, 1857, edited by Dr. Safi Ahmad, under *British Aggression in Awadh*, Meerut, 1969.

3. John Beams, 'On the Geography of India in the Reign of Akbar, Subah Awadh' *Journal of Asiatic Society of Bengal*, LIII, Part I (1884), pp. 215-32, with map.

4. W.C. Bennett, *A Report on the Family History of the Chief Clans of Roy Bareilly District*, Lucknow, 1870.

5. Francis Buchanan, *District Reports (1806-12)*, ed. and abridged by Montgomery Martin, *The History, Antiquities Topography*

and Statistics of Eastern India, 3 vols. London 1838: Indian reprint, 1976, 5 vols. The survey of Gorakhpur from Montgomery Martin's abridgement (vol. II) has been used.

6. Donald Butter, *Outlines of the Topography and Statistics of Southern District of Oudh and Cantonment of Sultanpur*, Calcutta, 1839, reprint Delhi, 1982.
7. Patrick Carnegy, *Notes on the Land-revenue Assessment of Upper India*, London, 1874.
8. *Foreign Department Secret Consultations*, 1780, National Archives of India, Delhi.
9. C.A. Elliott, *The Chronicles of Onnao*, Allahabad, 1862.
10. Syed Moinul Haq, 'The Story of the War of Independence, 1857-58', *Journal of Pakistan Historical Society*, vol. V. part I, January 1957.
11. *A Gazetteer of the Province of Oudh*, 3 vols., Allahabad, 1877.
12. Walter Hamilton, *The East India Gazetteer*: containing particulars, Descriptions of the Empire, Kingdoms, principalities, provinces, cities, Towns, Districts, fortresses, Harbours, Rivers, Lakes & C. *of Hindustan and the adjacent countries*, 2 vols, London, 1828.
13. Bishop Reginald Heber, *Narrative of a Journey Through the Upper Provinces*, 1824-25, London, 1828.
14. G. Hutchinson, *Narratives of the Mutinies in Oude*, Calcutta, 1859.
15. Innes, *Lucknow and Oude in the Mutiny*, London, 1896.
16. J.W. Kaye, *History of the Sepoy War in India*, 1857-58. London, 1880.
17. W.H. Lawrance, 'Kingdom of Oudh' published in *Calcutta Review*, 1845, (iii).
18. Karl Marx, 'Lord Canning's Proclamation and Land Tenure in India, *Daily Tribune*, No. 5344 of 7th June 1858, New York, the article is included in *The First Indian War of Independence*, Progressive Publishers, Moscow, 1952.
19. G.B. Melleson, *A History of Indian Mutiny*, London, 1878-80.

20. Captain Mundy, *Pen and Pencil Sketches*, London, 1833.
21. James Rennell, *A Bengal Atlas Containing Maps of the Theatre of War & Commerce on that Side of Hindustan*, London, 1781.
22. Syed Athar Abbas Rizvi, (ed.) *Freedom Struggle in Uttar Pradesh*, Vol. I, Lucknow, 1960.
23. R.D. Reeves, *Sleeman in Oudh*, Sleeman's diary of his tour of Oudh, edited and abridged with introduction and notes. London, 1971. This volume has been used for the informative introduction by Reeves.
24. W.H. Saleeman, *A Journey Through the Kingdom of Oudh during 1849-50*, 2 vols., London, 1858. R.D. Reeves's introduction to an abridgement of this work is indispensible for understanding the background to the original Diary.
25. Edward Thornton, *A Gazetter of the Territories under the Government of the East India Company and of the Native States on the Continent of India,' 4 vols.*, London, 1854.
26. J.V. Valentia, *Voyages and Travels in India, Ceylone the Red Sea, Abbysiniya and Egypt*, 1802-6, 3 vols. London, 1809.

B. Modern Works

(i) *Records of the Court Cases Revenue and Judicial Departments*:

1. *Board of Revenue Papers*, Lucknow, The Files of Rae Bareli District relating to 1861/62 and of *Oudh General* relating to 1858 have been used.
2. Letter No. 504 of 13th July, 1861 from the Deputy Commissioner of Paratapgarh to the Commissioner and Superintendent of Baiswara Division Resubmitting *Moafi* Register Nos. 1 to 22 of Shah Husain 'Ata received with his Docket No. 1936 of 20th November, 1860.
3. *Case File of Regular Suit No. 12 of 1880* in the Court of Sub-Judge Partapgarh, Shah Muhammad Usman Ghani 'Ata vs. Shah Muhammad Mehdi 'Ata. The suit ended in dismissal in 1882.
4. *Memorandum by the Hon'ble Sayed Mahmud on the Muhammadan Endowment at Salone* in the District of Rae Bareli

(Oudh)—dated Allahabad, the 20th August, 1884, *General Department, North-Western Provinces and Oudh,* 1885, File No. 102, proceeding no. 5, serial no. 10, pp. 19-64 [including three long appendices].

5. Gift-deed dated 26-12-1938 executed by Shah Muhammad Naim 'Ata in favour of Saiyid Shah Muhammad Husain Jafri in the office of sub-Registrar, *tehsil* Salon, Rae Bareli.

6. *Case File of Regular Suit No. 5 of 1945* in the Court of Sub-Judge Pratapgarh, Shah Muhammad Naim 'Ata vs. Sunni Central Board of Wqfs U.P. The suit ended in compromise on 2.5.1946.

7. *Case File of Regular Suit No. 1 of 1950* in the Court of Civil Judge Rae Bareli, Sunni Central Board of Waqfs U.P. vs. Shah Muhammad Naim 'Ata. The Suit was partly decreed on 31.7.1953 in terms of Scheme of Administration which is still in operation.

8. *Case File of Regular Suit No. 31 of 1966* in the Court of Additional Civil Judge Lucknow, Saiyid Shah Ahmad Husain Jafri vs. Shah Shabbir 'Ata & Others. The Suit was decreed in favour of the plantiff of 12.12.1984.

9. *Allahabad Weekly Cases,* Vol. X, Allahabad, 1984, pp. 928-32.

10. *Indian Law Reports,* (Lucknow Series), Vol. II Allahabad, 1927, pp. 109-132.

(ii) ***Works of Reference :***

1. Darogha Haji 'Abbas' 'Ali, *An Illustrated Historical Album of Rajas and Ta 'alluqadars of Oudh,* Allahabad, 1880.

2. Department of Revenue and Agriculture, Government of India, *Agricultural Statistics of India,* Calcutta, Issues of years 1884-85 and 1885-86 have been used.

3. Report from the Select Committee on East India Finances with proceedings, Minutes of evidences 1973, *British Parliamentary Papers; Colonics East India,* Vol. XXI, IUP Shannon, Ireland, 1970.

4. W. Crooke, *The Tribes and Castes of North-Western Provinces,* 1896.

5. H.M. Elliot, *Memoirs of the Races of the North-Western Provinces, of India etc.* ed. by J. Beams, 2 vols, London, 1869.
6. Abdul Hay, *Nuzhatul Khwatir*, (Arabic), vol. 5, Hyderabad, 1911.
7. O.H.K. Spate & A.T.A. Learmonth, *India and Pakistan: A General and Regional Geography*, 3rd ed., London, 1967.
8. H.R. Nevill, *District Gazetters of the United Provinces of Agra and Oudh*, various vols, one for each district, Lucknow.
9. *Report of the U.P. Zamindari Abolition Committee*, 2 vols, Allahabad, 1950.
10. J.A. Voeleker, *Report on the Improvement of Indian Agriculture*, London, 1893.
11. G. Watt, *The Dictionary of Economic Products of India*, 6 vols. London, 1889.
12. H.H. Wilson, *A Glossary of Judicial & Revenue Terms of British India*, London, 1875.

(iii) *Other Publications*:

1. Qeyamuddin Ahmad, *The Wahabi Movement in India*, Patna, 1966.
2. Muzaffar Alam, *The Crisis of Empire in Mughal North* : Awadh and Punjab, 1707-48, Delhi, 1986.
3. Muzaffar Alam, 'Religion and Politics in Awadh Society 17th and early 18th Centuries in *Islam and Indian Regions*, ed. Anna Libera Dallapiccola and Stephanic Zingel A. Lallemant, Stuttgait, 1993.
4. M. Athar Ali, *Mughal Nobility under Aurangzeb*, Bombay, 1966.
5. M. Athar Ali, 'Provincial Governors under Aurangzeb—An Analysis, '*Medieval India-A Miscellany*, I, Aligarh, 1967.
6. M. Athar Ali, 'Provincial Governors under Shahjahan—An Analysis, *Medieval India—A Miscellany*, III, Aligarh, 1974.
7. K.M. Ashraf, 'Muslim Revivalists and the Revolt', in P.C. Joshi's (ed.), *Rebellion, 1857: A Symposium*, Delhi, 1957.
8. A.A. Azmi,'*Ta'alluqadars* in the Kingdom of Awadh', Paper read in *Indian History Congress*, (1965), Cyclostyled volume

in the Seminar Library of the Centre of Advanced Study in History, AMU, Aligarh.

9. A.A. Azmi,'Position of Agriculture and Economy of the Nawabi Oudh, *Proceedings of the Indian History Congress* (hereafter as *PIHC*) 1967 (Patiala), session, pp. 82-90.
10. Richard B. Barnett, *North India Between Empires: Awadh, the Mughals and the British, 1720-1801*, Berkeley, 1980.
11. Purendu Basu, *Oudh and the East India Company*, Lucknow, 1942.
12. Rafat Bilgrami, 'Some Mughal Revenue Grants to Family and *Khanqah* of Saiyid Ashraf Jahangir, *Medieval India—A Miscellany*, II, Bombay, 1972, pp. 298-335.
13. G.D. Bhatnagar, *Oudh under Wajid Ali Shah*, Varansi, 1968.
14. Gautam Bhadra, 'Four Rebels of Eighteen Fiftyseven, *Subaltern Studies*, vol. IV (ed.) Ranjit Guha, Delhi, 1985.
15. C.A. Bayly, 'The Pre-History of Communalism? Religious Conflicts in India, 1700-1860, *Modern Asian Studies*, 19(II), 1985, pp. 172-203.
16. Bernad S. Cohn, 'Structural Changes in Indian Rural Society, 1595-1885, in *Land Control and Social Structure in India*, ed. R.E. Frykenburg, Madison, 1969.
17. *Cambridge Economic History of India*, eds. Tapan R. Chaudhary and Irfan Habib, 1982.
18. Abrar Husain Faruqi, *Masir-i-Dilawari*, (in Urdu) Lucknow, 1965.
19. Michael H. Fisher, *A Clash of Cultures, Awadh, the British and the Mughals*, Delhi, 1987.
20. Irfan Habib, *Agrarian System of Mughal India*, Bombay, 1963.
21. Irfan Habib, *An Atlas of the Mughal Empire*, New Delhi, 1982.
22. Irfan Habib, *Essays in Indian History Towards a Marxist Perception*, Tulika, Delhi, 1995.
23. Irfan Habib, '*Zamindar* in the *Ain*,'PIHC, (1958).
24. Irfan Habib, 'Aspects of Agrarian Relations and Economy in

a Region of Uttar Pradesh during the 16th Century,'*IESHR*, IV (iii), 1967.

25. Irfan Habib, 'Medieval Popular Montheism and its Humanism: The Historical Setting, *Social Scientist*, vol. 21, Nos. 3-4, March-April, 1993.
26. Irfan Habib, 'The Coming of 1857', in *Red the Earth, that year, that year, 1857*, History of India Series, *SAHMAT*, Delhi, 1997, pp. 1-13.
27. Kamaluddin Haider, *Sawanihat-e-Salatin Awadh* (in Urdu) Lucknow, 1879.
28. Syed Moinul Haq, *The Great Revolution of 1857*, Karachi, 1968.
29. Ibn Hasan, *Central Structure of the Mughal Empire*, Delhi, 1970.
30. Nurul Hasan, *Thoughts on Agrarian relation in Mughal India*, Delhi, 1973.
31. Nurul Hasan, '*Zamindars* under the Mughals, '*Land-Control and Social Structure in Indian History*, ed. L.F. Frykenberg, London, 1969.
32. Iqbal Husain, 'A Calendar of Khairabad Documents; 16th-19th Centuries, *Islamic Culture*, Vol. LIII No. (I) ed. (ii), Hyderabad, 1979.
33. Iqbal Husain, 'Lucknow Between the Annexation and the Mutiny, *U.P. Historical Review*, II (i), Allahabad, 1982.
34. Iqbal Husain, 'Fazle Haq of Khairabad- A Scholarly Rebel of 1857, '*PIHC*, 48th Session, 1987.
35. Zakir Husain, 'Some Original Tughlaq Documents and their Significance, *PIHC*, 1989, pp. 219-29.
36. P.C. Joshi (ed), *Rebellion, 1857 : A Symposium*, Delhi, 1957.
37. Muhammad Islamullah Khan, *Political Relations of Awadh Dynesty with East India Company, 1764-1856*, dissertation submitted at Claremont Graduate School and University Centre, London, for the award of Ph.D., 1967, (Microfilm in the Department of History, AMU).
38. Zahiruddin Malik, 'The problems of *faujdari* jurisdiction in Baiswara', Paper read in *Indian History Congress* (1973),

Cyclostyled volume in the Seminar Library of Centre of Advanced Study in History, AMU, Aligarh.

39. Ghulam Rasul Mehr, *Saiyid Ahmad Shahid*, (in Urdu), Lahore, 1954.

40. Ghulam Rasul Mehr, *Atharah Sau Sattawan ke Mujahid*, (in Urdu), Lahore, 1957.

41. W.H. Moreland, 'The Agricultural Statistics of Akbar's Empire *Journal U.P. Historical Society*, 11 (1), 1922.

42. W.H. Moreland, *India at the Death of Akbar*, London, 1920.

43. Shireen Moosvi, *The Economy of the Mughal Empire*, Delhi, 1987.

44. Shireen Moosvi, 'Colonialism and Resistance in U.P., 1764-1857, Presidential Address, 8th Session of *U.P. History Congress*, Varanasi, Feb, 1994, (Cyclostyled copy).

45. Shireen Moosvi, 'The City of Jaunpur under Akbar', Cyclostyled paper presented in the 9th session of *U.P. History Congress*, March, 1996.

46. Rudrangshu Mukherjee, *Awadh in Revolt, 1857-1859, A Study of Popular Resistance*, Delhi, 1984.

47. Saiyid Abul Hasan 'Ali Nadvi, *Sirat-i Saiyid Ahmad Shahid*, (in Urdu), 2 vols. Lucknow, 1939.

48. Seyyad Hossain Nasr, *Sufi Essays*, London, 1992.

49. K.A. Nizami, *Tarikh-i-Mashaikh-i-Chisht*, Delhi, 1953.

50. Muhammad Ayub Qadri, *Jang Azadi 1857, Waqiat aur Sakhsiyat*, (in Urdu),Karachi, 1976.

51. Jagdish Raj, 'The Revenue System of the Nawabs of Oudh, *Journal of Economic and Social History of the Orient*, 1959.

52. Shaikh Abdul Rasheed, 'Miratul Auza, *Proceedings of Indian Historical Records Commission*, 1954.

53. S.N.R. Rizvi, *Atharahvi Sadke Zamindar, Poorvi Uttar Pradesh Mien*, (in Hindi), PPH, 1989.

54. Noman Ahmad Siddiqi, *Land-revenue System of the Mughals*, Aligarh, 1971.

55. Majid H. Siddiqi, *The Agrarian Unrest in North India, The United Provinces* (1918-1922), Delhi, 1978.

56. Intizamullah Shahabi, *East India Company aur Baghi 'Ulema*, (in Urdu), Delhi, (n.d.).

57. Intizamullah Shahabi *Ghadr ke Chand Ulema*, (in Urdu) Delhi, (n.d.)

58. S.N. Sen, *Eighteen Fiftyseven*, New Delhi, 1957.

59. A.L. Srivastava, *First Two Nawabs of Awadh*, First edition, 1933, IInd edition, Agra, 1954.

60. A.L. Srivastava, *History of Shuja-ud-daulah*, 2 vols. Ist edition, 1939; IInd edition, Agra, 1961.

61. John A. Subhan, *Sufism: its Saints and Shrines*, Lucknow, 1960.

62. K.K. Trivedi, 'Changes in Caste Composition of the *zamindar* class in Western Uttar Pradesh; 1595-c 1900., *Indian Historical Review*, 11, (1) 1975.

Index